THE

POETS LAUREATE OF ENGLAND.

THE
POETS LAUREATE
OF
ENGLAND.

BEING

A HISTORY OF THE OFFICE OF POET LAUREATE,

*BIOGRAPHICAL NOTICES OF ITS HOLDERS, AND A
COLLECTION OF THE SATIRES, EPIGRAMS, AND LAMPOONS
DIRECTED AGAINST THEM.*

BY

WALTER HAMILTON,

FELLOW OF THE ROYAL GEOGRAPHICAL AND ROYAL HISTORICAL SOCIETIES,
AUTHOR OF "A HISTORY OF NATIONAL ANTHEMS AND PATRIOTIC
SONGS," "A MEMOIR OF GEORGE CRUIKSHANK," ETC.

" Who would not be
The Laureate bold,
With his butt of sherry
To keep him merry,
And nothing to do but to pocket his gold ?"
BON GAULTIER.

LONDON :
ELLIOT STOCK, 62, PATERNOSTER ROW.
1879.

REPUBLISHED BY GALE RESEARCH COMPANY, BOOK TOWER, DETROIT, 1968

Library of Congress Catalog Card Number 68–30621

PR505
.H3
1968

CONTENTS.

PREFACE.

FULL five hundred years have passed since Geoffrey Chaucer assumed the title of Poet Laureate, and he, the great forerunner of our poet kings to be, can still attract fond readers to admire his knowledge of our common nature, his genial humour, and his kindly heart. From Chaucer to Tennyson, in almost uninterrupted succession, a long line of poets may be traced upon whom the laurels have been conferred : the selection of the poet king has not always been a wise one, and yet the list contains many names we would not gladly miss. Chaucer and Spenser, Ben Jonson, Dryden and Rowe, Warton, Southey, and Wordsworth, these were all men of mark in their day, whilst he who owns the laurels now eclipses all who came before him.

It is therefore somewhat remarkable that so little should hitherto have been written about the office of Poet Laureate, possessing as it does several features which are generally considered interesting. Its antiquity, its close connection with Royalty and the great events of our history, the literary celebrity of many of its holders, and the curious privileges once held along with the title, salary, and butt of sack.

The odes it was once the custom to compose for the King's birthday, and New Year's day, were sung to music composed by the Court musician, in the great council chamber of St. James's Palace, before the King, Queen, and Court. These are no longer exacted, but they were regularly supplied by the Laureates from the time of Thomas Shadwell down to the year 1813, when on the death of Henry James Pye it was resolved to leave the odes at the poet's option.

It is perhaps to be regretted that no collection of the Laureate official odes and poems has ever been published. Their poetical merits are certainly not generally of a high class, but the historical facts they allude to might be of interest to the antiquary, and the philological student could in them trace back our language through many of its curious variations. Or, if we might take the complete works of our Laureates, both in prose and verse, since Chaucer's time, without reference to any other writers, we should have a tolerably comprehensive and complete history of the English language, poetry, drama, morals, politics, and religion, extending over more than five centuries.

A few of the official odes have been inserted, occasionally as examples of style, but more frequently as illustrative of the poets' connection with the office, for it need scarcely be said that the aim here has been to deal more particularly with the history of the Laureates as Laureates, rather than as Poets; Colley Cibber's merits as a Poet might have been dismissed in one line, and that not a flattering one, if poetical criticism alone had been intended; but his wearing the bays, and the literary squabbles arising from his promotion, could not be so summarily passed over in any work purporting to treat of the Poets Laureate.

It is an admitted fact that, with a few exceptions, the Laureates have been surpassed as poets by their contemporaries, and we therefore miss from the list many men who would have honoured the office by their names. Shakespeare, Milton, Pope and Byron, as Laureates, would have far more than compensated for the loss of Ben Jonson, Davenant, Cibber and Southey, although these were by no means the dullest of the race.

Nahum Tate was by birth an Irishman; with that exception all the Laureates have been English.

The earlier holders of the office derived their chief fame from their dramatic works, many of them indeed, especially Ben Jonson, Davenant and C. Cibber, being directly interested in theatrical enterprises. The Drama then afforded a much quicker and more certain path to wealth and fame than the sale of poetry, readers of which were then far less numerous than the patrons of the Stage. These circumstances explain to a certain extent the discrepancy existing between the value attached to the writings of some of the Laureates by contemporary critics, compared with the more discriminating decisions of posterity.

Thomas Shadwell, famous in his day as the author of many extremely popular comedies, was appointed to the post, to replace " glorious John Dryden," and the appointment was favourably received; now that it is more the fashion to read poetry, Dryden is greatly admired, whilst the merits of Shadwell as a dramatist are forgotten, only his wretched verses being occasionally referred to, as an excuse to pile ridicule and contempt on their unlucky author.

Ben Jonson being the first Laureate appointed by Royal Letters Patent, with his name the more detailed sketches in this volume commence, yet the record would have been incomplete had it contained no reference to his predecessors, the *Volunteer Laureates* as they have been generally styled. These men were all eminent in their day, and most of them are still honoured by the lovers of our early literature. When, indeed, the works of Chaucer, Gower, and Spenser shall have sunk into oblivion, it may be safely conjectured that the English language itself will be a thing of the past.

Samuel Daniel (1562—1619), the last of these Volunteer Laureates, deserves to be better remembered than he is. He was the son of a music master, and having a taste for both music and poetry, he acquired considerable renown in his time, was a favourite at Court, held several appointments under Elizabeth and James, and was the respected friend of the greatest literary men of the day. With Shakespeare, Ben Jonson, and Michael Drayton, he had more or less intimate relations, for he was concerned in the production of masques and plays, in which they also were interested. Daniel at length felt himself eclipsed by rising stars, and retired from the literary world, bidding it farewell in some lines affixed to his tragedy of *Philotas*, which are not destitute of pathos and manly dignity:—

> " And I, although among the latter train,
>   And least of those that sung unto this land,
> Have borne my part, though in an humble strain,
>   And pleased the gentler that did understand ;
> And never had my harmless pen at all
>   Distained with any loose immodesty,
> Nor ever noted to be touched with gall,
>   To aggravate the worst man's infamy ;
> But still have done the fairest offices
>   To virtue and the time."

Nor did he claim for his muse greater merit than it deserved; few amongst his successors have sinned less against modesty and good taste, than this poor old writer of the rough outspoken Elizabethan period.

Poetical inspiration is fitful and intermittent; he is the true genius who seizes the volatile spirit ere it evaporates; commencing that only which he feels he has the power to complete, whilst the inspiration lasts. Many passages of the greatest beauty are lost to the world, stored away in tedious volumes of second-rate poetry, whilst if, as in the case of many songs and ballads, the subject is well chosen and the treatment elegant and concise, the work is far more likely to acquire popularity and immortality, than a longer poem of even equal merit.

The songs of Burns, and Milton's "L'Allegro," Wordsworth's "We are Seven," and Southey's "Battle of Blenheim," are more generally read, and far more widely popular, than the longer works of those authors, beautiful as most of them undoubtedly are.

Were Ben Jonson's dramatic works now to be destroyed the loss would, perhaps, be less regretted than if his lines to Celia were torn from our memory; even the loss of a syllable would be a public misfortune.

> " Drink to me only with thine eyes,
>   And I will pledge with mine ;
> Or leave a kiss but in the cup,
>   And I'll not look for wine.
> The thirst that from the soul doth rise,
>   Doth ask a drink divine :
> But might I of Jove's nectar sup,
>   I would not change for thine.
>
> " I sent thee late a rosy wreath,
>   Not so much honouring thee,
> As giving it a hope that there
>   It could not withered be.
> But thou thereon didst only breathe,
>   And sent'st it back to me :
> Since when it grows, and smells, I swear,
>   Not of itself, but thee.''

Another instance is to be found in Edmund Waller.
Which of his longer poems would we not willingly resign
rather than blot out this sweet little epigram on a lady's
girdle :—

> " That which her slender waist confined,
>   Shall now my joyful temples bind ;
>   No monarch but would give his crown,
>   His arms might do what this has done.
>
> " It was my heaven's extremest sphere,
>   The pale which held that lovely deer.
>   My joy, my grief, my hope, my love,
>   Did all within this circle move !
>
> " A narrow compass ! and yet there
>   Dwelt all that's good, and all that's fair ;
>   Give me but what this riband bound,
>   Take all the rest the sun goes round."

Waller has no right to a place here; but who so hard-
hearted as to blame me for quoting the above, even
though examples might equally as well have been
selected from the Laureates.

Even Davenant, who wasted his powers on the tedious
Gondibert, could be tender and playful at times; how
perennial are love and raillery; who would judge that
more than 200 years have passed since he wrote the
following lines " On a Soldier going to the Wars."

> " Preserve thy sighs, unthrifty girl,
>   To purify the air ;
>   Thy tears to thread, instead of pearls,
>   On bracelets of thy hair.

" For I must go where lazy Peace
        Will hide her drowsy head ;
And, for the sport of kings, increase
        The number of the dead.

" But first I'll chide thy cruel theft ;
        Can I in war delight,
Who, being of my heart bereft,
        Can have no heart to fight ?

" Thou know'st the sacred laws of old
        Ordain'd a thief should pay,
To quit him of his theft, seven-fold
        What he had stolen away.

" Thy payment shall but double be ;
        O then with speed resign
My own seducèd heart to me,
        Accompanied with thine."

Tennyson's poetry will eventually be treated in much
the same way as posterity has dealt with that written by
the more admired of his predecessors. His longer works
will become standard classics, read by thoughtful students,
and the few people who really care for good poetry, and
who can and will spare the time to ponder over its
beauties. Some of his grandest passages will appear as
disjointed extracts in school books, and ladies' albums,
whilst by the general public his name will be remembered chiefly in connection with the brief and more
trivial productions of his pen ; and poems by which he
now sets little store, will then probably be chosen as
examples of his skill.

This is perhaps a somewhat sorrowful reflection, yet,

judging by experience and analogy, it is the only result to be expected.

In a work dealing with such an extended period it would obviously have been impossible to give exhaustive biographical details of each of the poets; the endeavour has been to select preferably such topics and occurrences for record, or remark, as were more intimately connected with the office which gives its title to the whole.

Some errors of omission may thus be easily accounted for; ignorance, alas! may claim its share; whilst for some missing poems the only possible apology for their absence is, that our forefathers delighted in a style of expression so broad, so literal, so free, as to defy imitation, and render quotation impossible in a work intended for general perusal.

Errors of commission I am less anxious about; dates and facts have been carefully selected and compared with the best authorities; it has been a labour of love for a long time past, and any friendly hints or corrections will be gratefully received, and used in a later edition.

Pope once wrote an account of the office of Poet Laureate, and most appropriately it was a burlesque history, for its dignity at that time was a burlesque, its holder was a burlesque actor, and the comedies he wrote were burlesques of human life; yet was Cibber never so truly successful in burlesque as when composing what he meant for serious odes on New Year's day, and the King's birthday.

The following pages have a more serious import; it was not with intent to ridicule the ancient office and its holders that they were penned. Yet, while asserting that this is not a burlesque history, I must admit that it has narrowly escaped being a history of burlesque.

As from the earliest times those who held the office have been attacked by their less fortunate contemporaries, to which assaults the Laureates have ever been ready to reply, it is obvious that any account of the holders of the laurel wreath would have been incomplete had it omitted these literary feuds, and the lampoons and epigrams they occasioned.

The smartest and wittiest of these were to be found in the works of our greatest satirists; *Mac Flecknoe*, *The Dunciad*, and Byron's *Vision of Judgment* had to be quoted, with many other works of a similar nature, but of less note, and these passages, together with the replies they occasioned, have brought the ludicrous side of the question into somewhat greater prominence than was originally intended.

Is it necessary to apologise for their introduction? I trust not, for those who love wit and satire will not object to meet with these jests which once delighted our ancestors; whilst to the matter-of-fact student it is only necessary to observe that every attention has also been given to the more serious portions of the work, and I can truly boast (what few historians can) that I have not invented a single fact, even under the greatest temptation.

A history of English parody and burlesque has still to be written; it is a subject of more importance than is generally supposed, and that it can be made both instructive and amusing readers of M. Octave Delepierre's learned work, *La Parodie*, will readily admit.

That book being in French, has, of course, only a limited circle of readers in this country, besides which, as it ranges over the literature of the principal European nations, it has too wide and general a scope to permit of more than a superficial glance at the subject in the chapter devoted to parodies of English poetry.

I had the pleasure of supplying M. Delepierre with some of the raw material used in that division of his history, together with notes on a few of the more obscure points, and, making allowances for the little space at his disposal, and the difficulty of writing in French on English parodies, the result is certainly a success. Indeed, it is doubtful if any account at present exists of this neglected by-path of English literature at all approaching his in completeness. Isaac Disraeli's meagre article has hitherto been deemed sufficient; William Hone advertised his intention to publish a history of the subject, and he certainly possessed ample materials for the work, which unfortunately he did not live to complete.

As to the selection of the parodies herein contained, the chief difficulty consisted in deciding how few, not how many, to quote.

Having at my disposal a large collection of these

b 2

interesting literary trifles, it was necessary to adopt some
rule as to their use.   As far as possible therefore nothing
in the nature of burlesque has been admitted unless it
contains reference to the life, works, and opinions of a
Poet Laureate, or was of interest in connection with
the office.   This arrangement has prevented the quotation of Canning's amusing parodies of Southey's style,
and the still more clever burlesques of Wordsworth and
Southey contained in that most exquisite collection, *The
Rejected Addresses*, written by James and Horace Smith.
The poetry of the anti-Jacobin is now somewhat out of
date, but *The Rejected Addresses* are for all time; "The
Baby's Débût," after Wordsworth, and "The Rebuilding,"
in imitation of Southey's "Kehama," are equal to any
of the poems in the collection.

Some of the satires here quoted are perhaps hardly
worthy of a place; anxiety to let no fish slip from the
net is the chief excuse for their preservation.

They prove that from the earliest times the Laureates
have been subject to the attacks of their less fortunate
rivals, and occasionally they throw a light on the history
and traditions of the office.   Without these little satires
and epigrams (now collected for the first time) the lives of
such second-rate men as Eusden, Tate, or Whitehead,
would scarcely tempt a modern reader's curiosity.

I am indebted to the courtesy of the Hon. Spencer
C. P. Fane, C.B., for an opportunity of inspecting the
interesting warrants and other documents preserved in

the Lord Chamberlain's Office. Amongst these was a memorandum concerning the Poet Laureates appointed from 1590 (Edmund Spenser) to the death of Robert Southey on the 21st March, 1843.

In this document occurs the following curious note in reference to John Dryden :—

" Soon after the accession of James II. (1685) Dryden turned Papist, and on the accomplishment of the Revolution was deprived of the office, which was conferred upon Richard Flecknoe.

" Richard Flecknoe, originally a Jesuit. The office of Poet Laureate, of which Dryden had been deprived on account of his religion, was conferred upon Flecknoe.

" Died 1678."

To which date in another handwriting is affixed the note : " This could not be, as the Revolution was not till 1688 ; perhaps 1688 should be the date."

The date 1678, as that of Richard Flecknoe's death, is correctly given ; that he was ever a Poet Laureate this date sufficiently disproves, but the origin of the erroneous entry of his name on the list of Laureates can only be explained on the following grounds :—

In November, 1681, a bill of high treason was presented against Lord Shaftesbury, which, to the delight of the Whigs, and the great discomfiture of the Court, the grand jury ignored.

When the foreman pronounced the decision with the word *Ignoramus* the hall rang with cheers, long sustained by the multitude outside, and in the evening the City was illuminated by bonfires, and a medal was struck to celebrate and perpetuate the victory of the popular cause. To ridicule this enthusiasm, and the hero of it, Dryden wrote a poem, entitled *The Medal*, at the express wish of Charles II., who, it is said, also designed the plan. Be that as it may, the poem was published in March, 1682, and Dryden received for it one hundred broad pieces from the king.

Amongst the numerous retorts made by Whig writers was the famous *Medal of John Bayes*, written by Thomas Shadwell, a savagely satirical and personal attack on Dryden. This did not long remain unanswered, for in October, 1682, appeared Dryden's *Mac Flecknoe; or a Satire on the True Blue Protestant Poet, T. S.*, a poem of two hundred and seventeen lines of the bitterest invective our language is capable of expressing.

In the plan of this satire it was necessary that Dryden should make use of the name of some very inferior poet lately deceased, one in fact who

> " In prose and verse was owned without dispute
> Through all the realms of *nonsense* absolute."

He selected one Richard Flecknoe, described him as the king of dulness, on his death-bed bequeathing his mantle and his muse to his poetic son Shadwell, re-christened Mac Flecknoe, the son and heir of Richard Flecknoe.

The *sobriquet* clung to Shadwell with that persistency characteristic of nicknames, although few can be found so far-fetched as this one was.

Richard Flecknoe, who would have been for ever forgotten immediately after his death but for the use
Dryden thus made of his name, was an Irishman, and
in his youthful days had been a Roman Catholic priest.
On the Restoration he relinquished that profession, and
took to poetry, of which he composed a considerable
quantity, that obtained for him no other reward than
ridicule. Andrew Marvel met him in Rome, and wrote
of him as a poet and musician, ever reciting his verses,
and, when the hearer was tired, turning to his lute.
Of his person—

> " This basso-relievo of a man
> Who, as a camel tall, yet easily can
> The needle's eye thread without any stitch ;
> His only impossible is to be rich.
>   *   *   *   *   *   *   *
> Lest his too noble body, growing rare,
> Should leave his soul to wander in the air,
> He therefore circumscribes himself in rhymes,
> And, swaddled in his own papers seven times,
> Wears a close jacket of poetic buff,
> With which he does his third dimension stuff."

He died in 1678 at an advanced age, and had therefore been dead four years when Dryden took his name
to bestow it on Shadwell; when in 1688 the Revolution deprived Dryden of his office, Shadwell obtained
it, and probably the appointment was ridiculed by some
envious contemporary as having been granted to Flecknoe
(meaning Mac Flecknoe), thus giving rise to this curious
entry in the record at the Lord Chamberlain's office of the

appointment as laureate of a man who had been ten years in his grave.

Party spite has occasionally interfered with the success of the poets' works, but has only had a temporary effect when those works possessed any real merit; posterity is more liberal-minded as a rule than contemporary criticism, and generally interests itself but slightly in the political opinions of a dead author, provided his books be interesting.

Thus Southey may be called a turncoat or a patriot according to one's views of politics; as a young man he was ridiculed by Canning in *The Needy Knife-grinder* for being a Republican and a Pantisocracist; in later years he was scolded by Byron and Macaulay for his bigoted Tory writings, and taunted with insincerity :—

> " He lied with such a fervour of invention,
> There was no doubt *he* earned his Laureat pension."

In a somewhat different manner Wordsworth divides opinions—one portion of the world's population insist on it that Wordsworth was the greatest poet of the nineteenth century, the other portion contends that—he was not. These, gentle reader, are matters of taste; you know the old proverb, and should your views on these or other similar topics differ from mine, I pray your pardon and compassion; even that compassion you would extend towards a luckless individual afflicted with colour blindness, who cannot realise the joy reserved for *you;* who knows not the beauties of the glowing summer skies, nor sees the splendour of each varying tint in the evanescent rainbow that springs aloft on a showery May day.

And now may I venture to address a few words to those mighty potentates—THE CRITICS ?

Alas! I only dare to cry, as ye are strong be merciful. It is an easy task to be lenient, and a grateful one when you see that the author has taken considerable pains to make the book fulfil the promise of his title-page.

> " I swear by your true friend, my muse, I love
> Your great profession, which I once did prove.
> And did not shame it with my actions then
> No more than I dare now do with my pen."

Use, then, O friendly censor, no more deadly weapon of attack than the ivory paper knife you plunge at random, like a taster, into the folds of my book.

Blame me not if the flavour do not suit your palate, for here is no pretension to the poetry of a Hogg, nor the philosophy of Bacon.

WALTER HAMILTON.

394, BRIXTON ROAD, LONDON,
December, 1878.

THE POETS LAUREATE OF ENGLAND CHRONOLOGICALLY ARRANGED.

POETS LAUREATE.	BIRTHPLACE.	WHERE EDUCATED.	DATE OF APPOINTMENT.	DEATH AND BURIAL.
GEOFFREY CHAUCER	London 1328	Cambridge (?)....	 1368	25 Oct., 1400, Westminster Abbey.
SIR JOHN GOWER	Yorkshire 1320	....	 1400	...... 1402, St. Mary Overy, Southwark.
HENRY SCOGAN	....	Poet Laureate to Henry IV.	......	....
JOHN KAY	....	Poet Laureate to Edward IV.	......	....
ANDREW BERNARD	Toulouse........	Poet Laureate to Henries VII. & VIII.	November, 1486	...... 1523 ......
JOHN SKELTON	Norwich ... 1460	Oxford & Cambridge	 1489	June, 1529, St. Margaret's Church, Westminster.
ROBERT WHITTINGTON	 1480	Oxford.........	 1512	...... 1530 (?) ......
RICHARD EDWARDS	Somersetshire 1523	Corpus Christi, Oxford.	 1561	...... 1566 .....
EDMUND SPENSER	London 1553	Pembroke Hall, Cambridge.	February, 1590	16 Jan., 1599, Westminster Abbey.
SAMUEL DANIEL	Taunton.... 1562	Magdalen Hall, Oxford.	 1598	13 Oct., 1619, Beckington.

NOTE.—The above have been styled *Volunteer Laureates.*

The following received Royal Letters Patent :—

BENJAMIN JONSON	London, 11 June,1573	St.John's, Cambridge	3 Feb, 1615-16	6 Aug, 1637, Westmt. Abbey.
SIR WILLIAM DAVENANT .	Oxford . Feb, 1605	Lincoln College. . . .	13 Dec. . 1638	7 Apr., 1668, Westminster Abbey.

During the Commonwealth the Office was in abeyance.

JOHN DRYDEN	Northamptonshire, 9 Aug, 1631	Trinity College, Cambridge.	18 Aug., 1670	1 May, 1700, Westminster Abbey.
THOMAS SHADWELL . . .	Norfolk 1640	Caius Coll., Cam. . .	1688	Nov., 1692, Chelsea Church.
NAHUM TATE.	Dublin 1652	Trinity Coll., Dublin	1692	12 Aug, 1715 ......
NICHOLAS ROWE.	Little Beckford 1673	Westminster School	1715	6 Dec, 1718, Westmt. Abbey.
REV. LAURENCE EUSDEN .	Yorkshire	Trinity Coll., Cam.	24 Dec. . . 1718	27 Sept, 1730.
COLLEY CIBBER	London, 6 Nov., 1671	Grantham Grammar School.	3 Dec. . . 1730	12 Dec.,1757,Westmt. Abbey
WILLIAM WHITEHEAD . . .	Cambridge . . 1715	Clare Hall, Cambridge.	19 Dec. . . 1757	14 Apr., 1785, South Audley-street Chapel.
THOMAS WARTON	Basingstoke . 1728	Trinity Coll., Oxford	May . . . 1785	21 May,1790,Trin.Coll., Oxon
HENRY JAMES PYE . . .	London, 10 July,1745	Magdalen College, Oxford.	 1790	11 Aug., 1813, Pinner.
ROBERT SOUTHEY	Bristol, 12 Aug.,1774	Balliol College, Oxford.	4 October 1813	21 Mar, 1843, Crosthwaite Churchyard.
WILLIAM WORDSWORTH . .	Cockermouth, 7 Apr., 1770	St.John's,Cambridge	6 April . . 1843	23 Apr., 1850, Grasmere Churchyard.
ALFRED TENNYSON . . .	Somerby, Lincoln-shire 1809	Trinity College, Cambridge.	19 Nov. . . 1850	....

INTRODUCTION.

THE custom of crowning poets is said to be nearly as ancient as poetry itself; it certainly existed at a period long anterior to the knowledge of letters in Britain; and in order to fully understand the nature of the office of Poet Laureate, it is necessary to give a brief account of the ceremonies observed in foreign countries.

The Greeks and Romans, in their pompous public ceremonies, crowned their favourite bards with laurel; and when Domitian held the Capitoline Games, he himself placed the laurel wreath upon the head of the successful author. And this custom continued to be observed until Theodosius abolished it, about 393 A.D., as a remnant (though surely a harmless one) of paganism. The Romans publicly conferred the honour of laureation upon Francis Petrarch in 1341, after he had voluntarily undergone an examination in history, literature, and philosophy. Robert, King of Naples, a great admirer of Petrarch, urged the Roman Senate to offer the laurel to the poet, and the notification of its intention to do so was sent to Petrarch at Vaucluse in August, 1340. Petrarch set out for the Neapolitan Court, where he demanded a public examination, offering to reply to all questions in history,

literature, or philosophy, that might be proposed to him
during three days.

He came through the examination with great *éclat*, and
the king presented him with his state robe, desiring him
to wear it on the day he should be crowned.   Petrarch
then proceeded to Rome, and on the 8th April, 1341,
received a crown of laurel on the Capitoline Hill, being
proclaimed Poet Laureate and historiographer.

After reciting a sonnet, he went to the church of St.
Peter, placed his chaplet on the high altar, and then
returned home.

The following is the formula used on the occasion by
the Count d'Anguillara when he placed the laurel on
Petrarch's brow :—

" We, Count and Senator for us and our College, declare FRANCIS
PETRARCH, great poet and historian, and for a special mark of his
quality of poet, we have placed with our hands on his head *a crown
of laurel*, granting to him, by the tenor of these presents, and by the
authority of King Robert, of the Senate and the people of Rome, in
the poetic as well as in the historic art, and generally in whatever
relates to the said arts, as well in this holy city as elsewhere, the
free and entire power of reading, disputing, and interpreting all
ancient books, to make new ones, and compose poems, which, God
assisting, shall endure from age to age."

The Emperor of Germany presented Pope Pius II. with
the laurel at Frankfort, in consequence of his having
composed some elegies and a satire.

One of this Pope's successors—Leo X.—named Camillo
Querno *Archipoeta*.   The inauguration was attended by
much burlesque ceremony, which affected the poet to tears.
The crown consisted of a spray of the time-honoured
laurel, with vine leaves, emblematical of Bacchus, God of
Wine and the Fine Arts, and cabbage, the leaves of which,
according to an old superstition, were an antidote to

drunkenness, but history records that in this instance they failed to keep the poet sober. His chief work, an epic poem of great length, entitled *Alexias*, he recited to an audience of Roman nobles, and incautiously boasted his power to make verses for a thousand poets, when he was reminded that he also drank sufficient for a thousand other arch-poets.

> " Archipoeta facit versus pro mille poetis ! "
> " Et pro mille aliis archipoeta bibit ! "

His perquisites were to be the leavings of the Pope's dishes and flagons, and all the circumstances attending his appointment are so absurd, that his name would have long since been forgotten by Englishmen but for the well known lines in Pope's *Dunciad :—*

> " Not with more glee, by hands Pontific crown'd,
> With scarlet hats wide waving circled round,
> Rome in her Capitol saw Querno sit,
> Thron'd on seven hills, the anti-Christ of wit."

Pope Clement VIII. invited Torquato Tasso (author of *Jerusalem Delivered*) from Mantua to Rome, intending to confer the laureate crown upon him in the Capitol. Tasso arrived in Rome in November, 1594, and was received by Clement with very great distinction: " I give to you the laurel," said the Pope, " that it may receive as much honour from you as it has conferred upon those who have had it before you." The public ceremony was delayed until the spring; but during the winter Tasso's health rapidly declined, and he died on the very day appointed for his coronation, the 25th April, 1595, at the age of 52.

In Spain the title has been occasionally used, the University of Seville having established the custom ; and Cervantes somewhat contemptuously alludes to it, when he makes Sancho Panza say : " Forgive me, honest Dapple, and entreat Fortune, in the best terms thou canst use, to deliver us from this vexatious misery in which we are equally involved ; in which case I promise to put a crown of laurel upon thy head, so as thou shalt look like a poet-laureate ; and withal, to give thee a double allowance of provender."—*Don Quixote*, Part II., Book IV.

In the Empire of Germany the office appears to have been much more regularly maintained, and latterly the title was so lavishly bestowed as to bring it into contempt, and numerous satires were directed against those who received, and those who conferred the dignity.

Apostolo Zeno, the Venetian composer, and father of the Italian Opera, was one of the most notable men who received the title *Il Poeta Cesareo ;* his successor was the still more celebrated Metastasio, upon whom the title was conferred by the Emperor Charles VI., with a pension of 4,000 guilders.

In Italy and Germany the honour of laureation was usually conferred by the State or some University, and was by no means limited to one poet at a time, as has usually been the case in England.

Thus the University of Strasbourg, which had the special privilege of appointing Poets Laureate, exercised this prerogative with more frequency than discrimination. The form of creation of three Poets Laureate by the Chancellor of the University of Strasbourg, in 1621, was as follows :—

" I create you, being placed in a chair of state, crowned with laurel and ivy, and wearing a ring of gold, and the same do pronounce and constitute, POETS LAUREATE, in the name of the Holy Trinity, the Father, Son, and Holy Ghost.   Amen."

The French have styled some of their early poets *Regal* —Ronsard for instance—but they never created a distinct office, or granted a pension, which omissions have given rise to some amusing epigrams.

During the Middle Ages a curious institution existed in France, called the *Floral Games*, which filled the poetry of that nation with allegorical images drawn from floral and botanical subjects. These poetical contests were originated, or revived, about 1498 by Clementina Isaure, Countess of Toulouse, and the games took place annually in the very appropriate month of May. In the gardens of the Luxembourg Palace at Paris there is a fine statue of this lady, who is styled "Clemence Isaure, *Fondatrice des Jeux Floraux.*"

The Countess published an edict which assembled all the poets of France to display their talents under the inspiring shade of artificial arbours, dressed with flowers; and he who produced the best poem was rewarded with a violet of gold. There were also several inferior prizes made of silver.

The conquerors were crowned with natural chaplets of their own respective flowers, each one choosing his titulary flower, which was supposed to act as his inspiring genius in the regions of Parnassus. During the ceremony degrees were also conferred. He who had won a prize three times was created a *Docteur en gaye science*, for so the poetry of the Provençal Troubadours was denominated. The instrument of creation was in verse. This fantastic institution soon became common throughout France, and these romantic rewards, supposed to be distributed with the most impartial attention to merit, infused a slight emulation which tended in some measure to revive the languishing genius of French poetry.

The City of London had for many years an officer entitled the *City Poet*, whose talents were to be devoted to the interests of the metropolis, and the glorification of its Mayors. The following is a list of some of the principal holders of the office :—

	BIRTH.	DEATH.
John Heywood	—	1565
George Peele	1552	1598
John Webster	Early part 17th century	
Thomas Middleton	1570	1626
Anthony Munday...	1554	1633
Ben Jonson	1573	1637
Thomas Dekker	—	1641
John Taylor (the Water Poet) ...	1580	1654
John Tatham	—	1658
John Ogilvy	1600	1676
Thomas Jordan	Middle of 17th century	
Matthew Taubmann	—	1685
Elkanah Settle	1648	1724

It will be seen that the City Poets were many of them men of considerable genius. Heywood, Webster, Peele, Ben Jonson, Middleton—notable as dramatists—and Thomas Jordan, a very prolific author, who for many years wrote the City Pageants, and Odes on the appointment of the Lord Mayor.

Elkanah Settle, the last of the City Poets, was the author of *A Panegyric on the Loyal and Honourable Sir George Jefferies, Lord Chief Justice of England*, 1683—at whose name people shudder even now. Settle died in 1724, and is chiefly worthy of recollection in connection with Pope's witty lines, descriptive of Lord Mayor's Day a century and a half ago. The bitter satire of the sixth line has probably never been surpassed, not even by Pope himself :—

> " 'Twas on the day when Thorold, rich and grave,
> Like Cimon, triumph'd both on land and wave

(Pomps without guilt, of bloodless swords and maces,
Gold chains, warm furs, broad banners, and broad faces),
Now night descending, the proud scene was o'er,
But lived, in Settle's numbers, *one day more;*
Now mayors and shrieves all hush'd and satiate lay,
Yet eat, in dreams, the custard of the day;
While pensive poets painful vigils keep,
Sleepless themselves to give their *readers sleep*."

The last lines refer to the yearly panegyric upon the
Lord Mayors, which it was the poet's duty to compose;
but that part of the show being at length frugally
abolished, the employment for a City poet was at an end,
and no successor to Settle was appointed.

From very ancient records it appears that the old Scan-
dinavian nations not only had royal bards, but that the
Irish and Welsh kings were constantly attended by their
poets. By some rules dating from 940, it is shown that
the bards of the Welsh kings were domestic officers, to
each of whom the king allowed a horse and a woollen
robe, and the queen a linen garment. Amongst other
curious fees and immunities attached to the office of royal
bard mention is made of the following:—

" The Governor of the Castle was privileged to sit next to him in
the hall, on the three principal feast days, and to place the harp in
his hand, and on those days the poet was to receive the steward's
robe as a fee. The bard was to sing a song in the queen's chamber
if desired ; he was to have an ox or a cow from the booty taken
from the enemy ; and when the king's army was in array, he was to
sing the song of the British kings. When invested with the office
the king was to present him with a harp (according to some authorities the gift was a chessboard) of the value of 120 pence, and the
queen was to give him a ring of gold. When the king rode out of
the castle, five bards were to accompany him ; if the poet asked a
favour, or gratuity of the king, he was fined an ode or a poem ; if
of a nobleman or chief, three ; if of a vassal *he was to sing him to
sleep*."

Rejoice ye shades of Eusden and of Tate! The Welsh
bards were early connected with the Irish, and so late as
the eleventh century continued to receive instruction from
them. In 1078 Gryffith ap Conan, King of Wales, placed
the bards under certain rules and restrictions, and drew up
very stringent laws for their protection. Thus whoever
even slightly injured a bard was fined six cows and 120
pence, and the murderer of one of these highly-prized
individuals was to be punished by the enormous fine of
120 cows. It is easy therefore to understand the horror
and indignation which the wholesale slaughter of their
bards by a murderous English king must have caused to
the Cambrian people.

Many of the regulations for the Irish poets were of a
similar character, and all point strongly to the high favour
in which they were held; it was considered an act of
sacrilege to seize their estates, even in times of the
greatest national distress, and to kill a bard was the most
heinous of crimes. In those parts of Britain most subject
to Roman rule, many of these old national customs fell
into disuse, and soon became obsolete, but in those districts where the Celtic element predominated, the bards
retained much of their old ascendency, long after the
order of the Druids was extinct. The Welsh, favoured by
the inaccessibility of their country, were able to preserve
many customs, which Englishmen and Scotchmen, constantly invaded and harassed by various foreign powers,
were unable to retain; their bardic festivities were
observed by the Welsh until a comparatively late period,
whilst their language, one of the oldest and purest in
Europe, survives to the present time, the practise of it
being zealously encouraged by numerous respectable and
intensely national societies.

Concerning Ossian, it is impossible here to enter into the controversy which Macpherson's version created, but there seems little room to doubt that some portions of these poems were composed by old Gaelic bards, orally preserved, handed down by tradition, and dating from a very early period.

The origin of the definite office, or title, of Poet Laureate in England, is involved in considerable obscurity ; most writers on the subject have contented themselves with the very meagre information contained in Selden's work on *Titles of Honour*, and few have been able to add anything really reliable to what is contained in that book.

The learned John Selden's remarks on the subject contain mention of several poets whose liveliest works will be more fully noticed in a future chapter. The following is an abstract of his account of the office :—

He commences with an account of the manner in which the ceremony of investing a poet with the laurels was performed at Strasbourg in 1616, by Thomas Obrechtus, the Count Palatine. Joannes Paulus Crusius, the recipient, attended at the time and place appointed by the public proclamation of the Count, and the assembly being full, Crusius commenced the proceedings by the recital of a petitioning epigram.

The Count followed with a long oration in praise of the art of poetry, and concluded by addressing Crusius in Latin. The poet thereupon recited a poem of 300 verses, on a subject chosen by himself. These verses were called in the ceremony of the creation, *specimen pro impetranda Laurea.*

Obrechtus then displayed his patent as Count Palatine received from the Emperor, citing from it the power conferred upon him of creating Poets Laureate. An oath of allegiance to the Emperor and his successors was then administered to Crusius, after which the Count Palatine crowned him with laurels, and proclaimed him *Poetam et Vatem Laureatum.* A gold ring was placed upon his finger, and the Count made a speech, exhorting Crusius to uphold the dignity conferred upon him. Crusius replied in another poetical recitation expressive of his thanks, upon which the ceremony ended.

In his remarks about the office, Selden says that in the German empire the custom of giving crowns of laurel to the poets had been in use about 150 years, and was either performed by imperial authority under the Emperor's own hand, or by the Counts Palatine, or by others having the necessary authority. They were crowned with the branches of the tree of their old patron Phœbus. The first poet laureate of Germany was Conradus Celtes Protuccius, who was created by Frederick III. This laureate afterwards received a patent from Maximilian I., naming him Rector of the College of Poetry and Rhetoric in Vienna, with power to confer the laurels on approved students. In later times the title was so lavishly and indiscriminately bestowed as to bring it into great ridicule.

Selden next states that he had met with no example of the laureation of poets in France, but gives a description of the crowning of Petrarch at Rome. As the later Roman Empire derived its custom of crowning its poets from the old Roman ceremony, so England probably received the idea of creating laureates from the later empire.

John Skelton had the title of laureate under Henry VIII., and at the same time Robert Whittington, " Grammaticæ magister et protonates Angliæ in florentissima Oxoniensi Academia Laureatus." Under Edward IV. one John Kay, dedicates his " Siege of Rhodes " to the king, calling himself " his humble poet Laureate." And

John Gower, a famous poet under Richard II., has his statue in St. Mary Overy Church crowned with ivy mixed with roses. Selden concludes his rambling account of the origin of the office thus:—"And thus have I, by no unreasonable digression, performed a promise to you my beloved BEN JONSON. Your curious learning and judgment may correct where I have erred, and adde where my notes and my memory have left me short.

You are—

> "Omnia Carmina doctus
> "Et calles Mython plasmata et Historiam,"

and so you both fully know what concerns it, and your singular excellence in the art most eminently deserves it."

Thomas Warton, who, in his recondite history of English poetry gives much valuable information about the office and its early holders, is the next authority to be consulted.

Warton says that the title of Poet Laureate was certainly a distinction originally conferred by the universities for skill in Latin versification; poetical merit in the vulgar tongue was entirely beside the question. From time immemorial there had been a dependent in the royal household called the King's Poet, or King's Versificator. Little information can be obtained concerning the persons who first held this appointment, although the names of several men, who under our Norman kings acted as bards, are mentioned. Warton says that the Poet Laureate to the kings of England is undoubtedly the same that was styled the *King's Versifier*, and to whom one hundred shillings were paid as his annual stipend in the year 1251; but when or how that title commenced, and whether this officer was ever solemnly crowned with laurel at his first investiture, both Selden and Warton have left undetermined.

It is certain that the holders of the ancient title of *Versificator* wrote their poems in Latin; thus, Gulielmus Peregrinus, royal poet to Richard I., accompanied his master to the Crusades, and sang his achievements in a Latin poem, which he dedicated to Herbert, Archbishop of Canterbury, and Stephen Turnham, a warrior in the expedition. He was living about the year 1200; and Robert Baston (who died in 1310), held the same appointment under Edward II., who carried him to witness the siege of Stirling Castle, upon which operation Baston composed a poem in Latin hexameter verse; but being unfortunately captured by the Scotch, they compelled him to write a panegyric on Robert Bruce, which he also performed in Latin, and in similar metre, a noteworthy instance of poetical tergiversation.

Chaucer and Gower were but self-styled laureates; nor is it till the reign of Edward IV. that we come to an officially appointed laureate, as it is said John Kay was, although it seems doubtful whether his appointment might not also have been a university degree. It is extraordinary that he should have left no poetry to prove his pretensions in some degree to this office, with which it is said he was invested by the king on his return from Italy. The only composition he has transmitted to posterity is a prose translation of a Latin history (written by the Vice-Chancellor of the Knights of Malta) of the Siege of Rhodes. This quaint old book was printed by Caxton in 1490, and is excessively rare; it was entitled "*The Dylectable Newesse and Tythynges of the Gloryous Victorye of the Rhodjans agaynst the Turkes.* Translated from the Latin of G. Caoursin by *Johan Kaye (Poete Laureate). W. Caxton, Westminster.*" The dedication runs thus:—

" To the most excellente—most redoubted, and most crysten king ;
King Edward the fourth, Johan Kay hys humble poete laureate and
most lowley servant : kneyling unto the ground sayth salute."

Considerable confusion has been created on the subject
of early laureations in consequence of certain degrees in
grammar which were anciently granted at the universities
(but more particularly at Oxford); on those occasions a
wreath of laurel was presented to the new graduate, who
was afterwards usually styled *poeta laureatus*. From the
Oxford University registers it appears that on the 12th
March, 1511, Edward Watson, student in grammar, obtained the laurels on the condition that he should compose
a Latin poem in praise of his university. In the following
year Richard Smyth obtained the same dignity, with the
proviso that he should affix 100 Latin hexameter verses to
the gates of St. Mary's Church. Maurice Byrchenshaw,
another laureate, was desired to write the same number of
verses, and to promise not to read Ovid's *Art of Love*
with his pupils. These scholastic honours appear to have
given rise to the appellation *Poeta laureatus*, poet laureate, and Warton enumerates several instances of the
recipients of this title at Oxford. Amongst other less
known names, he mentions John Skelton, who was laureated about 1489, and in the year 1493 was permitted to
wear his laurel at Cambridge :—

" Nay, Skelton wore the laurel wreath,
And passed in scholes ye knoe."

Robert Whittington was honoured with the university
laurel in 1512, and was the last recipient of a rhetorical
degree at Oxford. He wrote some panegyrics on Henry
VIII. and Cardinal Wolsey, but it is very doubtful
whether he was ever royally appointed a poet laureate.

There is, however, no doubt that Andrew Bernard

derived the title and pension direct from the Crown about 1486, and it is no small proof that the officer was expected to be a good Latin poet, that all the pieces written by Andrew Bernard, in the character of Poet Laureate, are in Latin, although he held the office as late as the reign of Henry VII.

However our English language was then in a transition state, and Hallam says that all letters, even of a private nature, were written in Latin by the English till the beginning of the reign of Edward I. soon after 1270, when a sudden change brought in the use of French.

This was not altogether a matter of fashion, being rendered necessary by the great diversity of dialect and spelling that existed. An historian writing in 1380 says, "Hit semeth a grete wonder that Englyssmen have so grete dyverste in their owin langage in sowne, and in spekyin of it, which is all in one ilonde." And it appears that men of different counties frequently spoke such dissimilar dialects as to be unable to converse intelligibly together so late as the reign of Elizabeth.

Warton is of opinion that it was not customary for the Royal Laureates to write in English, until the reformation had begun to diminish the veneration which had hitherto been felt for Latin, and a better sense of things had taught our poets to cultivate the mother tongue which Spenser and Shakespeare found sufficient for their uses.

Although there exist no historical records of the origin of the appointment, there are many paragraphs in the elder poets recognising its existence; it seems probable, however, that until the time of Bernard very little regularity was observed, either in the use of the title, or the pecuniary emoluments which accompanied it.

From the appointment of Bernard to that of Ben

Jonson a series of laureates held office, often without pension, and usually without any definite or legal form of creation.

Ben Jonson's predecessors are therefore generally styled the *Volunteer Laureates*—a title which Savage assumed many years afterwards, much to the annoyance of Colley Cibber—to distinguish them from those who have received Royal Letters Patent.

Since the first grant of Letters Patent to Jonson in 1619 to the present day, we have had an unbroken race of officially appointed and pensioned poets laureate; of their duties, pay, and perquisites, more will be said hereafter. Our laureates have never been solemnly crowned in public, as has been the custom in some foreign countries, nor have any examinations ever been held to inquire into the fitness of persons for the post. Being a Court appointment, political feeling more than poetical taste has generally influenced the selections; and it is a somewhat singular fact that two of the greatest poets who have held the appointment—Dryden and Southey—never would have obtained it, had they not previously been guilty of the most complete and shameless political apostasy.

It will be seen that the list of those who have borne the laurels in England contains many familiar and honoured names, and also includes a few authors whose works are unknown to the general reader. In the few instances where the literary merit of a laureate has been very inferior, some interest is attached to the history of the individual in his connection with the office, and it is hoped that the following remarks may draw attention to works now greatly neglected, containing much historical information, many passages of quaint and amusing description, wit of the keenest, humour of the driest, and poetry of the most fanciful. Even those laureates whose writings are most contemned have been the cause of wit in others; to them it is we owe the finest satirical poems in the language: *Mac Flecknoe* and *The Dunciad, The Rehearsal,* and some of the wittiest passages in *English Bards and Scotch Reviewers ;* thus the names of a Tate, Eusden, or a Pye will be preserved for ever, like flies in amber—

> " The things, we know, are neither rich nor rare,
> But wonder how the devil they got there."

Several of our laureates have enjoyed considerable fame during their lifetime for poems of only ephemeral interest; others there are, whose works have now become obsolete in style and language; while it will be seen that a few have owed their appointment entirely to the influence of patrons, regardless of their fitness for the post.

The official duties were always light; they consisted in the composition of an ode to the Sovereign on his, or her, birthday, another on New Year's Day, and an occasional poem to celebrate important national events, written entirely at the poet's option both as to the subject and his treatment of it. Since Southey happily ceased to perform even these small services, the office has remained a complete sinecure, for although Mr. Tennyson has written a few Court poems, they have appeared at long and most irregular intervals. This fact is scarcely to be regretted when we remember what Whitehead says of the Laureate who

> " Obliged by sack and pension,
> Without a subject or invention,
> Must certain words in order set,
> As innocent as a gazette—
> Must some meaning half disguise,
> And utter neither truth nor lies,"

Having thus given an outline (necessarily an imperfect one) of the origin of the office of poet laureate, the biographical accounts of its holders will now follow, commencing with the *Volunteer Laureates.*

It is not intended to enter into detailed criticisms of their poetical works, nor to weary the reader with a too minute inquiry into the ordinary events of that every-day life which a poet must lead, in common with lesser mortals. The particular points to which attention will be drawn, are those relating to the poets' connection with the office, and the events marking their tenure of it ; the literary attacks they were subjected to, the envy, malice, and detraction they had to bear, illustrated by numerous satirical epigrams and curious lampoons which have never yet been collected together.

THE VOLUNTEER LAUREATES.

" Ev'n now, confess'd to my adoring eyes,
  In awful ranks thy gifted sons arise.
  Tuning to knightly tale his British reeds,
  Thy genuine bards, immortal Chaucer leads :
  His hoary head o'erlooks the gazing quire,
  And beams on all around celestial fire."
  T. WARTON.—*The Triumph of Isis.*

GEOFFREY CHAUCER, the ornament of the Courts of Edward
III. and Richard II., was born in London about 1328. There
is some doubt at which of the universities he studied, but
Warton claims him for Oxford. In the *Court of Love,* Chaucer
speaks of himself as of *Cambridge,* clerk ; this, whilst no
proof that he was educated at Cambridge, might be
admitted as an argument that he did not study at Oxford.

He went with the invading army of Edward III. to
France, and was taken prisoner at the siege of Retters in
1359. On regaining his liberty he travelled into Italy,
where he was introduced to Petrarch at a wedding party,
at which Froissart the chronicler was present, and most
probably Boccaccio also.

He had held some minor court appointments under
Edward III., to whose son, John of Gaunt, he was dis-
tantly related by marriage, and in 1368 he was appointed
Gentleman of the Privy Chamber, with a grant of twenty

marks, equal to a little more than £200 of our present coinage. He was afterwards made Comptroller of the Customs of Wine and Wool in the Port of London, and received a pitcher of wine daily from the royal table, an allowance which was commuted by Richard II. for a pension of twenty marks granted by letters patent.

Having adopted the doctrine of Wickliffe, he fell under the displeasure of the Court, was imprisoned, and had to dispose of both his pensions of twenty marks each, in 1388, but having renounced his heretical doctrines, and exposed his confederates, he regained the favour of the king. He held at various times the office of Clerk of the King's Works in the Palace of Westminster, in the Royal Manors of Shene, Kennington, Byfleet, and Clapton, and in the mews at Charing; in 1380 he superintended the restoration of St. George's Chapel, Windsor. He finally retired to the Royal Manor of Woodstock (on which Blenheim House now stands) where he gave himself up to literary pursuits, and composed *The Canterbury Tales*, which have delighted so many generations of his countrymen. Many of Chaucer's fables are derived from *Il Decamerone* of Boccaccio; he has somewhat improved them by putting them into verse; he has preserved all the indelicacy of the originals, but it must not be forgotten that our forefathers were an outspoken race of men, and that much of the language they generally used would be considered very coarse by the superfine superficials of to-day, who know nothing of the origin and development of our modern English, which may truly be said to have lost in vigour in almost every instance where it has gained in refinement on the Chaucerian dialect. As pictures of life in England 500 years ago Chaucer's writings are invaluable to the student, and he merits the deepest reverence of every lover of English literature, as the first writer of any pretension who adopted the mother tongue for his poetry, and proved incontestably that it admitted of great descriptive power, noble expression, and keen wit.

The deeply-seated love for Chaucer's works is evidenced by the numerous societies constantly occupied in the elucidation of the circumstances of his life, and of doubtful passages in his poems. Unfortunately for the general reader his wit and gaiety are much dimmed by the obsolete dialect, and antique orthography. Notwithstanding all the keys and glossaries which have been written, Addison justly remarks:—

> " Long had our dull forefathers slept supine,
> Nor felt the raptures of the tuneful nine,
> Till Chaucer first, a merry bard, arose,
> And many a story told in rhyme and prose ;
> But age has rusted what the poet writ,
> Worn out his language and obscured his wit :
> In vain he jests in his unpolish'd strain,
> And tries to make his readers laugh in vain."

Although neither Chaucer, nor his successor, Gower, was officially appointed Laureate, it is certain the former used the title until his death, when Gower assumed it. Chaucer died in London on the 25th October, 1400, and was buried in the great south cross aisle of Westminster Abbey, which has since fitly been called Poet's Corner, and is now crowded with the monuments of men who have adorned the language which Chaucer called into existence. In 1555 one Nicholas Brigham, an Oxford student, deposited the bones of Chaucer under a new tomb, which he erected at his own cost, and inscribed with a new epitaph, in the chapel of Bishop Blase in the Abbey (or St. Peter's Church, as old writers always style it): this tomb still exists.

SIR JOHN GOWER was born in Yorkshire about 1320, and was of good family and possessions. He was a member of the Inner Temple, and it is said by Leland that he was made Chief Justice of the Court of Common Pleas, but this is very doubtful. Like his friend Chaucer, he was an adherent of the Lancaster branch of the Royal Family, by whom he was befriended. His greatest work, a moral, metaphysical, and sententious poem, is divided into three parts, which are called *Speculum Meditantis, Vox Clamantis,* and *Confessio Amantis,* only the last being in English.

Richard II., meeting Gower rowing on the Thames near London, invited him into the Royal barge, and after much conversation requested him to *book some new thing.* In compliance with this request Gower composed the *Confessio Amantis,* or *Lover's Confession,* which was first printed by Caxton in 1483. The remainder of his writings have never been printed for public use, although the Roxburgh Club printed his sonnets (fifty in number) in 1818. Gower's style is more serious and didactic than Chaucer's, with a greater affectation of learning, and his treatment of even the most lively subjects is solemn and sedate.

Gower died in 1402. He went totally blind some years before his death; he was buried in St. Mary Overy, Southwark, where his monument still remains in tolerably good preservation.

Of JOHN KAY, Poet Laureate to Edward IV., nothing more is known than what has already been related in the introduction. The only work of his now extant is the translation of the *Siege of Rhodes.*

ANDREW BERNARD (better known as "Master Bernard, the Blind Poet"), a native of Toulouse, and an Augustine monk, was successively Poet Laureate to Henry VII. and Henry VIII. He was also Historiographer Royal, * and preceptor in grammar to Prince Arthur, the elder brother of Henry VIII. In an instrument dated November 1486 the King granted a salary of ten marks to Andrew Bernard, Poet Laureate, until he can obtain some equivalent appointment. He afterwards received several ecclesiastical preferments, and was made Master of St. Leonard's Hospital at Bedford. In accordance with the traditions of the office, all the poems he wrote as *Laureate* are in Latin. They consist of "An Address to Henry VIII. for the Most Auspicious Beginning of the Tenth Year of His Reign;" "An Epithalamium on the Marriage of Francis the Dauphin of France, with the King's Daughter;" "A New Year's Gift for the Year 1515;" and some Latin hymns. His most important prose work was a history, which he brought down to the time of the capture of Perkin Warbeck.

JOHN SKELTON, a very remarkable individual, and most original writer, was born about 1460, as is supposed, in Norwich. He was of a good family, which came originally from Armathwaite, in Cumberland. After a course of study at both the Universities, he proceeded to Louvain, where he was created one of the University Laureates.

---

* The offices of Poet Laureate and Historiographer Royal were subsequently held conjointly by several authors, as in the case of Dryden, and afterwards Shadwell. The office of Historiographer has frequently been unoccupied. Thomas Rymer, the celebrated antiquary, succeeded Shadwell, being appointed on 23rd December, 1692. G. P. R. James, the novelist, who died in 1860, was Historiographer Royal for several years.

He received the like honour from Oxford about the year 1489 :—

> " At Oxford, the University,
> Advanced I was to that degree ;
> By whole consent of their Senate,
> I was made Poet Laureate."

He was also permitted to wear a special robe of white and green, the king's colours, decorated with gold and silk embroidery, the name of the poetical muse being worked upon it, as appears from his own description :—

> " Why were ye, Calliope,
> Embroider'd with letters of gold ?
> SKELTON LAUREATE, ORATOR REGIUS,
> Maketh this answer :—
> Calliope,
> As ye may see,
> Regent is she of poets all,
> Which gave to me
> The high degree
> Laureate to be of fame royal.
> Whose name enrolled
> With silk and gold
> I dare be bold thus for to wear.
> Of her I hold,
> And her household,
> Though I wax old
> And somewhat sere,
> Yet is she fain,
> Void of disdain,
> Me to retain
> Her serviture.
> With her certain
> I will remain
> As my souverain
> Most of pleasure."
>
> *Maulgré touz malheurs.*

Although he was principally famous in his time as a classical scholar, his powerful satirical writings in the vernacular were extremely popular with the lower orders, especially as they were mainly directed against the vices, luxury, and oppression of the priesthood, at a time when public opinion was being strongly agitated about the corruptions and malpractices of the Roman Catholic clergy.

Notwithstanding Skelton wrote thus, he was himself ordained a priest in 1498, and presented to the living of Diss in Norfolk, but in this position his open and fearless attacks upon the monks and friars could not long pass unnoticed.

With something of the wit of Rabelais, and all his scurrility and coarseness, he not only ridiculed the superstition and hypocrisy of priestcraft in his writings and conversation, but ventured at length to preach against them from the pulpit. For this conduct he was severely censured by Nykke, Bishop of Norwich; it has been stated that he was suspended and imprisoned, but this is not known with any certainty.

He next attacked Cardinal Wolsey in a poem entitled "Why come ye not to Court," which contains bitter censures on the pomp, and overweening pride, of the powerful cardinal.

Orders were given for the arrest of Skelton, who only escaped imprisonment by taking shelter in the Sanctuary of Westminster, where he was kindly entertained by Abbot Islip.

"Why come ye not to Court," contains the following passage, descriptive of Cardinal Wolsey's behaviour at the deliberations in the Star Chamber, which Shakespeare may have had in his mind when he drew his splendid delineation of the great prelate :—

> " In the Chamber of Stars
> All matters there he mars ;
> Clapping his rod on the board
> No man dare speak a word,
> For he hath all the saying
> Without any renaying ;
> He rolleth in his records,
> He saith, How say ye, my lords ?
> Is not my reason good ?
> Good even, good *Robin Hood !*
> Some say yes, and some
> Sit still as they were dumb ;
> Thus thwarting over them
> He ruleth all the roast ;
> With bragging and with boast ;
> Borne up on every side
> With pomp and with pride.
> To kepe his flesh chaste
> In Lente, for his repaste
> He eateth capons stewed,
> Pheasant and partridge mewed ;
> Spareth neither maid nor wife,
> This is a 'postle's* life !"

In another part of the poem he openly prays :—

> " God save his noble grace,
> And grant him a place
> Endless to dwell
> With the devil of Hell !
> For I undertake
> He would so brag and crack
> That he would then make
> The devils to quake !"

---

* An apostle.

Well might Southey say of him—

" The power, the strangeness, the volubility of his language, the audacity of his satire, and the perfect originality of his manner, made Skelton one of the most extraordinary writers of any age or country."

In Percy's *Reliques of Ancient English Poetry* will be found an elegy on Henry, the fourth Earl of Northumberland.   It has a Latin preface, and is headed—

" *Poeta Skelton Laureatus libellum suum metrice alloquitur.*"

" *Skelton Laureat upon the dolorous dethe and much lamentable chaunce of the moost honorable Erle of Northumberlande.*"

This nobleman, whilst endeavouring to raise a subsidy demanded by the avaricious Henry VII., was murdered by the enraged populace, in his house at Cocklodge, near Thirsk, in Yorkshire, April 28, 1489.   The poem is very interesting, both from its literary merits, and from the remarkable picture it gives of the feudal pomp and ceremonies of the time in which it was written :—

> " He was envyronde aboute on every syde
> Withe his enemys, that were stark mad, and wode ;
> Yet whils he stode he gave them woundes wyde ;
> Alas for routhe ! what thouche his mynde were goode,
> His corage manly, yet ther he shed hys bloode !
> All left alone, alas ! he fawte in vayne ;
> For cruelly amonge them ther he was slayne."

Skelton may be considered one of the earliest of our dramatic authors.   He wrote " *The Nigramansir* (Necromancer), a morall interlude and a pithie, plaid before the king on Palme Sunday," and " Magnificence, a goodlie interlude and a merrie, devysed and made by Myster Skelton, Poet Laureate," also " *Necromantia*, a Dialog of the Poete Lucyan, for his fantasye faynd for a mery pastyme, and furst by him compiled in the Greeke tongue, and after translated oute of Greeke into Latin, and oute of Latin into Englysh, for the erudicion of them which be disposed to lerne the tonges."

In *The Crowne of Laurell*, Skelton attempted a higher style of poetry, and both for subject and treatment it is considered his best poem, although the allegory is somewhat tedious. He describes the palace of Fame with its thousand gates, and introduces the *poets laureate*, or learned men of all nations, assembled before *Pallas*. The list shows the authors, ancient and modern, who were most admired in Skelton's time. They are—Quintilian, Theocritus, Hesiod, Homer, Cicero, Sallust, Ovid, Lucian, Statius, Persius, Virgil, Juvenal, Livy, Ennius, Aulus Gellius, Horace, Terence, Plautus, Seneca, Boethius, Maximian, Boccaccio, Quintus Curtius, Plutarch, and Petrarch, the catalogue is closed by Gower, Chaucer, and Lydgate, who first adorned the English language, in allusion to which part of their characters, their apparel is said to shine beyond the power of description, and their tabards to be studded with diamonds and rubies. That only these three English poets are here mentioned may be considered as a proof that only these three were yet thought to deserve the name, and Skelton concludes the description of their gorgeous apparel with the words, " They wanted nothing but the Lawrell."

Skelton had been tutor to Prince Henry, by whom, when he came to the throne as Henry VIII., he was made Royal Orator, and many of his Latin poems are inscribed :—

"*Per Skeltonida, Laureatum, oratorem regium.*"

He remained in the Sanctuary, at Westminster, until his death, in June, 1529. He was buried in the Church of St. Margaret's, Westminster; the following epitaph was placed over his tomb :—

> *Joannes Skeltonus,*
> *Vates Pierius, hic situs est.*

Much of the odium Skelton incurred may be ascribed to the bitter religious feuds of the troubled time in which he lived, and to the active share he took in bringing about the Reformation. Added to this was the fact that although a priest, he was married and had a child. The most licentious conduct would have been easily pardoned by his brother priests, but to break the rule of the Church by entering into matrimony was held a more heinous crime than the breach of all the ten commandments. The *Quarterly Review*, speaking of the Rev. A. Dyce's edition of *Skelton*, remarks that Pope's well-known couplet—

> " Chaucer's worst ribaldry is learned by rote,
> And *beastly Skelton* Heads of Houses quote,"

is not altogether just. Skelton, especially in his gay and frolicsome mood, is, no doubt, occasionally indelicate, but with none of that deep-seated licentiousness which taints some periods of our literature; and the laureate of those days may fairly be allowed some indulgence for the manners of his time, when, to judge from the letters of Henry VIII. to Anne Boleyn, there was no very fine sense of propriety even amongst the highest of the land. And as to the gross epithet which Pope has associated with his name, he deserves it far less than Pope's own bosom friend. There is more " beastliness " in a page of Swift than in these two volumes of Skelton. There is, in truth, a very whimsical analogy between these two clerical personages. Skelton must fill a very considerable place in every history of our literature. As a poet he cannot be ranked high; yet, with the exception of the love sonnets of Surrey and Wyatt, he is the only English verse writer between Chaucer and the days of Elizabeth who is *alive*. Of late years much of the prejudice against Skelton has been explained away, and that he possessed a poetical fancy, combined with much sweetness of expression, may be seen by a perusal of *Merry Margaret*, an exquisite little poem, particularly when we consider the rugged language and coarse style then in use. It commences—

> " Merry Margaret, as midsummer flower,
> Gentle as falcon, or hawk of the tower ;
>> With solace and gladness,
>> Much mirth and no madness,
>> All good and no badness.
>>> So joyously,
>>> So maidenly,
>>> So womanly,
> Her demeanour in everything,
> Far, far, passing, that I can indite,
>> Or suffice to write,
> Of merry Margaret, as midsummer flower,
> Gentle as falcon, or hawk of the tower."

The most remarkable features of Skelton's poetry are his marvellous ear for rhyme, the keenness of his satire, the correctness of his descriptions, and the humorous gaiety of his narratives. He was also celebrated for the numerous specimens he composed in that strange jumble of Latin, French, and English, known as *Macaronic* verse ; these are now only interesting to the enthusiastic student of the curiosities and frivolities of literature. Shortly after his death a small volume appeared, entitled " *Merry*

Tales, newly imprinted and made by Master Skelton, Poet Laureate." It is very doubtful whether Skelton really wrote them ; for, being known as the wit of the time, his name was probably thought a good recommendation for a jest book. The first tale relates to Skelton, and is a fair specimen of the quaint humour of the period :—

" TALE I.

" *How Skelton came late home to Oxford from Abingdon.*

" Skelton was an Englishman, born as Scogan° was, and he was educated and brought up at Oxford, and there he was made a Poet Laureate. And on a time he had been at Abingdon to make merry, where he had eat salt meats ; and he did come late home to Oxford, and he did lie in an inn named the 'Tabard,' which is now the ' Angel,' and he did drink and went to bed. About midnight, he was so thirsty and dry, that he was constrained to call to the tapster for drink ; and the tapster heard him not. Then he cried to his host, and his hostess, and to the ostler for drink, and no man would hear him. ' Alack !' said Skelton, ' I shall perish for lack of drink ! What remedy ? ' At the last he did cry out, and said ' Fire ! fire ! fire ! ' when Skelton heard every man bustle himself upward, and some of them were naked, and some were half asleep and amazed, and Skelton did cry ' Fire ! fire ! ' still, that every man knew not whither to resort. Skelton did go to bed, and the host and hostess, and the tapster with the ostler did run to Skelton's chamber with candles lighted in their hands, saying, ' Where, where, is the fire ? ' ' Here, here, here,' said Skelton, and pointed his finger to his mouth, saying, ' Fetch me some drink to quench the fire, and the heat, and the dryness in my mouth ; ' and so they did.

" Wherefore it is good for every man to help his own self in time of need with some policy or craft, so be it there be no deceit or falsehood used."

The orthography of the above extract has been modernised for the greater convenience of the reader.

---

* Alluding probably to Henry Scogan, poet to Henry IV.

RICHARD EDWARDS, who held various Court appointments in the early years of Queen Elizabeth's reign, acted as Court poet, and has by some been styled laureate. He was born in Somersetshire, about 1523, and studied at Corpus Christi, Oxford; he afterwards became member of Lincoln's Inn. In 1561 he was appointed a gentleman of the Royal Chapel and master of the singing boys there. He was the author of the first English tragedy upon a classical subject, *Damon and Pythias*, which was acted before Elizabeth by the boys of the Royal Chapel, and of a play called *Palamon and Arcite*, which was played before the Queen in Christ Church Hall, Oxford, in 1566. He also wrote some poems, published in 1573, in a collection called *A Paradise of Dainty Devices*. In a word, as Warton says, he was the "first fiddle, the most fashionable sonneteer, the readiest rhymer and the most facetious mimic of the Court."

Thus his chief popularity appears to have been due to his pleasing natural gifts, by which, of course, posterity is in no way benefited; but one little poem of his is still well known, as from its simple beauty and pathos it deserves to be. It is founded on the maxim of Terence :—

"Amantium Iræ amoris integratio est,"

and narrates a train of thought arising from the little incident told in the first verse :—

"In going to my naked bed, as one that would have slept,
I heard a wife sing to her child, that long before had wept.
She sighed sore, and sang full sweet, to bring the babe to rest,
That would not cease, but cried still, in sucking at her breast.
She was full weary of her watch, and grieved with her child,
She rocked it, and rated it, until on her it smil'd ;
Then did she say, 'Now have I found the proverb true to prove,
The falling out of faithful friends renewing is of love."

This has been set to music, and is one of the most beautiful and popular of our old madrigals.

Edwards died in, or about 1566 ; the following extract is from an elegy to his memory, written by George Turberville:—

> " Ye learned muses nine, and sacred sisters all,
>   Now lay your cheerful cithrons downe
>   And to lamenting fall.
> For he that led the daunce, the chiefest of your traine,
>   I meane the man that Edwards hight,
>   By cruell dethe is slaine.
>   Ye courtiers chaunge your cheere,
>   Lament in wasteful wise ;
>   For now your Orpheus has resignde,
>   In clay his carcas lies.
> Oh ruth ! he is bereft, that, whilst he lived here,
>   For poet's penne and passinge wit
>   Could have no Englishe peere."

Edmund Spenser.

> Sage Spenser waked his lofty ray
> To grace Eliza's golden sway,
> O'er the proud theme new lustre to diffuse,
> He chose the gorgeous allegoric muse,
> And call'd to life old Uther's elfin tale,
> And rov'd thro' many a necromantic vale,
> Portraying chiefs that knew to tame
> The goblin's ire, the dragon's flame,
> To pierce the dark enchanted hall,
> Where Virtue sate in lonely thrall.
> From fabling Fancy's inmost store
> A rich romantic robe he bore ;
> A veil with visionary trappings hung,
> And o'er his virgin-queen the fairy texture flung."
>   T. Warton.   *Ode to the King*, June 4th, 1787.

Spenser was born about 1553, in East Smithfield, near the Tower of London.

" At length they all to merry London came,
  To merry London, my most kindly nurse,
  That to me gave this life's first native source ;
  Though from another place I take my name,
  An house of ancient fame."

Although his parents were in humble circumstances, they were related to several good families, to whose influence Spenser was probably indebted for much of the Court favour he eventually obtained.

From a curious manuscript in the possession of Colonel Towneley, it appears that he was a scholar at the Merchant Taylors' School :—

" Gownes given to certeyne poor schollers of the Schools about London, in number 32, vizt. St. Paul's, Merchant Taylors', St. Anthony's Schole, St. Saviour's Grammar Schole, and Westminster Schole."

First on the list of the scholars of Merchant Taylors who had gowns is Edmund Spenser, and another entry records the gift of ten shillings.

" April 28, 1569. To Edmund Spenser, scholler of the Merchante Taylors' schollers at his gowinge to Pembroke Hallin Cambridge, x. s."

From this fact, and his being a sizar at Cambridge, it is evident that he was in straightened circumstances, which is further shown by a note, dated—

" Nov. 7, 1570. To Richard Laugher and Edmonde Spenser, two poore scholars of Pembrock Haule, vj. s. a peace, in the whole xij s., by the hands of Mr. Thomas New, fellow of the same house."

He " proceeded B.A." in 1573, and " commenced M.A." in 1576. There appears to have been some unpleasantness between him and the college authorities; he was not elected to a fellowship, but quitted Cambridge after he had taken his master's degree.

On leaving college, he went to reside in the north of

England for some time, but being unsuccessful in a love suit, he came to London, where he obtained the valuable friendships of the noble Sir Philip Sidney, and the powerful Earl of Leicester.

In an age when interest was all-powerful, a man with such patrons was not likely to remain long without a Court appointment, and Spenser soon obtained the post of secretary to Lord Grey, Lord-Deputy of Ireland. In 1581 he was named Clerk to the Irish Court of Chancery, and received a grant from the Crown of the lease of the Abbey of Enniscorthy, County Wexford. But in less than a year Spenser made over this property to a man named Synot, and returned to England. This step he is supposed to have taken from poverty; restless, extravagant, and grasping, ever obtaining grants from the Crown, he was yet always poor, and always complaining. It must however be remembered, that in those turbulent times, life in Ireland could not have been very enjoyable for an Englishman, and must have been little better than exile to a man of Spenser's temperament.

In 1586, a few months before the death of his kind friend Sidney, Spenser obtained a second grant of land in Ireland, consisting of a portion of the estates forfeited by the Earl of Desmond, for treason. This property consisted of upwards of 3,000 acres of land, with the Castle of Kilcolman, in the county of Cork, held at a small rental, on the conditions of personal residence and cultivation of the estate. Whilst he resided at Kilcolman, he was visited by Sir Walter Raleigh, and there he wrote the first portion of that work which was to make his name for ever famous.

The first part of *The Faerie Queene* was published in 1590, and was thus dedicated

" To the most high, mightie and magnificent Empresse, renowned for pietie, vertue, and all gratious government, ELIZABETH, by the Grace of God Queene of Englande, Fraunce and Ireland, and of Virginia,"

as was also the second edition.

Much of the allegorical machinery of the poem was obviously designed to flatter the Queen, and her vanity prompted her to reward the poet with a grant of £50 a year, commencing in February, 1591, and in *Piers Penni-lesse*, 1590, he is spoken of as the new laureate.

But such a man as Spenser was sure to have enemies as well as friends at Court; amongst these was the astute Lord Burleigh, who was opposed to the political party by whom Spenser was protected and befriended.

When, therefore, the Queen informed Burleigh of her intention to pension the poet, he scornfully remarked, " What; all this for a rhyme?" to which Elizabeth evasively replied, " Then give him what is reason!" The conversation was repeated to Spenser by some good-natured friend, and after he had waited a considerable time for his allowance, he handed the Queen a little epigram on the subject :—

> " I was promised on a time
> To have reason for my rhyme ;
> But from that time unto this season,
> I have had nor rhyme nor reason."

The hint had the desired effect, the pension was paid, and this fact is the only justification for styling Spenser the " Court Poet," as he never received the grant of a title, nor does he appear to have assumed one, as some of his predecessors had done.

In *Mother Hubberd's Tale*, Spenser wrote some bitter lines about the cares of a courtier's life, which certainly came with a bad grace from one who owed all his success

in life to Court patronage ; for in those days authorship was
but a pastime, not a profession.   Whatever heartburnings
other hangers on at courts may have experienced, Spenser
surely had no right to cry :—

> " So pitiful a thing is suitor's state !
> Full little knowest thou that hast not tried
> What hell it is in suing long to bide :
> To lose good days that might be better spent,
> To waste long nights in pensive discontent :
> To speed to-day, to be put back to-morrow ;
> To feed on hope, to pine with fear and sorrow ;
> To have thy princes grace, yet want her peers ;
> To have thy asking, yet wait many years ;
> To fret thy soul with crosses and with cares ;
> To eat thy heart through comfortless despairs ;
> To fawn, to crouch, to wait, to ride, to run,
> To spend, to give, to want, to be undone."

Spenser's querulous disposition is little qualified to add
to our admiration for him as a poet, and his contemporaries
mention his character with something akin to contempt.
Phineas Fletcher sarcastically remarks :—

> " All his hopes were crossed, all suits denied ;
> Discouraged, scorned, his writings vilified ;
> Poorly, poor man, he lived ; poorly, poor man, he died."

The first two lines of course are purely ironical.   Yet
the man who wrote so pitifully of his treatment at
Court, was always encroaching on his neighbours' rights
at home, with whom he was frequently embroiled in law-
suits ; his harshness to the poor on his estate caused him
to be bitterly hated by them, and shows him to have been
deficient in that tenderness of heart which might have
atoned for his littleness of character.

The dislike he had inspired bore bitter fruit, for when
Tyrone's rebellion broke out in 1598, Kilcolman Castle
was one of the first houses to be sacked and burnt.

Spenser, with his wife and two children, escaped with difficulty, but one little child perished in the flames; yet, notwithstanding this fearful retribution, it is recorded that for many years afterwards Spenser's memory was held in detestation in the neighbourhood.

Spenser returned to London in sorrow and ill-health, and died a few months later in King Street, Westminster, on the 16th January, 1599, and was buried with considerable ceremony in Westminster Abbey, by the side of Chaucer. His funeral was attended by the most eminent poets of the day, and the expenses were defrayed by the Earl of Essex.

A monument was erected to his memory by the Countess of Dorset in 1620; this was repaired by the authorities of his college in 1788, when certain errors in the dates were rectified.

Spenser's *Faerie Queene* (although incomplete) so far eclipses his other poetical works, that they run the risk of being nearly forgotten, numerous and beautiful though they are. Amongst them is a pastoral elegy on Sir Philip Sidney, and an "Epithalamium" on his own courtship and marriage.

The following beautiful sonnet contains a train of thought eminently characteristic of the poet, whose greatest successes appear to have been always embittered by a tinge of discontent, or blended with some bitterness :—

> " Sweet is the Rose, but growes upon a brere ;
> Sweet is the Junipere, but sharpe his bough ;
> Sweet is the Eglantine, but pricketh nere ;
> Sweet is the Firbloome, but his braunche is rough ;
> Sweet is the Cypresse, but his rynd is tough ;
> Sweet is the Nut, but bitter is his pill ;
> Sweet is the Broome-flowre, but yet sowre enough ;
>   And sweet is Moly, but his root is ill.

> So every sweet with soure is tempred still ;
> That maketh it be coveted the more ;
> For easie things that may be got at will,
> Most sorts of men doe set but little store :
> 　　Why then should I accoumpt of little paine
> 　　That endlesse pleasure shall unto me gaine ! "

Amongst his prose works is a " Discourse on the State of Ireland," which was not published until long after his death. It contains much that is considered sound political economy, although it advocates the exercise of arbitrary power, in such a manner as had, in his own person, led to bloodshed and ruin.

> " A silver trumpet Spenser blows,
> 　And, as its martial notes to silence flee,
> From a virgin chorus flows
> 　A hymn in praise of spotless Chastity.
> 'Tis still !　Wild warblings from th' Æolian lyre
> Enchantment softly breathe, and tremblingly expire."
> 　　　　　　　　　　　　　　　　　KEATS.

SAMUEL DANIEL, who was called the *Atticus* of his day, was Volunteer Laureate during the early years of the first James's reign.　He was born near Taunton in Somersetshire in 1562, and was educated at Magdalen Hall, Oxford.　He resided at Wilton, under the patronage of the Countess of Pembroke, and afterwards became tutor to the Lady Anne Clifford, daughter of the Countess of Cumberland, and seems to have been a general favourite with the nobility.　He was considered one of the most virtuous and honourable men of the time, and enjoyed the friendship of Spenser and Jonson.　He was Gentleman Extraordinary, and one of the Grooms of the Privy Chamber to Queen Anne, wife of James I.　Daniel wrote a *History of England to the reign of Edward III.,* a poem on the *Civil Wars* (Ben Jonson remarks of this *there is not one battle in the book*), and some minor poetical effusions; whilst for the entertainment of the Court he wrote the following masques and tragedies:— *The Tragedie of Cleopatra,* 1599; *The Tragedie of Philotas,* 1605; *The Queen's Arcadia,* acted at Christ Church, Oxford, August, 1605; *Tethy's Festival, or the Queen's Wake,* acted at Whitehall, June 5th, 1610; *Hymen's Triumph;* and *The Vision of the Twelve Goddesses.*

In the composition of *Masques,* a peculiar style of entertainment then much in fashion at Court, he was at length quite eclipsed by the superior genius and wit of his rival Ben Jonson, who possessed greater dramatic art. Daniel therefore quitted the Court in some disgust about three years before his death. Ben Jonson was then appointed Laureate, and, as if to add to Daniel's chagrin, received a settled pension. Daniel whilst Court poet had received no direct income from that post, and was naturally displeased that Jonson should not only take this title during his lifetime, but should also receive the grant of a special pension.

When he took his leave of poetry he alluded in his closing address to the labours of his past life, by which he had endeavoured to improve the tastes and morals of the age, and to the fact of having outlived his popularity, and being obliged to give way to younger men. He died at Beckington, near Philip's Norton, on October 13th, 1619, and was buried in the church of that parish.

Coleridge speaks of him as " the admirable Daniel," and indeed all writers concur in his praise, Ben Jonson, his powerful rival, not excepted, who remarked " that he was a good, honest man, had no children, and was no poet;"

the latter part of the sentence is, however, totally in-
applicable to the author of the following beautiful

Sonnet on Sleep.

" Care-charmer Sleep, son of the sable night,
   Brother to Death, in silent darkness born,
Relieve my anguish, and restore the light,
   With dark forgetting of my care, return.
And let the day be time enough to mourn
   The shipwreck of my ill-advised youth ;
Let waking eyes suffice to wail their scorn,
   Without the torments of the night's untruth.
Cease, dreams, the images of day-desires,
   To model forth the passions of to-morrow;
Never let the rising sun prove you liars,
   To add more grief, to aggravate my sorrow.
Still let me sleep, embracing clouds in vain,
   And never wake to feel the day's disdain.

Whilst the following lines, extracted from his tragi-
comedy, *Hymen's Triumph*, show that although Daniel
may not have possessed the power of creating strong
dramatic situations, he could at least write poetry well
worthy of the age in which he lived, and of being remembered in this :—

Ulysses and the Syren.

SYREN.

Come, worthy Greeke, Ulysses, come,
   Possesse these shores with me,
The windes and seas are troublesome,
   And here we may be free.
Here may we sit and view their toyle
   That travaile on the deepe,
Enjoy the day in mirth the while,
   And spend the night in sleepe.

ULYSSES.

Faire nymphe, if fame and honour were
    To be attained with ease,
Then would I come and rest with thee,
    And leave such toiles as these.
But here it dwels, and here must I
    With danger seek it forth ;
To spend the time luxuriously
    Becomes not men of worth.

SYREN.

Ulysses, O, be not deceiv'd,
    With that unreall name.
This honour is a thing conceiv'd,
    And rests on other fame.
Begotten only to molest
    Our peace, and to beguile
(The best thing of our life) our rest,
    And give us up to toyle.

ULYSSES.

Delicious nymphe, suppose there were
    Nor honour, nor report,
Yet manlinesse would scorne to weare
    The time in idle sport :
For toyle doth give a better touch
    To make us feel our joy ;
And ease findes tediousness as much
    As labour yeelds annoy.
    ❋   ❋   ❋   ❋   ❋   ❋

Daniel was the last of the Volunteer Laureates, for although Michael Drayton has been sometimes called by that title, he does not appear to have had any just claim to it.

Ben Jonson, who succeeded Daniel, held the office by virtue of Royal Letters Patent, and with him, therefore, commences the history of the officially appointed Poets Laureate.

THE POETS LAUREATE.

BEN JONSON,

(1619—1637.)

" Then Jonson came, instructed from the school,
　To please in method, and invent by rule,
　His studious patience and laborious art,
　By regular approach essay'd the heart ;
　Cold approbation gave the lingering bays,
　For those who durst not censure, scarce could praise.
　A mortal born, he met the gen'ral doom,
　But left, like Egypt's king, a lasting tomb."

Dr. Johnson.

OF the early life of Ben Jonson (or Johnson, as his name was then commonly spelt) but little is known, except that he was the posthumous son of a minister of the Reformed Church, and was born in 1573 (Gifford says 1574, but this is probably an error), in Hartshorn-lane, Charing-cross.

He was educated at Westminster School, under Master Camden, the antiquary, whence, it is said, he proceeded for a short time to St. John's, Cambridge, of which circumstance, however, the College books make no mention. His step-father, Thomas Fowler, was a bricklayer by trade, and Jonson appears to have served a short apprenticeship under him; but as it is said that he was seen in the exercise of his trade, building the garden wall of Lincoln's

Inn, Chancery-lane, with a trowel in one hand and a copy
of Virgil in the other, it is highly probable that he was
but an indifferent workman with bricks and mortar,
whatever success he may have attained with his pen. It
is evident that the building trade was not to his taste,
for he quitted it very shortly, and went as a Volunteer
to the army then serving in Flanders, where he distinguished himself by his bravery in the field; and
although but a youth, he slew an enemy in single
combat, and bore off his arms as trophies, a circumstance to which he afterwards referred with pride, in
the lines

To True Soldiers.

" Strength of my country, whilst I bring to view
Such as are miscalled captains, and wrong you
And your high names, I do desire that hence
Be nor put on you, nor you take offence.
I swear by your true friend, my muse, I love
Your great profession, which I once did prove,
And did not shame it with my actions then,
No more than I dare now do with my pen."

Unfortunately for Jonson, his courageous disposition
was accompanied by an obstinate pugnacity, impatience of
contradiction, overbearing pride, and great self-assertion—
an unlucky combination of qualities to which he owed
most of the misfortunes he experienced in a rough and
stormy life.

Gifford, in his memoir, somewhat softens down these
harsh outlines by remarking " that Jonson, far from being
vindictive, was one of the most placable of mankind. He
blustered, indeed, and talked angrily, but his heart was
turned to affection : his enmities appear to have been short-
lived, whilst his friendships were durable and sincere."

On his return from the army, he directed his attention to the stage, and wrote his first play, *Every Man in his Humour,* which was very successful. It was produced at the Globe theatre, in Southwark, and Shakespeare played a chief part in it. Jonson also tried the boards, but was not at all successful as an actor. About the same period that this comedy was produced, in 1598, Jonson fought a duel with a fellow-actor named Gabriel Spenser, whom he killed, being himself wounded in the encounter.

In Mr. Collier's *Memoirs of Edward Alleyn,* the founder of Dulwich College, he inserts a letter from " Philip Henslowe to Mr. Edward Alleyne, at Mr. Arthure Langworthes, at the Brille, in Sussex," dated the 26th September, 1598, which contains the following remarkable passage :—

" Sence you weare with me I have lost one of my company, which hurteth me greatly, that is Gabrill, for he is slayen in Hogesden fylldes (Hoxton Fields) by the hands of Bengemen Jonson, bricklayer, therefore I wold fayne have a littell of your counsell yf I could."

For this crime he was thrown into prison, and narrowly escaped hanging; whilst thus confined, and in fear of death, his thoughts very naturally turned upon religion, and " taking the priest's word for it," as he said, he became a Roman Catholic, of which church he remained a member for twelve years.

On regaining his liberty, Jonson composed some plays, and many masques and pageants for the court entertainments of James I.; but it was not long before he gave that monarch affront through some unguarded expressions he introduced in the comedy of *Eastward Hoe !*

What were the objectionable passages cannot now be settled with any certainty; whether it was that his expressions were construed into a satire on the lavish patronage the Scotch received from the King, and his courtiers; or whether it was that Jonson ridiculed the indiscriminate sale and granting of knighthoods and baronetcies, which was unpleasant to the King, is a disputed point. But the following speech which occurs in the first scene of the fourth act of *Eastward Hoe!* seems sufficient to explain the displeasure of so arbitrary a man as James :—

" 1*st Gentleman.*—On the coast of Dogges, sir ; y'are i'th Isle o' Dogges, I tell you. I see y'ave been washed in the Thames here, and I believe ye were drowned in a tavern before, or else you would never have toke boat in such a dawning as this was. Farewel, farewel ; we will not know you, for shaming of you. *I ken the man weel ; he's one of my thirty-pound knights.*"

Chapman and Marston, Jonson's co-partners in the work were apprehended, and poor Jonson, with characteristic magnanimity, gave himself up to participate in the punishment of his friends.

They were all three sentenced to have their ears and noses slit, but by the interposition of their friends they escaped this mutilation on their undertaking to mutilate the play by erasing the objectionable passages.

Great were the rejoicings on the liberation of Ben and his friends, and a merry banquet was given in honour of the event, at which Camden and Selden were present.

At the conclusion of this festival, Jonson's mother drank to his health and long life, at the same time producing a packet of poison, which she had intended to have administered to her son and herself, had the barbarous sentence of the court been carried out.

In the course of the next few years Jonson produced the most celebrated of his plays, which made him very popular with the frequenters of the theatre ; in the estima-

tion of the audiences of that time he held a much higher
place than did his friend and patron, Shakespeare. He
was also brought much into notice at Court, from having
composed many masques for the king and nobility.
About 1610, he publicly returned to the Protestant Church,
and at his first communion drank off the whole cup
of wine in token of his hearty reconciliation to his
original religion.

The death of James's eldest son, Prince Henry, in 1612,
caused a cessation of Court entertainments, and during
this period of partial release from his dramatic labours,
he accompanied Sir Walter Ràleigh's son to France, in
the capacity of tutor, a post for which his free social habits
rendered him totally unfit.

Young Raleigh does not appear to have acted in a
gentlemanly manner, for having succeeded in making
Jonson "dead drunk," he had him drawn about the streets
of Paris on a car, with many ill-natured jests at his
expense; and by some biographers it is said he finally
had Jonson carried in a buck-basket to Sir Walter, with
the message that " their young master had sent home his
tutor." But this is an idle tale, as Sir Walter was at
this time a prisoner in the Tower of London. This
brutal frolic Jonson described to Drummond of Hawthornden, whom he visited during a pedestrian excursion
into Scotland in 1618.

But after his return from France, and previous to his
visit to Drummond, Jonson went, in company with Michael
Drayton, to Stratford-on-Avon (early in 1616), and it is
recorded that an exceedingly " merry meeting " with
Shakespeare took place. What a subject for an historical
painting : the big, burly Jonson, dusty and travel-stained,
walking down the quaint, sunny street of old Stratford,

arm in arm with his antiquarian friend, the author of
Polyolbion, whilst the handsome Shakespeare, fresh from
the cool retreat of his study, walks quickly up with out-
stretched hands to welcome them to New Place, where
hearty hospitality awaits them, and a choice bottle of
canary especially for Ben.

> " But that which most doth take my muse and me,
> Is a pure cup of rich canary wine,
> Which is the Mermaid's now, but shall be mine ;
> Of which had Horace or Anacreon tasted,
> Their lives, as do their lines, till now had lasted."

These are the words in which Jonson invited a friend
to supper; but this proof is not needed to show that he
was a hard drinker and a jovial companion, and it is probable that the festivities at New Place were somewhat
more merry than wise. Perhaps Shakespeare's more delicate organisation suffered from slight excesses, which his
more hardened companions entered into without thought,
and survived without pain. Shakespeare died very soon
afterwards of a fever, which Ward, in his *Diary,* distinctly
attributes to the excitement and festivities attendant upon
this visit.

Ben Jonson wrote some pathetic lines on the death of
his old friend, to whose kindness he owed much of his
success in life. The terms " gentle Shakespeare " and
" Sweet Swan of Avon," now generally applied to Shakespeare, first occur in these poems :—

> " This figure that thou here seest put,
> It was for gentle Shakespeare cut."

And,

> " Sweet Swan of Avon ! what a sight it were
> To see thee in our water yet appear,
> And make those flights upon the banks of Thames,
> That did so take Eliza and our James ! "

Whilst Jonson was at Hawthornden, Drummond made notes of much of his conversation, merely for his own satisfaction; his conduct in so doing has been much abused, as being a breach of the laws of hospitality. Drummond, however, had no intention to publish the notes, and those who love the memory of our old authors will easily forgive him, and wish that there had been other Drummonds and Boswells, that we might know more of the thoughts and conversations of such men, for instance, as Spenser, Shakespeare, or Milton.

The following are a few of the heads of a conversation betwixt the famous poet, Ben Jonson and William Drummond, of Hawthornden, January, 1619.

He was a Master of Arts in both Universities. He married a wife who was a shrew, yet honest to him. It was Sir James Murray who accused him to the King in the matter of *Eastward Hoe!* (before alluded to).

He wrote all verses first in prose, as his master, Camden, taught him, and said that verses stood by sense, without either colours or accent. He proceeded to give his opinion of various poets, contemporaries and others, somewhat freely.

Thus, of Shakespeare, "He wanted art, and sometimes sense, for in one of his plays he brought in a number of men, saying they had suffered shipwreck in Bohemia, where there is no sea near by 100 miles."

Drummond, after recording the outspoken opinions of Jonson, adds his ideas of the poet himself, in the following candid sentences:—

" Ben Jonson was a great lover and praiser of himself, a contemner and scorner of others, given rather to lose a friend than a jest ; jealous of every word and action of those about him, especially after drink, which is one of the elements in which he lived ; a dis-a dissembler of the parts which reign in him ; a bragger of some good that he wanted ; thinketh nothing well done but what either he or some of his friends have said or done. He was passionately kind and angry ; careless either to gain or to keep. He was for any religion, as being versed in both ; oppressed with fancy, which had over-mastered his reason, a general disease of many poets. His inventions are smooth and easy, but above all he excelleth in a translation. When his play, *The Silent Woman,* was first acted, there were found verses after on the stage against him, concluding that that play was well named *The Silent Woman,* because there was never one man to say *Plaudite* to it."

In 1616 King James appointed Jonson, Poet Laureate, with an annual salary of 100 marks (equal to about £67), and promised him the reversion of the office of Master of the Revels.

In the same year he published a collection of his plays and poems in a folio volume, entitled *The Works of Benjamin Jonson.* This title was by many considered too pompous, and gave rise to the question :—

" Pray tell me, Ben, where does the myst'ry lurk ?
　　What others call a Play, you call a Work,"

which was thus wittily answered :—

" The author's friend thus for the author says ;
　　Ben's plays are works, when others' works are plays."

Jonson prudently declined the honour of knighthood, which the King also offered to bestow upon him. With his uncertain and comparatively small income, he felt he could not adequately support the title, whilst as a distinction it was of little value, so indiscriminately had it been disposed of.

He spent much of his time visiting the nobility, probably superintending the performances of his masques.

E

His life at this period was passed in happy alternations of gay conviviality, and peaceful study and composition. His expenditure, it is true, was somewhat improvident; but this was the height of his prosperity, and his friends have admiringly recorded his almost princely hospitality, and open-handed generosity.

As City Poet, Jonson received a pension of one hundred nobles* (value 6s. 8d. each), and the Earl of Pembroke sent him £20 every New Year's Day, to buy books with.

Notwithstanding his extravagant style of living, he formed a valuable library, which was unfortunately destroyed by fire, together with his MSS. of several valuable works, including a life of Henry V., some plays, a grammar of the English language, and an account of his journey into Scotland.

His *Execration upon Vulcan* humorously expresses his vexation at this irreparable calamity :—

> " And why to me this, thou lame lord of fire ?
> What had I done that might call on thine ire ?
> Or urge thy greedy flames thus to devour
> So many my years' labours in an hour ?
> I ne'er attempted, Vulcan, 'gainst thy life ;
> Nor made least line of love to thy loose wife ;
> Or in remembrance of thy affront and scorn,
> With clowns and tradesmen kept thee closed in horn.

---

* Martis Secundo die Septembris, 1628. Hamersly, Mayor, Rep. No. 42, f. 271. "Item—this daie Beniamyn Johnson, Gent., is by this court admitted to be the Citties Chronologer in place of Mr. Thomas Middleton, deceased, to have hold exercise and enioye the same place, and to have and receive for that his service, out of the Chamber of London, the some of one hundred nobles per annum to contynue duringe the pleasure of this court and the first quarters payment to begin att Michaelmas next."

'Twas Jupiter that hurled thee headlong down,
And Mars that gave thee a lantern for a crown.
Was it because thou wert of old denied,
By Jove, to have Minerva for thy bride ;
That since, thou tak'st all envious care and pain
To ruin every issue of the brain ?
Thou might'st have yet enjoyed thy cruelty
With some more thrift, and more variety :
Thou might'st have had me perish piece by piece,
To light tobacco, or save roasted geese,
Singe capons, or crisp pigs, dropping their eyes ;
Condemned me to the ovens with the pies ;
And so have kept me dying a whole age,
Not ravished all hence in a minute's rage."

The death of his patron, James I., reduced Jonson to
the necessity of again writing for the stage, which, it is
evident from many passages in his poems, was a distasteful
task, notwithstanding the great success which had attended
some of his dramatic productions :—

" And since our dainty age,
Cannot endure reproof,
Make not thyself a page
To that strumpet, the stage ;
But sing high and aloof,
Safe from the wolf's black jaw, and the dull ass's hoof."

Of Jonson's plays, his comedies were the most admired,
although several were unsuccessful in acting. His two
tragedies, founded on classical models, cost him much
labour, but were ill-appreciated by the unlearned ; " as it
was never acted, but most negligently played by some, the
king's servants, and more squeamishly beheld and censured
by others, the king's subjects," was printed by Jonson
on the title-page of one of these plays, *The New Inn*,
whose ill success his pride would allow him no other
excuse for.

Dryden says :—

> " Thus Jonson did mechanic humour show,
> When men were dull, and conversation low,
> Then Comedy was faultless, but 'twas coarse,
> Cobb's tankard was a jest, and Otter's horse."

This refers to what have been termed the Comedies of Character, upon which Jonson's fame as a dramatist is chiefly founded; in the allusion to Captain Otter, he has selected a character from *Epicene, or the Silent Woman*, one of the most amusing of Jonson's comedies.

In 1629, when Jonson was distressed by sickness and poverty, Charles I. made him a present of £100, which the poet acknowledged in the epigram commencing :—

> " Great Charles, among the holy gifts of grace
> Annexed to thy person and thy place,
> 'Tis not enough (thy piety is such)
> To cure the called king's evil with thy touch ;
> But thou wilt yet a kinglier mastery try,
> To cure the poet's evil, poverty."

Shortly afterwards he sent the king the following petition, which was acceded to, as Charles raised his pension from 100 marks to 100 pounds, with a tierce of canary :—

> " THE HUMBLE PETITION OF POOR BEN ;
> TO THE BEST OF MONARCHS, MASTERS, MEN,
> KING CHARLES.

> " —— Doth most humbly show it,
> To your Majesty, your poet.

> That whereas your royal father,
> JAMES the blessèd, pleased the rather,
> Of his special grace to *letters*,
> To make all the MUSES debtors
> To his bounty, by extension
> Of a free poetic pension,

A large hundred marks annuity,
To be given me in gratuity
For done service, and to come :
  And that this so accepted sum,
Or dispensed in books or bread
(For with both the MUSE was fed)
Hath drawn on me, from the times,
All the envy of the *rhymes,*
And the rattling pit-pat noise
Of the less poetic boys,
When their popguns aim to hit,
With their pellets of small wit,
Parts of me (they judged) decayed ;
But we last out still unlayed.
  Please your Majesty to make
Of your grace, for goodness sake,
Those your father's *marks,* your *pounds ;*
Let their spite, which now abounds,
Then go on, and do its worst ;
This would all their envy burst ;
And so warm the poet's tongue,
You'd read a snake in his next song."

The warrant by which King Charles increased Jonson's pension is dated March, 1630, and is the first patent regularly issued for the post of Poet Laureate.

It directs that the pension shall be

" Paid out of the said Exchequer, at the Feast of the Annunciation of the Blessed Virgin Mary, the Nativity of St. John the Baptist, St. Michael the Archangel, and the Birth of our Lord God, quarterly, as by the said letters patent more at large may appear. Know yee nowe, that wee, for divers good considerations vs at this present especially movinge, and in consideration of the good and acceptable service, done vnto vs and our said father by the said Benjamin Johnson, and especially to encourage him to proceede in those services of his witt and penn, which wee have enjoined vnto him, and which we expect from him, are graciously pleased to augment and increase the said annuitie or pension of one hundred marks, vnto an annuitie of one hundred pounds of lawful money of England for his life. . . . And further know yee, that wee of our more especial grace, certen knowledge and meer motion, have given and granted, and by these presents for vs, our heires and successors, do give and graunt vnto the said Benjamin Johnson, and his assigns, one terse of Canary Spanish wine yearly ; to have, hold, perceive, receive, and take the said terse of Canary Spanish wine vnto the said Benjamin Johnson and his assigns during the term of his natural life, out of our store of wines yearly, and from time to time remayninge at or in our cellers within or belonging to our palace of Whitehall." Endorsed—*Expl. apud Westm. vicesimo-sexto die Martii anno R. Caroli quinto.*

Dr. Johnson says that this pension of £100 was adequate for the conveniences of life at that time, being the same salary as was paid to the king's physician. But treasury payments in King Charles's days were far from punctual, and the wine which was promised from the royal cellars was often as much in arrear as the pension. Jonson complained of this neglect in some epigrams directed against the king's household, and in one, dated 1630, he says :—

> " What can the cause be, when the king hath given
>   His poet sack, the household will not pay ?
> Are they so scanted in their store ? or driven
>   For want of knowing the poet, to say him nay ?
> Well, they should know him would the king but grant
>   His poet leave to sing his household true ;
> He'd frame such ditties of their store and want,
>   Would make the very Greencloth to look blue ;
> And rather wish in their expense of sack,
>   So the allowance from the king to use,
> As the old bard should no canary lack ;
>   'Twere better spare a butt, than spill his muse.
> For in the genius of a poet's verse,
> The king's fame lives. Go now, deny his tierce !"

These forcible and very uncourtierlike lines were ill adapted for the petition of a suitor, and Jonson did not receive his wine until he had written another epigram in a much more submissive strain.

Towards the close of his career he was associated with Inigo Jones in the production of several Court masques, but the partnership led to a very unkindly feeling between the two artists. A quarrel took place, which, according to some writers, originated in the paltry question of the precedence of names on the title-page of a masque, and Jonson was so ill-advised as to write several bitter lampoons against the great architect, who was then in high favour at Court :—

> " —— Sir Inigo doth fear it, as I hear,
> And labours to seem worthy of this fear,
> That I should write upon him some sharp verse,
> Able to eat into his bones, and pierce
> The marrow. Wretch ! I quit thee of thy pain,
> Thou 'rt too ambitious, and dost fear in vain :
> The Libyan lion hunts no butterflies ;
> He makes the camel and dull ass his prize.
> If thou be so desirous to be read,
> Seek out some hungry painter, that, for bread,
> With rotten chalk or coal, upon the wall
> Will well design thee to be viewed of all
> That sit upon the common draught or strand ;
> Thy forehead is too narrow for my brand."

Jonson's conduct in this affair was more glaringly imprudent than it had ever been, even in the hot-blooded days of his youth, and friends and foes were alike amazed at his intemperate language ; for he was at this time almost entirely dependent on his Court and City pensions for support, and it must be remembered that the masques partook more of the nature of spectacles and pageants than of plays, and that the costumes, decorations, and machinery designed by Jones were probably thought more highly of, than the few verses, songs, and choruses which Jonson composed as a medium for the introduction of Inigo Jones's inventions. Jonson saw his error, and recalled several of the satires; but he was too late in making this *amende*, for Jones had taken deadly offence, and at once brought all his powerful influence to work to ruin his adversary. Many passages in Jonson's poems and plays which were supposed to reflect upon Jones were ordered to be left out, Jonson was dismissed from the Court entertainments, and his pension was stopped. Another misfortune followed shortly afterwards; the City authorities resolved to withhold the annual pension of 100 nobles hitherto paid to Jonson as City Poet. This punishment may also have been brought about through the influence of Inigo Jones, but the motive assigned in the City records is the failure of Jonson to furnish the poetical offerings expected from him :—

"Whitmore, Mayor, Rep. No. 46, *f.S. Jovis decimo die Novembris*, 1631. Item—It is ordered by this Court that Mr. Chamberlen shall forbeare to pay any more fee or wages unto Beniamine Johnson, the Citties Chronologer, until he shall have presented unto this Court some fruits of his labours in that place."

Upon this Ben wrote to the Earl of Newcastle: "The barbarous Court of Aldermen have withdrawn their chanderly pension for verjuice and mustard, 33*l.* 6*s.* 8*d.*"

The City pension was not, however, long withheld, for in September, 1634, it was ordered to be restored, and also "that Mr. Chamberlen shall satisfie and pay unto him his arrerages thereof."

The last years of Jonson's life were embittered by a complication of painful disorders, which compelled him to keep the house, whilst his want of prudence in money matters often reduced him to great distress. His wife had been dead for many years, all his children had died young, and amongst the most beautiful and pathetic of his poems, are his epitaphs to their memory. In his last illness he was tended by a female, whose relationship to him is unknown, although he may have been married a second time ; there is an entry in the register of St. Giles's Church, Cripplegate, of the marriage of Ben Johnson and Hester Hopkins, on the 27th July, 1623, and Mr. Collier suggests that this may have been the poet, a somewhat hazardous assumption, as the name of Johnson was not an uncommon one.

He died on the 6th August, 1637, " in the house under which you pass to go out of the churchyard into the old palace," at Westminster. He was buried in the Abbey, in an upright position, and although a subscription was set on foot to purchase a monument, its erection was delayed by the breaking out of the Civil War. The present medallion in Poet's Corner was set up in the middle of the last century by a " person of quality," whose name was desired to be concealed. By a mistake of the sculptor, the buttons were placed on the left hand side of the coat, hence the following epigram, which is neither very true nor very poetical :—

> " O ! Rare Ben Jonson
>   What a turncoat grown !
>   Thou ne'er wast so
>   Till cut in stone.
>   Then let not this disturb thy sprite
>   Another age shall set thy buttons right."

Ben Jonson's epitaph was a genuine idea, and the result of a happy thought of a friend of Davenant and Suckling. Aubrey says : " Jonson lies buryed in the north aisle in the path of square stone (the rest is lozenge), opposite to the scutcheon of Robertus de Ros, with this inscription only on him, in a pavement square, blew marble, about 14 inches square,

O RARE BEN JONSON,

which was donne at the charge of Jack Young (afterwards knighted), who, walking there when the grave was covering, gave the fellow eighteenpence to cutt it."

In Mr. F. Buckland's *Curiosities of Natural History* there is an account given of the poet's tomb being opened, when his skeleton was found in an upright position, and his skull, still having red hair adhering to it, was carefully replaced.

There is something in Ben Jonson's name suggestive of conviviality, we think of him with "mountain belly and rocky face" in connection with canary and claret, dogmatically yet wittily giving his opinion on his favourite classics, as naturally as we think of the merry Curé of Meudon sitting in his armchair convulsing us with laughter, and surprising us with his learning.

What clubs are to authors in our day, taverns were in Jonson's time, less refined, less luxurious, but probably far more hearty, social, and convivial resorts. Hard drinking was the rule, and many anecdotes are handed down to us of the excesses committed by the wits and poets.

Tradition has preserved a good-humoured account of the first interview, at a tavern, between Bishop Corbet (then a young man) and Ben Jonson. Corbet was sitting alone, and Ben, who had just brought himself up to the "pitch of good fellowship," desired the waiter to "take that gentleman a quart of *raw* wine; and tell him," he added, "I *sacrifice* my service to him."

"Friend," replied Corbet, "I thank him for his love; but tell him, from me, that he is mistaken, for *sacrifices are always burned.*" This pleasant allusion by the young wit to the mulled wine of the time did not fail to win the notice and esteem of the classical old poet.

Some one well acquainted with his habits, wrote an epigram upon his tragedy *Catiline :*—

> " With strenuous sinewy word that Catiline swells
> I reckon it not among men miracles.
> How could that poem heat and vigour lack,
> When each line oft cost *Ben* a cup of Sack ?"

Jonson's favourite haunts were the "Sun and Moon," in Aldersgate-street, and the "Mermaid," in Bread-street, whither also resorted Shakespeare, Fletcher, and Beaumont. The latter poet, writing to Jonson from the country, says :

> " What things have we seen
> Done at the Mermaid ! heard words that have been
> So nimble, and so full of subtle flame,
> As if every one from whom they came
> Had meant to put his whole art in a jest,
> And had resolved to live a fool the rest
> Of his dull life, then, when there hath been thrown,
> Wit able enough to justify the town
> For three days past,—wit that might warrant be
> For the whole City to talk foolishly
> Till that were cancelled ; and when that was gone,
> We left an air behind us, which alone
> Was able to make the next two companies
> Right witty ; though but downright fools, seem wise."

But in after years, and when associated with a younger set of poets, Jonson reigned supreme at the Apollo, the name given to the club held in the "Old Devil Tavern," at Temple Bar; its sign was St. Dunstan pulling the devil's nose.

> " And each true Briton is to Ben so civil
> He swears the muses met him at 'The Devil.'"
> —POPE.

This "Devil Tavern" was the favourite haunt of the wits and lawyers, and the latter placarded their chamber doors with the extraordinary announcement, "Gone to the 'Devil'!" somewhat prematurely, as their clients thought.

VERSES PLACED OVER THE DOOR AT THE ENTRANCE INTO THE APOLLO.

" Welcome all who lead or follow
To the Oracle of Apollo—
Here he speaks out of his pottle,
Or the tripos, his tower bottle :
All his answers are divine,
Truth itself doth flow in wine.
Hang up all the poor hop drinkers,
Cries old Sim, the king of Skinkers ; *
He the half of life abuses
That sits watering with the Muses.
Those dull girls no good can mean us ;
Wine it is the milk of Venus,
And the poet's horse accounted :
Ply it, and you all are mounted.
'Tis the true Phœbian liquor,
Cheers the brains, makes wit the quicker,
Pays all debts, cures all diseases,
And at once the senses pleases.
Welcome all who lead or follow,
To the Oracle of Apollo."

Ben Jonson drew up the *Leges Conviviales* for the guidance of members and visitors ; these rules were in Latin, and were engraved in letters of gold on a black marble slab, placed over the mantelpiece. Aubrey mentions that Mr. Lacy, the player, had seen him at these meetings :—

"That he was wont to weare a coate with slitts under the arm pitts. He would many times exceede in drink ; canarie was his beloved liquor. Then he would tumble home to bed, and when he

---

* Simon Wadloe, the landlord of " The Devil."

had thoroughly perspired, then to studie. Long since, in King James's time, I have heard my uncle Danvers say, who knew him, that he lived without Temple Barre at a combe-maker's shop about the Elephant and Castle. In his later time he lived in Westminster, in the house under which you pass as you go out of the churchyarde into the old palace, where he dyed."

BEN JONSON'S DRAMATIC WORKS.

TRAGEDIES.

Sejanus, His Fall. Acted 1603.
Catiline, His Conspiracy. 1611.
Mortimer's Fall. Unfinished.

COMEDIES.

Every Man in His Humour. Acted 1598.
The Case is Altered. Acted before 1599.
Every Man out of His Humour. Acted 1599.
Cynthia's Revels; or, The Fountain of Self Love. 1600.
Poetaster; or his Arraignment. 1601.
Volpone; or, The Fox. 1605.
Eastward Hoe. 1605. (In conjunction with Chapman and Marston.)
Epicene; or, The Silent Woman. 1609.
The Alchymist. 1610.
Bartholomew Fair. 1614.
The Devil is an Ass. 1616.
The Staple of News. 1625.
New Inn; or, The Light Heart. 1629.
The Tale of a Tub.
The Magnetic Lady; or, Humours Reconciled.
The Sad Shepherd, unfinished.

A number of masques for various Court entertainments on the coronation of King James; the reception of the

King of Denmark ; on the marriage of the Earl of Essex ;
on the marriage of Lord Haddington ; for the entertainment of Monsieur le Baron de Tout, Ambassador Extraordinary from the French king; and for many similar
festivities. The masques themselves are peculiar compositions, which can only be compared to the opening
scenes of modern pantomimes, with, however, many variations.

CHRISTMAS, HIS MASQUE, as it was presented at Court,
in 1616, contains the following characters, who are all to
be suitably attired :—Christmas and his ten children, Mis-
Rule, Caroll, Minc'd Pie, Gamboll, Post and Pair, New
Year's Gift, Mumming, Wassall, Offering, and Baby-Cockee;
Venus and Cupid are also introduced.   These characters
march about and sing ; there is a little dialogue and much
chorus, one verse of which forms a quaint prelude :—

> " Now God preserve, as you well do deserve,
>   Your Majesties, all two there ;
>   Your highness small, with my good Lords all,
>   And *Ladies*, how do you do there ? "

AN ODE FOR BEN JONSON.

> " Ah BEN !
> Say how, or when
> Shall we thy guests
>   Meet at those lyric feasts,
>   Made at the Sun,
>   The Dog, the Triple Tun ?
>   Where we such clusters had,
> As made us nobly wild, not mad ;
>   And yet each verse of thine
> Outdid the meat, outdid the frolic wine."

—HERRICK'S HESPERIDES.

SIR WILLIAM DAVENANT.

(1638—1668.)

" To my Friend Will Davenant."

" Thou hast redeemed us, Will, and future times
Shall not account unto the age's crimes
Dearth of pure wit ; since the great lord of it,
Donne, parted hence, no man has ever writ
So near him, in 's own way.   I would commend
Particulars ; but then, how should I end
Without a volume ?   Every line of thine
Would ask (to praise it right) twenty of mine."

— Sir John Suckling.

Sir William Davenant, who succeeded Ben Jonson as
Laureate, held the office during one of the most eventful
periods of English history, and his life partook of the
successes and reverses of the Royalist party, to which he
was firmly attached.

His works mark the boundary which separates the old
romantic poets from the modern school of writers ; and
his exertions in connection with the Drama changed
the theatre from the condition of a booth at a fair, destitute of actresses, scenery, properties, or comfort, to
the brilliant saloon, having a well-appointed stage, handsome scenery, ingenious machinery, and appropriate properties.

Davenant was born at Oxford, in February, 1605; his father, "a grave, melancholy man," kept the "Crown Inn," at which house Shakespeare occasionally lodged on his journeys between London and Warwickshire. Davenant's mother, who was a beautiful woman of good wit and conversation, was fond of the poet's society, and scandal made so free with her reputation as to assert that Shakespeare was the father of her son.

When some one ventured to speak of James the First as the "modern Solomon" to Henry IV. of France, that monarch replied, "Aye, Solomon the son of David," alluding to Mary Stuart's favourite, Rizzio the musician; and a somewhat similar anecdote is related by Pope of Davenant when a boy. He was running eagerly from school to meet Shakespeare, who was then in Oxford, when he was met by an old townsman, who asked whither he was going so hastily; "To see my Godfather, Master William Shakespeare." "That's a good boy," replied his old friend, "but have a care that you do not take God's name in vain!"

Aubrey relates that Davenant would sometimes, when he was pleasant over a glass of wine with his most intimate friends (one of whom was Sam Butler, the author of *Hudibras*) say, "that it seemed to him that he writ with the very same spirit that Shakespeare did," and was contented enough to be thought his son; adding that Davenant's mother was of "very light report."

Davenant's imitation of the Bastard's conduct in *King John* is ridiculed by Sir Walter Scott, who says, "I think the pretension can only be treated as Phœton's was according to Fielding's farce:—

"'Besides, by all the village boys I'm shamed,
You the sun's son, you rascal? you be damned!'"

But the question is not now to be solved; there is no very great reason to deny Sir William's assertion, for both in person and in genius he more nearly resembled the great poet, than the dull sober old Vintner; and it is certain that he entertained the greatest respect for Shakespeare; one of his earliest poetical efforts was " An Ode in Remembrance of Master William Shakespeare," a loving and appreciative tribute to his memory.

From the grammar-school of his native parish, where he received the rudiments of his education, Davenant proceeded to Lincoln College, he afterwards went to London, and became page to the Duchess of Richmond. Whilst in her service, and subsequently in that of Sir Fulke Greville, Lord Brooke, Davenant acquired that taste for the stage, which never afterwards left him; he also formed friendships with some eminent and powerful men, who aided him in the production of his earliest dramatic compositions.

As these were eminently successful, he was employed to write masques and pageants for the Courts, which were provided with scenery and decorations by Inigo Jones, and in the performances of which the leading courtiers and even the Queen took part.

Brought thus closely in contact with the most refined and intellectual people of the Court, Davenant's wit and gaiety were soon noticed, and made him a general favourite. The Queen exerted her influence to obtain for him the office of Laureate, which since the death of Jonson had been unoccupied, and Davenant received the appointment on 13th December, 1638. His rival, Thomas May, says:—" He continued very steadfast in his old road, adhered to his old principles, and his old friends, writing from time to time new poems, exhibiting new plays, and

F

having the chief direction and management of the Court diversions, so long as the disorders of those times would permit."

But the troubles of the Civil War commenced, the Court and Commons were up in arms, and as Davenant was professionally dependent on the Court, and was known as a staunch Royalist, the Parliament apprehended him; twice he escaped, but was recaptured; he made a third attempt, and succeeded in reaching France. There he placed his services at the Queen's disposal, and greatly assisted her in the energetic efforts she was making in her husband's cause.

In 1643 an expedition was fitted out to assist the Cavaliers, and Davenant was appointed Lieutenant-General of Ordnance; he distinguished himself by his bravery, and received the honour of knighthood for his services at the siege of Gloucester.

But the Royal cause was on the wane. Davenant retired to Paris, residing for some time in the Louvre with his friend Lord Jermyn; he became a Roman Catholic, and devoted his time to his longest and most important poem—*Gondibert.*

In 1650 he again tempted fortune, by organising a scheme to colonise Virginia; but the vessel in which he sailed was captured by the watchful Parliamentary cruisers, and the unlucky poet was conveyed a close prisoner, to Cowes Castle, Isle of Wight, and his character as a determined opponent of the Parliament rendered his position one of the greatest danger. His friends exerted themselves to the utmost on his behalf; but it was specially owing to the intercession of John Milton that Davenant's life was spared,—an obligation he never forgot; and when at a future day the Royalists were in power, and Milton was to be sacrificed for his party, Davenant paid his debt of gratitude by obtaining a pardon for the grand old Republican. Although his life was spared, Davenant spent two years in prison, being removed from the Isle of Wight to the Tower of London.

During his captivity his active mind was occupied by his poem, the first part of which, published in 1651, had been written in the Louvre, from whence the preface was dated, whilst the postscript was given from Cowes Castle, where he was then confined, expecting his immediate execution. He says:—

"I am here arrived at the middle of the third book. But it is high time to strike sail and cast anchor, though I have run but half my course, when at the helm I am threatened with *death;* who, though he can visit us but once, seems troublesome; and even in the innocent may beget such gravity as diverts the music of verse. Even in a worthy design, I shall ask leave to desist, when I am interrupted by so great an experiment as *dying;*—and 'tis an experiment to the most experienced; for no man (though his mortifications may be much greater than mine) can say *he has already died.*"

This poem may be, as D'Israeli asserts, one to delight philosophers, but it is certainly very little suited to modern taste. It was given to the world, with a long and curious commendatory preface by Thomas Hobbes, the great theologian, and was highly praised by Cowley and Waller; the latter says of it:—

> "Thy matchless book,
> Wherein those few that can with judgment look,
> May find old lore in pure fresh language told,
> Like new stamped coin made out of angel gold;

Such truth in love as the antique world did know,
In such a style as courts may boast of now ;
Which no bold tales of gods or monsters swell,
But human passions, such as with us dwell.
Man is thy theme ; his virtue, or his rage,
Drawn to the life in each elaborate page."

But the critics complained that the elaborate panegyric
of Hobbes raised their expectations too high, and the
following epigram was published

Upon the Preface.

" Room for the best of poets heroic
If you'll believe two wits and a stoic.
Down go the *Iliads*, down go the *Æneidos ;*
All must give place to Gontiberteidos.
For to *Homer* and *Virgil* he has a just pique
Because one's writ in Latin, the other in Greek ;
Besides an old grudge (our critics they say so)
With *Ovid*, because his surname was *Naso*,
If fiction the fame of a poet thus raises,
What poets are you that have writ his praises !
But we justly quarrel at this our defeat,
You give us a stomach, he gives us no meat.
A Preface to *no* book, a porch to no house,
Here is the mountain, but where is the mouse ? "

The covert allusion to Davenant's nose is one of the
numerous cruel sarcasms levelled at him in reference to
a personal defect. It is uncertain whether the injury to his
nose was the result of the dissipated life he led, or
whether from the more honourable cause of a wound he
received in battle. Aubrey asserts the former, and all
the satirists follow him, whilst Sir John Mennis, a friend
of Davenant's, has the following equivocal lines on the
subject :—

" For Will has in his face the flaws
    Of wounds received in 's country's cause,
They flew on him, like lions passant
And tore his nose, as much as was on't,
They called him superstitious groom,
And Popish dog, and cur of Rome,
But this I'm sure was the first time
That Will's *religion* was a crime."

Sir John Suckling, in *A Sessions of the Poets*, gives a humorous account of the various authors who apply to Apollo for the laurels. In the poem, which is too long to be given in full, he refers eulogistically to Jonson and Davenant; Apollo is about to bestow the wreath upon the latter, but is deterred by a whimsical question of precedent relating to Davenant's nose :—

" A session was held the other day,
    And *Apollo* himself was there, they say—
The laurel that had so long been reserv'd,
Was now to be given to him best deserv'd.

" Therefore the wits of the town came thither,
    'Twas strange to see how they flocked together,
Each strongly confident of his own way,
That day thought to carry the laurel away.
    *   *   *   *   *   *
" The first that broke silence was good old *Ben*,
    Prepared before with Canary wine,
And he told them plainly he deserved the Bays,
For his were called Works, where others were but Plays ;

" And bid them remember how he had purged the stage
    Of errors that had lasted many an age ;
And he hoped they did not think the *Silent Woman*,
The *Fox* and the *Alchymist* outdone by no man.

" Apollo stopt him there, and bade him not go on,
    'Twas merit, he said, and not presumption
Must carry 't ; at which Ben turned about,
And in great choler offered to go out.

*   *   *   *   *   *   *   *

" *Will Davenant*, asham'd of a foolish mischance
   That he had got lately travelling in *France*,
   Modestly hop'd the handsomeness of 's muse
   Might any deformity about him excuse.

" Surely the company would have been content,
   If they could have found any precedent ;
   But in all their records, either in verse or in prose,
   There was not one Laureate without e'er a nose.

" Suckling next was call'd, but did not appear ;
   But straight one whispered Apollo i' th' ear,
   That of all men living he cared not for 't,
   He loved not the muses so well as his sport,

" And prized black eyes, or a lucky hit
   At bowls, above all the trophies of wit ;
   But Apollo was angry and publicly said,
   'Twere fit that a fine were set upon 's head."

At length Apollo bestows the laurel upon a fat
alderman, and the poem ends in a somewhat abrupt
and unsatisfactory manner.

Until disfigured by the loss of his nose, Davenant had
been considered a very handsome man, he must, therefore,
have been deeply grieved not only by the taunts of his
rivals, but by the insults he received even in the public
streets. Thus having one day refused an old woman
charity, he was surprised to hear her loudly pray heaven
to spare his eyesight. Struck by the novelty of her cant
expressions, he gruffly told her that his eyesight did not
fail him. To which she replied, " that she prayed it never
might, as he had nothing to rest his spectacles upon."

Annoyed at the sarcasms levelled at his book by
frivolous coxcombs, and *soi-disant* wits, and more particularly by an anonymous collection of verses, published
by a club of *The Author's Friends*, as they styled

themselves, Davenant retorted in angry and unguarded language, and brought down upon himself another epigram, entitled

A LETTER SENT TO THE GOOD KNIGHT.

"Thou hadst not thus been long neglected,
But we, thy four best friends, expected,
Ere this time, thou hadst stood corrected ;
But since that planet governs still,
That rules thy tedious fustian quill,
'Gainst nature and the Muses' will ;
When, by thy friends' advice and care,
'Twas hoped, in time, thou wouldst despair
To give ten pounds to write it fair ;
Lest thou to all the world would show it,
We thought it fit to let thee know it ;
Thou art a damn'd insipid poet!"

But Davenant had another failing, which laid him open to the attacks of epigrammatists. This was his desire to be thought of noble descent, for which purpose he adopted a new mode of writing his name,—D'Avenant, as though the D' implied the possession of family estates, in the manner of the old French prefix, *De*.

"Some say by *Avenant* no place is meant,
And that our Lombard * is without descent ;
And as, by *Bilk*, men mean there's nothing there,
So come from *Avenant* means from *nowhere*.
Thus *Will*, intending *Davenant* to grace,
Has made a notch in 's name, like that in 's face."

Towards the end of 1652 Davenant was released from the Tower, and as he had been knighted for services rendered to the Royal cause at the siege of Gloucester, his release by the Parliament, without trial, occasioned

---

* The scene of *Gondibert* is laid in Lombardy.

some surprise. The offence of having held arms, with distinction, against the Commonwealth was not usually passed over so lightly, and the opportunity for spiteful sarcasms was not lost by his envious brother poets, who wrote various uncomplimentary explanations of the mystery. The epigram *Upon Fighting Will* is one of the best of these attacks :—

> " The king knights Will for fighting on his side ;
> Yet when Will comes for fighting to be tried,
> There is not one in all the armies can
> Say they e'er felt, or saw, this fighting man.
> Strange that the knight should not be known i' th' field,
> A face well charg'd, though nothing in his shield :
> Sure Fighting Will like *basilisk* did ride
> Among the troops, and all that *saw* Will died ;
> Else, how could Will, for fighting, be a knight,
> And none alive that ever saw Will fight ? "

On regaining his liberty, his thoughts reverted to the stage as a means of existence, but the Puritan party, still in the ascendant, looked upon the Drama with horror and disgust, and it was only by much interest and manœuvring that he at length obtained permission to give " entertainments" of a very modified form, resembling slightly the nature of a drama, but still more like a modern opera. The first of these performances took place in May, 1656, at Rutland House, and being successful, was followed by others of a similar description, until the Restoration in 1660.

Shortly after the restoration he obtained a patent from the king for a theatre in Lincoln's Inn Fields, which flourished under the especial patronage of James, Duke of York, and the actors were sworn in by the Lord Chamberlain as the *duke's servants,* in contradistinction to the king's servants, who performed at the Cockpit, in Drury Lane.

In the spring of 1662, Davenant opened his house with the plays of *The Siege of Rhodes* and *The Wits*, having new scenes and decorations, of a kind which, both for novelty and splendour, had never before been seen in England. The performances commenced at three o'clock in the afternoon, and there was an announcement that " notwithstanding the great expense necessary to scenes, and other ornaments in this entertainment, there is a good provision made of places for a shilling."

Here he produced several of his own plays, and, in conjunction with Dryden, remodelled, and it may be said spoilt, *The Tempest, Macbeth,* and *Julius Cæsar.*

> " For Shakespeare's magic could not copied be,
> Within that circle none durst walk but he.''

As a lessee he was obliged to cater for the public, and whatever may be the opinion of modern critics as to his alterations, it must not be forgotten that Davenant was mainly instrumental in reviving a taste for Shakespeare, whose works were then rapidly sinking into oblivion.

Davenant's eventful life was now drawing to a close, at a time when fortune seemed inclined to make some amends to the aged poet for the struggles and reverses of his youth. His theatre was prospering, his pieces were highly esteemed at Court, although his great epic poem was far too intellectual and thoughtful to find many readers amongst the gay, frivolous *entourage* of Charles II.; but his greatest popularity was no doubt amongst the rapidly increasing class of theatre-going people, whose gratitude he had well merited by his constant efforts to increase their comfort, and provide them amusement. He died in Lincoln's Inn Fields, on the 7th April, 1668, and was buried in Westminster Abbey, with every mark of respect and esteem.

"I was at his funeral," says Aubrey; "he had a coffin of walnut-tree. Sir John Denham said it was the finest coffin that ever he saw." On his tombstone was inscribed—

O Rare Sir William Davenant!

but this, like most second-hand compliments, defeats its own purpose, and neither pleases, nor surprises.

Davenant was nominally Poet Laureate for about thirty years, but the political commotions which occurred at the commencement of that term rendered it impossible for him to obtain a regular payment of the pension attached to the office, which he virtually ceased to hold during the Protectorate, when Thomas May was in the ascendant.

In addition to the introduction of movable scenery, the improvement of stage machinery, and the rearrangement of the auditorium, Davenant was the first manager who introduced women on the stage. Female parts had hitherto been played by boys, but as during the Commonwealth the theatres were closed, the trained boys grew into men, and when they came to act again were quite unfitted for the representation of lovely woman.

This fact was humorously alluded to in the prologue written by Thomas Jordan, the City Poet, to introduce the first woman on the stage, in the exceedingly appropriate character, for such an occasion, of the hapless Desdemona :—

A Prologue, to introduce the first Woman that came to act on the stage, in the Tragedy called "The Moor of Venice."

"I came unknown to any of the rest,
    To tell the news ; I saw the lady drest ;

The woman plays to-day ; mistake me not,
No man in gown, or page in petticoat :
A woman to my knowledge, yet I can't,
If I should die, make affidavit on't.
Do you not twitter, gentlemen ? I know
You will be censuring : do it fairly, though ;
'Tis possible a virtuous woman may
Abhor all sorts of looseness, and yet play ;
Play on the stage—where all eyes are upon her ;
Shall we count that a crime, France counts an honour ?
In other kingdoms husbands safely trust 'em ;
The difference lies only in the custom.
And let it be our custom, I advise ;
I'm sure this custom's better than th' excise,
And may procure *us* custom : hearts of flint
Will melt in passion, when a woman's in't.
But, gentlemen, you that as judges sit
In the Star Chamber of the house—the pit,
Have modest thoughts of her ; pray do not run
To give her visits when the play is done,
With, ' *Damn me, your most humble servant, lady ;*'
She knows these things as well as you, it may be ;
Not a bit there, dear gallants, she doth know
Her own deserts,—and your temptations too.
But to the point :—in this reforming age
We have intents to civilise the stage.
Our women are defective, and so sized,
You'd think they were some of the guard disguised ;
For to speak truth, men act, that are between
Forty and fifty, wenches of fifteen ;
With bone so large, and nerve so incompliant,
When you call ' Desdemona,' enter giant.
We shall purge everything that is unclean,
Lascivious, scurrilous, impious or obscene ;
And when we've put all things in this fair way,
Barebones himself may come to see a play.''

Before Davenant introduced this novelty, a laughable
incident drew the king's attention to the necessity for it.

He was one day kept waiting for the play to commence, and sent for the manager to inquire the cause of the delay. "Please, your highness," was the apologetic reply, "the queen is not yet shaved, and she has to come on in the first scene."

In 1662 a clause was expressly inserted in the Royal Letters Patent to license this innovation, which, at first, met with considerable ridicule and opposition :—

"And for as much as many plays, formerly acted, do contain several profane, obscene, and scurrilous passages ; and the women's parts therein have been acted by men in the habits of women, at which some have taken offence ; for the preventing these abuses for the future, we do hereby strictly command and enjoin that from henceforth no new play shall be acted by either of the said companies containing any passages offensive to piety and good manners, nor any old or revived play containing any such offensive passages as aforesaid, until the same shall be corrected and purged by the said masters or governors of the said companies from all such offensive and scandalous passages as aforesaid. And we do likewise permit and give leave that all women's parts to be acted in either of the said two companies for the time to come may be performed by women, as long as these recreations, which by reason of the abuses aforesaid, were scandalous and offensive, may by such reformation, be esteemed not only harmless delights, but useful and instructive representations of human life, to such of our good subjects as shall resort to the same."

Little is known of Davenant's private life, except that it was a dissolute one ; his company was much sought after by the great, and he had the reputation of being a witty and brilliant conversationalist.

He was twice married ; his first wife, Anne, was buried March 5, 1654-5, at St. Andrew's, Holborn ; his second wife, who survived him, was interred in St. Bride's, Fleet Street, as appears from the burial register :—" Burial of widow of Sir William Davenant, Feb. 24, 1690—1. Lady Mary Davenant, old vault, fever."

Had Sir William Davenant lived in a more thoughtful and serious period of our history, it is probable that his *Gondibert* would have received great attention, and its success might have prompted him to further efforts in the same direction. But the Court of Charles the Second could be serious in nothing but vice ; the poem was laughed down, and will probably never be revived, although it contains some fine thoughts, and, strange to say, some passages which are frequently quoted.

In the Duke of Buckingham's celebrated farce *The Rehearsal* the leading character *Bayes* was originally called *Bilboa*, and was meant for a satirical portrait of Davenant, whose plays furnish many of the passages which are so cleverly parodied in this *jeu d'esprit* which gave Sheridan the first idea of *The Critic*.

But the performance of *The Rehearsal* was delayed until the end of 1671, some time after the death of Davenant, so the name of *Bayes* was substituted for *Bilboa*, and the characteristics of John Dryden were ridiculed; but the authors did not like to forfeit the strokes they had levelled at Davenant, to whom alone the well-known incident of the plaster for the nose could apply.

BAYES.—" You talk of time and tune. You shall see me do 't. Look you now ! Here I am dead." (Lies down flat on his face; as he rises up hastily, he tumbles and falls down again).

" Ah ! gadsookers, I have broke my nose. A plague of this damned stage with your nails and your tenter hooks, that a man cannot come here to teach you to act, but he must break his nose, and his face, and the devil and all. Pray, sir, can you help me to a wet piece of brown paper?"—*The Rehearsal*, Act. II., Scene 5.

However when the piece was performed, Lacy, who played *Bayes* mimicked the dull ponderous manner of Dryden in the most unmistakable way, and thus the piece became a kind of patchwork, being partly a satire on Davenant, and partly on Dryden, the plays of both authors being unsparingly parodied and ridiculed.

Mention has already been made of THOMAS MAY, the Parliamentary Historiographer, and although it does not appear that he was appointed to the post of laureate by the unpoetical party to which he was attached, yet, as he may be considered to have occupied the throne during the commonwealth, whilst Davenant was absent, or confined in prison, a few notes on his career are here inserted.

He was of an ancient family and was born in Sussex in 1594. He wrote several plays, but his reputation rests chiefly on his translation of Lucan's *Pharsalia*. He was for sometime in great favour with Charles I. at whose command he published in 1635 a poem in seven books, entitled "The Victorious Reign of Edward III." But Clarendon says that though he received much countenance, and a very considerable donation from the king, he deserted the Court party for that of the Parliament upon His Majesty's refusing to give him a small pension, which he had designed and promised to another very ingenious person. It appears from other authorities that the "pension" alluded to, was the office of queen's poet which May expected to receive but which was given to Davenant.

Fuller also accounts for his desertion of the Court on the ground that "his bays were not gilded richly enough." It does not appear to have occurred to these old writers that a spirit of patriotism might have prompted May, as it did many of the best men of the day, to enlist in the Parliamentary cause. That he was an upright, honourable man is shown by his *History of the Parliament* which valuable record of a singularly interesting period is written with great courage and impartiality, especially noteworthy when it is remembered that he was the secretary and historiographer of that Parliament whose acts he freely and fearlessly enumerates and criticises. May died suddenly on the 15th November, 1650, and was buried in Westminster Abbey. His death was said to have been caused by tying his night cap too tightly under his chin, and he, being very fat, was choked when he turned on his side. On the Restoration his body was removed to St. Margaret's Churchyard, and the monument which had been erected by Parliament to his memory was taken down and thrown aside.

SIR WILLIAM DAVENANT'S DRAMATIC WORKS.

TRAGEDIES.

Albovine, King of the Lombards. 1629.
The Cruel Brother. 1630.
The Just Italian. 1630.
The Platonick Lovers. T. C. 1636.
The Unfortunate Lovers. 1643.
The Fair Favourite. T. C.
The Law against Lovers. T. C.
The Siege. T. C.
The Distresses. T. C.
Macbeth. Altered from Shakespeare, 1674.
The Tempest „   „   „
Julius Cæsar „   „   „

COMEDIES.

Love and Honour.   **1649.**
The Wits.   1665.
The Rivals.   1668.
The Man's the Master.   **1669.**
News from Plymouth.
The Playhouse to be Let.
The Colonel.   Not printed.

There were also several masques; also, *The First Day's Entertainment at Rutland House, by Declamation and Musick, after the Manner of the Ancients,* 1656; and *The Siege of Rhodes, made a Representation, by the Art of Prospective in Scenes; and the Story sung in Recitative Musick, at the Back Part of Rutland House, in the Upper End of Aldersgate Street.* 1656.

JOHN DRYDEN.

(1670—1688.)

> " Waller was smooth ; but Dryden taught to join
> The varying verse, the full resounding line,
> The long majestic march, and energy divine."
>
> A. POPE.

JOHN DRYDEN, who holds the first place in the second rank of our classical poets, was certainly one of the greatest satirists in the language, and the first poet who joined argument with verse—a style of composition which Pope successfully imitated. Living in the stormy days which preceded and followed the Restoration, the revolution which Dryden effected in English literature and taste may be fitly compared to the changes through which our country passed, to emerge, at length, free from the baneful influence and vicious examples of the Stuarts, and richer, purer, and greater for the trials it had endured.

"What was said of Rome," remarks Dr. Johnson, "adorned by Augustus, may be applied by an easy metaphor to English poetry, embellished by Dryden. 'He found it brick, and he left it marble.'" His writings constitute the last of the so-called romantic school of poetry, and the first of the didactic and reasoning style which his pupil and admirer, Pope, brought to the height of polish and refinement. The strength of intellect and power of language—which Dryden possessed to a far greater extent than Pope—is shown as strongly by his prose-writings as by his poetry. The former consist principally of essays on poetry, and criticism in the form of prefaces, and are characterised by the purity of his English, the fitness of every word he uses to its position, and the originality of his style.

He has little or no sentiment, and more humour than wit. His poetry is argumentative or political, seldom fanciful or gay; and scarcely a tender or pathetic passage is to be found in all his poems. His plays (now never performed) are probably but seldom read; yet it must not be forgotten that by his contemporaries they were much admired, and brought him more profit and fame than all his poetry. A new tragedy by Dryden at the King's Theatre was the greatest of all attractions, and king, court, town, and the wits, all flocked to the first day's performance, as we may see by reference to Pepys' chatty "Diary." In comedy he may be said to have failed; he had not the sparkling wit, the power of repartee, or the graceful epigrammatic turn of expression the audiences of those days looked for in comedy, and which they found in the masterpieces of Congreve, Etherege, and Wycherley.

John Dryden was born on the 9th of August, 1631, in the parsonage of the small parish of Aldwincle All Saints, in Northamptonshire. He came of a good family, and this fact, which one would suppose to be of little interest to the general reader, is elaborately detailed in most biographies, with long genealogical notes. Not only is this the case with Dryden, but of every other poet in whose behalf a claim for gentle blood can be put in; as though the name of a Dryden or a Spenser *could* derive any further lustre from the accident of birth. There were various ways of spelling the family name, Dreydon and Dreyden had been in use, but Driden was the most usual form, and the poet adopted that orthography on the occasion of his marriage ; but at all other times he spelt his name—Dryden.

He was first sent to study at Westminster School, where he formed a lasting friendship with the celebrated and severe Dr. Busby.

In May, 1650, Dryden was elected to a scholarship in Trinity College, Cambridge, and took the degree of Bachelor of Arts in January, 1654.

Many years afterwards his rival, Shadwell, accused him of having been nearly expelled—

> " At Cambridge first your scurrilous vein began,
> Where saucily you traduced a nobleman,
> Who, for that crime, rebuked you on the head ;
> And you had been expelled had you not fled."
>
> THE MEDAL OF JOHN BAYES.

But the incident to which these lines refer occurred in 1652, several years before Dryden left the college, and the punishment of being "put out of commons for a fortnight," which is recorded against his name, shows that his crime was not considered a very heinous one.

A few months after he had taken his degree, his father died, leaving a small estate of the annual value of sixty pounds, of which two-thirds came to John Dryden, the remaining third going to his mother, with reversion to him at her death.

Although this income of forty pounds a year was equivalent to about three times the same nominal value in the present day, it was barely sufficient to keep Dryden at college; and the narrowness of his means is the reason usually assigned for his not taking the degree of Master of Arts, the fees of which dignity were very heavy. The degree was, however, afterwards conferred upon him by the Archbishop of Canterbury.

Before he finally quitted Cambridge, he suffered a misfortune which no doubt threw a shade over his future career, and tended to force him into the dissipated, reckless life he afterwards led. His cousin, Honor Driden, daughter of Sir John Driden, was young, beautiful, and an heiress, the poet endeavoured to win her affections, but without success, and the lady died unmarried.

Having resided seven years in Cambridge (which town he very much disliked) he removed to London in the summer of 1657, and was employed in some literary capacity (probably as secretary) by his relative, Sir Gilbert Pickering, one of the most rigid of Puritans, a member of the Protector's Council, and a man of such hasty temper, that he was known as "the Fiery Pickering."

> " The next step of advancement you began
> Was being clerk to Noll's lord chamberlain."

Thus from personal interest, as well as from family ties, Dryden became attached to the Protector's cause, for besides Sir Gilbert Pickering, who held offices under Cromwell, both Dryden's father, and his uncle, Sir John, had displayed great zeal for the Puritan party.

The Protector's death in 1658, whilst it destroyed the power of the great party to which Dryden had attached himself, gave him the subject for his first poem of any pretension, although he had at the age of seventeen written an elegy upon the death of his schoolfellow, Lord Hastings, which, overladen as it is with classical and pedantic allusions, has yet some fine lines. The verses upon the death of Cromwell, however, quickly attracted attention, and they certainly contain indications of his powers of thought and versification; some critics at once pronounced them superior to Waller's poem on the same subject, and most people were of opinion that Sprat's verses were far inferior to Dryden's.

HEROIC STANZAS,

consecrated to the glorious memory of his Most Serene and Renowned Highness, OLIVER, late Lord Protector of this Commonwealth, &c."

The following verses are the most remarkable for their panegyrics upon Cromwell:—

> " His grandeur he derived from heaven alone ;
>   For he was great, ere fortune made him so ;
> And wars, like mists that rise against the sun,
>   Made him but greater seem, not greater grow.
>
> *　　*　　*　　*　　*　　*　　*　　*
>
> " Such was our Prince ; yet owned a soul above
>   The highest acts it could produce to show ;
> Thus poor mechanic arts in public move,
>   Whilst the deep secrets beyond practice go.
>
> " Nor died he when his ebbing fame went less,
>   But when fresh laurels courted him to live :
> He seemed but to prevent some new success,
>   As if above what triumphs earth could give.
>
> *　　*　　*　　*　　*　　*　　*　　*
>
> " His ashes in a peaceful urn shall rest ;
>   His name a great example stands, to show
> How strangely high endeavours may be blessed,
>   Where piety and valour jointly go."

In the last verse the poet was singularly unfortunate in his predictions, for within a few months the Royalists returned, and vented a cowardly and malignant spite on Cromwell, by the exposure of his body upon Tyburn gallows, and his head over the entrance to Westminster Hall.

However, at the time that Dryden penned these verses there was a probability of the Commonwealth continuing under the presidency of Richard Cromwell; but General Monk brought back King Charles, to ornament the throne with his profligacy and extravagance, and amongst the first to hail the happy event was John Dryden, who at once espoused the Royal cause, much to the disgust of Pickering, who being a consistent Republican retired to his estates, leaving Dryden to push his way at Court.

Consequently Dryden's fortune at this period must have suffered some diminution, yet he still had his annuity; by writing to order for the booksellers he added a little to his income, and hoped that by adopting the views of the ruling faction his poetry would become fashionable. But he was as yet comparatively unknown as an author, and Shadwell, referring to Dryden's poverty at this period, says that " he lived in a lodging with a window no bigger than a pocket looking-glass, and dined at a *threepenny* ordinary, enough to starve a vacation tailor," and, again in the *Medal of John Bayes*:—

> " He turned a journeyman to a bookseller ;
> Writ prefaces to books for meat and drink,
> And as it paid, he would both write and think."

Coming from his rival, Shadwell, these lines may be considered as somewhat exaggerated.

Dryden now wrote a poem on the Restoration, entitled, "*Astræa Redux*, a poem on the Happy Restoration and Return of his Sacred Majesty Charles the Second," in which, after insulting the memory of the Protector, and blaming as crimes the very qualities he had previously praised as virtues, he proceeds to enumerate all the noble qualities Charles was supposed to possess, and impiously compares the Restoration to God's guidance of Moses, and Charles to King David, whose crimes, it is but fair to confess, he successfully imitated.

It was about this time that Dryden became acquainted with Sir Robert Howard, son of the Earl of Berkshire, a would-be poet and dramatic author, to whom Dryden addressed some fulsome verses in praise of his poems. They then co-operated in several literary productions; and for some years a close friendship existed between them.

Through his intimacy with Sir Robert, Dryden became acquainted with his sister, the Lady Elizabeth Howard, to whom he was married, on the 1st December, 1663, at St. Swithin's church. The entry of the license is as follows :—

" *Ultimo Novembris,* 1663.

"Which day appeared personally John Driden, of St. Clemt, Danes, in the County of Midd., Esq.,, aged about 30ty yeeres, and a batchelor, and alledged that hee intendeth to marry with Dame Elizabeth Howard, of St. Martin in the Fields, in the County aforesaid, aged about 25 yeeres, with the consent of her father, Thomas, Earle of Berke, not knowing nor believing any impediment to hinder the intended marriage, of the truth of the premisses he made faith and prayed license for them to bee married in the parish church of St. Swithin's, London.

"JOHN DRIDEN."

" Juratus, Hen. Smyth, Jun."

This was, in so far as Dryden was concerned, probably a *mariage de convénance ;* for, although he was of good family, his relatives were out of favour at Court, and therefore his alliance with an influential family was

greatly to his interest.   It is probable, also, that the Earl
of Berkshire made a settlement upon his daughter at her
marriage: Mr. Malone estimates its value as about sixty
pounds per annum.

Scandal had been busy with the lady's reputation, and
a letter is extant, written by the Lady Elizabeth to the
licentious Earl of Chesterfield, proving beyond reasonable
doubt that she had had an intrigue with him before her
marriage.   Her tastes were not coincident with the poet's,
nor were his friends admitted into her circle; she had a
violent temper, and was subject to fits of temporary
insanity, which gradually increased in intensity, until at
length her intellect entirely gave way.

The marriage was, therefore, in every sense an unhappy
one; and had not his wife survived him, Dryden intended
to have placed the following lines on her tombstone :—

> " Here lies my wife ; here let her lie ;
> She's now at rest—and so am I."

and sneers against the married state abound in his plays,
a species of wit much in fashion amongst the authors of
the court of Charles.

Dryden's conduct was not calculated to soften the
asperity of his wife's disposition.   Once, when she complained of the little time he passed in her society, and
expressed a wish that she might have been one of his
favourite books, he churlishly replied, " Well, then, you
should have been an almanac, for then I could change you
every year."   Besides the disparity of dispositions, Dryden
was notoriously profligate.   His connection with the
theatre brought him into the society of actresses at a
period when they were singularly pre-eminent for beauty
and immorality ; and the name of Mistress Ann Reeve is

inseparably connected with that of Dryden in many stinging satires of the day.

Several of Dryden's biographers, in their anxiety to screen the poet, have endeavoured to paint him blameless as a man. Every fact has been warped in order to prove that all his inconsistencies were perfectly disinterested; that the gross immorality of his writings was the fault of the period he lived in, and that his indecency was not improper, because he was contemporary with other writers more indecent than himself; that the profligacy of his life existed only in the lampoons written against him, and any awkward date, or stubborn fact, that jars with these suppositions is either entirely ignored, or explained away in the most sophistical manner. Surely it is possible to admire the *poetry* of Dryden, without seeking to justify its licentiousness, or its sickening adulation of the predominant faction. What need to distort facts with a view of proving Dryden to have been a spotless innocent, and all contemporary writers, liars?

Dryden's first play, the comedy of *The Wild Gallant*, was produced at the King's Theatre in 1663. It was a decided failure; but the king's mistress, Lady Castlemaine, encouraged him with her patronage. In order to further propitiate the lady, he wrote some verses in her praise, in which occur the following lines :—

> " You, like the stars, not by reflection bright,*
> Are born to your own heaven, and your own light ;
> Like them are good, but from a nobler cause,
> From your own knowledge, not from nature's laws.
> Your power you never use, but for defence,
> *To guard your own*, or others' *innocence.*"

---

* Dryden's astronomy seems at fault, as he asserts that the stars do not reflect the sun's light.

The last line is delicious, considering to whom it was applied. Well might Buckingham exclaim :—

> " Dryden, who one would have thought had more wit,
> The censure of every man did disdain,
> Pleading some pitiful lines he had writ
> In praise of the Countess of Castlemaine."

Dryden's next play was a tragi-comedy, entitled *The Rival Ladies*, part of which was written in rhyme, in the so-called heroic style introduced by Davenant; a style which consists in the portrayal of passions of the most violent description, in language so florid, and elevated above nature, as often to be beyond ordinary comprehension.

Most of Dryden's early plays belong to this school, and a somewhat acrimonious controversy arose between him and his friend, Sir Robert Howard, who justly ridiculed the system of rhyming in plays. Dryden maintained his position in his prefaces and poems, and friendly intercourse between the two poets was at an end for a time. Dryden afterwards became a convert to Howard's theory, that prose was the proper vehicle for stage dialogue.

In 1670 Dryden was appointed Poet Laureate and Historiographer Royal. The first office had been vacant since the death of Davenant in 1668, the second since the death of James Howell in 1666. The two appointments were now joined in one patent, dated 18th August, 1670, which conferred a salary of £200 a year, and a butt of canary wine from the king's cellars. As the salary was to be paid to Dryden from Midsummer Day, 1668, he was entitled to a very handsome sum on his appointment. In his hands the post was a mere sinecure, he wrote no Laureate Odes—his *Astræa Redux* and the *Panegyric upon the Coronation of Charles II.* having been written several years before he was invested with the laurels. Taking all the sources of Dryden's income into account, Sir Walter Scott estimates it to have reached £700 a year in 1670—more than equivalent to three times that amount in the present day—and shortly afterwards the official salary was raised to £300 a year, with a pension of £100 a year dependent on the king's pleasure.

It must, however, be borne in mind that King Charles's Exchequer was seldom punctual in its payments, and that at one time Dryden's pay was as much as four years in arrear.

Shortly after his appointment *The Rehearsal* was produced. This clever farce, written by the Duke of Buckingham, in conjunction with Sam Butler, Spratt, and Clifford, unsparingly ridiculed Dryden under the name of *Bayes*, and the actor of the part imitated his personal appearance, mimicked his dull heavy speech in delivering the numerous parodies of passages from his plays, and introduced his favourite oaths and expressions.

Thus it came about that the nick name of *Bayes* was ever after applied to Dryden, until Pope fastened it on Colley Cibber in the *Dunciad*.

Buckingham's dislike for the heroic plays and rhyming tragedies which monopolised the stage had long been known, and when *The Rehearsal* was first written in 1665 he had intended to place Davenant in the poetical pillory, but various circumstances conspired to delay its representation, until long after Davenant's death :—

> " I come to his farce, which must needs be well done,
> For Troy was no longer before it was won,
> Since 'tis more than ten years since this farce was begun."

As might have been expected, great opposition was shown on the first performance, but the town eagerly seized every satirical point, every parody was appreciated, and the farce was a complete success. Dryden's theatrical reputation was, however, too well founded for this satirical effusion to deter him from further dramatic composition. The income he derived from the stage was between £300 and £400 a year; he had a share and a quarter in Killigrew's house, for which he agreed to furnish three plays annually, but he found it impossible to fully carry out this onerous engagement, and had frequent squabbles with the manager in consequence of his breach of contract.

In 1679 an anonymous *Essay upon Satire* appeared, in which Rochester and the king's two mistresses were attacked in some vigorous lines. The authorship of the poem has never been clearly established, although the Earl of Mulgrave, who had had a desperate quarrel with Rochester, was probably its originator, but evidence of Dryden's pen is also found in parts of it; and Rochester, who was highly enraged at the lampoon, hired some ruffians, who set upon Dryden in Rose Alley, Long Acre, on the night of December 18th, 1679, and severely beat him.

Dryden was then living at the house which is now No. 137, Long Acre. Rochester died shortly afterwards; and it does not appear that Dryden obtained any redress for the outrage, although a reward was offered for the discovery of his assailants.

In the very unsettled and anxious times which immediately preceded the death of Charles II., Dryden espoused the party of the Duke of York; and yet, strangely enough, in all his writings at that period, he maintained the cause of the Protestant Church—a course which exposed him to much ridicule and abuse for inconsistency, but which was in reality the only period in his life when his principles prevailed over his interest.

On the death of Charles, he wrote a funeral poem, entitled *Threnodia Augustalis*, in which he impiously exclaims :—

> " False heroes, made by flattery so,
> Heaven can strike out like sparkles at a blow,
> *But ere a prince is to perfection brought*
> *He costs Omnipotence a second thought.*"

During the reign of James II., Dryden was a persistent and bigoted supporter of all the Court measures, and the attempts to reintroduce Popery were powerfully seconded by his poems ; for Dryden had adopted the Roman Catholic religion soon after the accession of James, a fact which Evelyn records in his Diary, alongside with the conversion of Mistress Nell Gwynne, quaintly adding that " such proselytes were no great loss to the Church."

There was no surer way to James's favour than to adopt his religion ; and, undeterred by the recollection of *Religio Laici, The Spanish Friar*, and numerous other writings, containing strong Protestant sentiments and bitter satires of Popery, Dryden adopted the religion of the dominant party, and wrote for it, as wittily, vigorously, and intolerantly, as he had a few months previously written against it.

Whether Dryden became a Papist or remained a Protestant, is now of little consequence, except to explain the startling inconsistencies which appear in his works. For, as Lord Macaulay says,—

" He knew little, and cared little about religion. He had during many years earned his daily bread by pandering to the vicious taste of the pit, and by grossly flattering rich and noble patrons. Self respect and a fine sense of the becoming were not to be expected

from one who had led a life of mendicancy and adulation. Finding
that if he continued to call himself a Protestant his services would
be overlooked, he declared himself a Papist.''

The poet's apologists deny that love of pay or place
influenced his perversion, and assert that the persuasions
of his wife and eldest son effected the change. But
Dryden had been for many years estranged from his wife,
and his son, brought up principally under her care, was a
mere boy, an undergraduate at Cambridge in 1686, the
year of Dryden's conversion.

It is extremely improbable, therefore, that these persons
effected so great and sudden a change on such a worldly,
calm, and calculating mind as Dryden's. But the very
first link in the chain is wanting, for it is only *suspected*
that Lady Elizabeth was at that time a Roman Catholic,
because her brother was one, and there is not the slightest
ground for the assertion that Charles Dryden was a Papist
before his father became one.

It has also been asserted that the pension was re-
granted to Dryden before his change of religion took
place. A few dates will disprove this : Charles II. died
in 1685, and for a year the extra pension of £100, which
was in reality a *personal* gift from Charles to Dryden, was
in abeyance. In January, 1686, Evelyn records Dryden's
proselytism, and on March 4, 1686, letters patent were
issued granting Dryden an additional pension of £100
a year, to date from the beginning of the reign, and it is
absurd to suppose that a man so parsimonious as James
was, should suddenly have resumed the payment of a
lapsed pension without some sufficient cause, such as was
to be found in Dryden's well-timed conversion.

It is certain that James did not act so generously
towards the other pensioners of his brother, and when on

his accession it was necessary to draw up new letters-patent for the offices of Poet Laureate and Historio-grapher, he was so economical as to cause the annual butt of canary to be omitted from the perquisites of the office, at which time it must be remembered Dryden was a Protestant. It was necessary to examine these facts at some length, not so much with a view of showing that Dryden changed his religion to gain a pension of £100 a year, as to expose the fallacious arguments used by his apologists in excusing an action which would require no apology, could we only believe it to have been sincere.

But the man who had alternately eulogised Cromwell, and welcomed the Restoration *à gorge déployée;* who had been a Puritan when young, then a staunch supporter of the Church of England, and finally became a Papist; who was ever ready to adapt himself to the party of the day, and to become a violent partisan of the most powerful faction, cannot well be deemed sincere in adopting a religion he had always ridiculed, at a time when such a change was exactly coincident with his interest.

In 1683 Dryden had been appointed collector of the Customs in the Port of London, and this grant was also renewed by James.

The publication in 1687 of the *Hind and Panther* openly announced his conversion. This poem, which Dr. Johnson calls "an allegory intended to comprise and to decide the controversy between the Romanists and Protestants" gave rise to some of the bitterest satires that were ever directed against Dryden. The most celebrated of these was a parody entitled *The Country and City Mouse,* written by Prior and Montague; and Shadwell, a rising dramatist, who acquired the name of the *True Blue Poet* from his steady adherence to his religious and political principles, also wrote against Dryden, but with such inferior verse and argument that the laureate could afford to say—

> " Losing he wins, because his name will be
> Ennobled by defeat, who durst contend with me."

But the next year came William of Nassau and the Revolution, and in 1689 Dryden was deprived of all his offices, because he could not, as a Roman Catholic, swear the oaths of allegiance, supremacy, and abjuration, prescribed by Act of Parliament to be taken by all holders of office.

To have recanted would have disgusted his friends without conciliating his foes, he therefore resigned his pension, and about the same time went to live in Gerrard Street, Soho.

Lord Macaulay says :—

" One of the first acts Dorset, as Lord Chamberlain, was under the necessity of performing, must have been painful to a man of so generous a nature, and of so keen a relish for whatever was excellent in arts and letters. Dryden could no longer remain Poet Laureate. The public would not have borne to see any Papist among the servants of their Majesties ; and Dryden was not only a Papist but an apostate. He was removed ; but he received from the private bounty of the magnificent chamberlain a pension equal to the salary which had been withdrawn. The deposed Laureate, however, continued to complain piteously, year after year, of the losses which he had not suffered."

In the following lines, taken from Blackmore's *Prince Arthur*, Laurus (a translation of the nickname Bayes) is meant for Dryden, and Sakil is the Lord Chamberlain :—

> " Laurus among the meagre crowd appeared,
> An old, revolted, unbelieving bard,
> Who thronged, and shoved, and pressed, and would be heard.

Sakil's high roof, the Muses' palace rung
With endless cries, and endless songs he sung.
To bless good Sakil, Laurus would be first ;
But Sakil's prince and Sakil's God he curst.
Sakil without distinction threw his bread,
Despised the flatterer, but the poet fed."

What must have added considerably to Dryden's vexation at this misfortune was the promotion of Shadwell,
his hated rival, whose personal appearance and poetical
works he had cruelly satirised in *Mac Flecknoe,* to the
office of poet laureate and historiographer royal.

Dryden recommenced writing for the stage, and in
the course of the next few years produced several plays
with varied success, the last, *Love Triumphant,* which
appeared early in 1693 was a complete failure. Schlegel,
whose judgment of Dryden's political and satirical poems
seems formed upon a superficial acquaintance with the
subject, gives us his opinion of Dryden's comedies (of
which compositions he is a more profound and reliable
critic than of poetry) " that they are incredibly bad " :—

" Dryden's plans are improbable, even to silliness ; the incidents
are all thrown out without forethought ; the most wonderful theatrical strokes fall incessantly from the clouds. He cannot be said
to have drawn a single character ; for there is not a spark of nature
in his dramatic personages."

Dryden also published some miscellaneous poems, and
several translations, but his great work, the translation of
Virgil, was not produced until 1697, when it succeeded
beyond the poet's expectation, as he states in a letter
dated September 3rd, 1697, to his sons, who were then
in Rome. In this letter also occurs the remarkable
passage :—

"Towards the latter end of this month, September,

H

Charles will begin to recover his perfect health, according to his nativity, which, casting it myself, I am sure is true, and all things have happened according to the very time that I predicted them."

Thus showing that a man possessed of one of the brightest intellects of the seventeenth century was a firm believer in astrology; and upon his death the horoscope of his son Charles, to which he alludes, was found in his pocket-book.

Dryden's friends were very anxious that he should dedicate his translation of Virgil to the king. To this he would not consent, although it was supposed that the compliment would have pleased "the Protestant hero."

Old Jacob Tonson, his publisher, was particularly annoyed at Dryden's firmness on this point; but he had his revenge, for in every engraving representing Æneas he caused him to be drawn like King William, with a prominent hooked nose.

This compliment to the king was known to be in opposition to Dryden's wish, and gave rise to much merriment :—

> " Old Jacob, by deep judgment swayed,
>   To please the wise beholders,
> Has placed old Nassau's hook-nosed head
>   On poor Æneas' shoulders :—
> To make the parallel hold tack,
>   Methinks there's little lacking ;
> One took his father pick-a-pack,
>   And t'other sent his packing."

This was not Dryden's first disagreement with his publisher, who was of a coarse and vulgar disposition, and treated authors with but little courtesy.

During the progress of the work, there were frequent

disputes about the payment of the subscribers' money, the bad coins that Tonson sent, and his tiresome demands "for more copy." On one occasion, Dryden sent back the messenger with the following fragment in place of the expected proofs :—

A CHARACTER OF JACOB TONSON.

" With leering looks, bull-faced, and freckled fair,
With two left legs, and Judas-coloured hair,
And frowsy pores that taint the ambient air—"

" Tell the dog," said Dryden, " that he who wrote these can write more."

Although he had now ceased writing for the stage his plays were still prominently before the public. Their immorality had been attacked by several writers, but more particularly by Sir Richard Blackmore, and Jeremy Collier, the nonjuring divine, who, in 1698, published his celebrated attack upon the licentiousness and profanity of the English comedies of the day.

This work is still the text-book of many people who regard the theatre with horror, forgetting that most of the evils it exposes have long since been removed, or very much abated. But, in Dryden's time, the reproaches were deserved, and by no plays more than by those of his composition.

Dr. Johnson, speaking on this subject, remarks that whilst—

" Blackmore's censure was cold and general, Collier's was personal and ardent ; Blackmore taught his reader to dislike, what Collier incited him to abhor."

To these attacks, Dryden somewhat feebly replied in a Prologue and Epilogue, written for the occasion of his own benefit in March, 1700, only a few weeks before his death.

Colley Cibber, then a rising young actor, and afterwards Poet Laureate, had to deliver both these orations, which he thus mentions in his autobiography :—

"These immoralities of the stage, had by an avowed indulgence been creeping into it ever since King Charles his time ; nothing that was loose could then be too low for it. In this almost general corruption, *Dryden*, whose plays were more famed for their wit than their chastity, led the way, which he fairly confesses,. and endeavours to excuse, in his epilogue to the *Pilgrim*, revived in 1700 for his benefit, in his declining age and fortune. This epilogue and the prologue to the same play written by *Dryden* I spoke myself."

In the Prologue, he contents himself with ridiculing Sir R. Blackmore, a minor poet, who was physician to King William, by whom he had been knighted :—

> " We know not by what name we should arraign him,
> For no one category can contain him.
> A pedant, canting preacher, and a quack,
> Are load enough to break one ass's back.
> At last, grown wanton, he presumed to write,
> Traduced two kings, their kindness to requite."

But beyond these loose personalities, he does not attempt to answer Blackmore's criticism on his plays. In the Epilogue, he replies to Collier a little more explicitly :—

> " Perhaps the parson stretched a point too far,
> When with our theatres he waged a war.
> He tells you, that this very moral age
> Received the first infection from the stage ;
> But sure, a banished court, with lewdness fraught,
> The seeds of open vice returning brought.
>
> *   *   *   *   *   *   *   *
>
> The poets who must live by courts, or starve,
> Were proud so good a government to serve ;
> And, mixing with buffoons and pimps profane,
> Tainted the stage for some small snip of gain,"

Had these excuses possessed even the merit of truth, they would not have exonerated the poet; for no man has a right to plead necessity for committing wanton and shameless immorality.

But Dryden led the taste of the town, and was for many years the acknowledged head of the literary world; he therefore, more than any other man of the day, had the power to direct the popular taste towards purity and morality; this he never attempted, not even in his translations and fables, where he interpolated loose descriptions, and gross allusions into the already sufficiently licentious tales of Chaucer and Boccaccio.

And yet these were amongst the last works he published, and were prefaced by an apology for the grossness of some of his writings :—

"I shall say the less of Mr. Collier, because in many things he has taxed me justly ; and I have pleaded guilty to all thoughts and expressions of mine which can be truly accused of obscenity, profaneness, or immorality, and retract them. Yet it were not difficult to prove that in many places he has perverted my meaning by his glosses."

The same preface contains some bitterly sarcastic remarks on Sir R. Blackmore, concluding thus "but I will deal more civilly with his two poems, because nothing ill is to be spoken of the dead; and therefore peace be to the manes of his (epic) Arthurs."

Of his contest with Collier, the general opinion was that Dryden's arguments, keen and witty as they were, did not explain away the parson's facts, consisting chiefly of passages quoted from Dryden's plays; and although the audiences at the theatres did not perceptibly diminish, nor the morality of the drama greatly improve, public attention was called to the debasing influence of exhibitions calculated chiefly to inflame the passions.

> " John Dryden enemies had three,
>   Sir Dick, old Nick, and Jeremy :
>   The doughty knight was forced to yield,
>   The other two have kept the field ;
>   But had his life been somewhat holier,
>   He'd foiled the Devil and the Collier."

When Sir Walter Scott was preparing his edition of Dryden, he wrote a letter, from which the following is an extract, justifying himself for giving Dryden's works to the public in an unmutilated form.   To have attempted to purify his works would have been nearly as difficult, and quite as absurd, as to endeavour to make a young ladies' edition of Rabelais.

"I will not castrate John Dryden," says Sir Walter ; " what would you say to any man who would castrate Shakespeare, or Massinger, or Beaumont, and Fletcher ? I don't say but that it may be very proper to select correct passages for the use of boarding schools and colleges, being sensible that no improper ideas can be suggested in these seminaries, unless they are intruded, or smuggled under the beards and ruffs of our old dramatists.   But in making an edition of the works of a man of genius for libraries and collections (and such I conceive a complete edition of Dryden to be), I must give my author as I find him, and will not leave out the page, even to get rid of the blot, little as I like it."

Dr. Johnson, whose political opinions inclined him to favour Dryden, thus sums up his character for literary morality :—

" His works afford too many examples of dissolute licentiousness, and abject adulation, but they were his trade rather than his pleasure. Of dramatic immorality he did not want examples among his predecessors, or companions among his contemporaries; but, in the meanness and servility of hyperbolical adulation, I know not whether, since the days in which the Roman Emperors were deified, he has even been equalled, except by Afra Behn in an address to Eleanor Gwyn."

Warton (himself a laureate) speaks quite as unreservedly of Dryden's failings, in his *Ode to the King*, June 4th, 1787 :—

> " At length the matchless Dryden came,
> To light the Muse's clearer flame ;
> To lofty numbers grace to lend,
> And strength with melody to blend ;
> To triumph in the bold career of song,
> And roll th' unwearied energy along.
> Does the mean incense of promiscuous praise,
> Does servile fear, disgrace his regal bays ?
> I spurn his panegyric strings,
> His partial homage, tun'd to kings."

Early in May, 1700, Dryden died in Gerard Street, from mortification caused by the flesh growing over a toe nail. Amputation of the leg was advised, to this Dryden would not consent, as it was improbable that he would long survive the operation.

His funeral procession started from the College of Physicians, it was led by a band of musicians, and the hearse was followed by a long train of coaches. Dr. Garth pronounced a Latin oration over the corpse, which was interred in Westminster Abbey.

In 1720 the Duke of Buckingham caused a bust of the poet to be placed in the Abbey, with a short inscription in which the date of Dryden's birth was wrongly given :—

J. DRYDEN.

Natus 1632.   Mortuus Maii I. 1700.

Joannes Sheffield, Dux Buckinghamiensis,

Posuit. 1720.

In 1731 the widow of the Duke of Buckingham removed the first bust, replacing it by a superior one, carved by Schumacher, which still surmounts the tomb.

It has been asserted that the funeral was delayed three weeks in consequence of an odious practical joke of Lord Jefferies (second son of the notorious judge of that name); but Dr. Johnson discredits the tale, and, indeed, it seems incredible that such an insult to the great poet, had it occurred, should not have been more fully explained by historians of the period.

In private life Dryden possessed many amiable qualities. He was extremely diffident and retiring with strangers; but his learning and advice were always at the disposal of his friends, and numerous anecdotes are related of his kindness to rising men of letters.   Among the most noteworthy of his *protégés* were Congreve, Southern, and Walsh.   He says of himself: " My conversation is slow and dull, my humour saturnine and reserved.   In short, I am none of those who endeavour to break jests in company or make repartees."

In reading, his delivery was remarkably devoid of expression, insomuch that he frequently marred the effect of his best lines by his tedious recital of them.

Colley Cibber particularly mentions this peculiarity :—

" As we have sometimes great composers of musick who cannot sing, we have as frequently great writers that cannot read.   Of this, *Dryden* our first great master of verse and harmony, was a strong instance.   When he brought his play of *Amphytrion* to the stage, I heard him give it his first reading to the actors, in which, though it is true, he delivered the plain sense of every period, yet the whole was in so cold, so flat and unaffecting a manner, that I am afraid of not being believed, when I affirm it."

Until the last few years of his life he had always been a very temperate man. When he became acquainted with Addison, he commenced to drink more than he was used to; such excesses of the table were, however, but little noticed at that period.

In person Dryden was short, stout, and fresh complexioned—he had early been known by the *sobriquet* of the *Poet Squab*—whilst his face was chiefly remarkable for the great distance between his eyes, and for a mole on the right cheek.

A letter, which appeared in the *Gentleman's Magazine* after his death, says : —

" I remember plain John Dryden before he paid his court with success to the great, in one uniform clothing of Norwich drugget. I have ate tarts with him and Madame Reeve at the Mulberry Garden, when our author advanced to a sword and Chedreux wig."

Towards the close of his career, Dryden was looked upon as an oracle, the undisputed monarch of the poetical world, his chair the throne to which aspiring wits came to pay homage. Addison attests his supremacy in the lines :—

" But see where artful Dryden next appears,
   Grown old in rhyme, but charming even in years ;
   Great Dryden next, whose tuneful muse affords
   The sweetest numbers and the fittest words."

and at Will's Coffee House, his almost daily resort, he was usually encircled by the most celebrated literary men of the day. His arm-chair was regularly placed for him in the balcony in summer, or in the warmest corner by

the fireside in winter. It was at one of these levees that
Pope, when a boy, saw the old poet, whose fame he was
destined to eclipse; and here probably Swift came to see
his famous relative, and to be told by him, " Cousin Swift,
you will never make a poet," words which the vindictive
dean never forgave, perhaps because he felt their great
truth.

Dryden's prophecy of Congreve's future greatness as a
poet was not so strikingly realised, for in the following
lines he seems to shadow forth a far higher rank than he
ever attained in the sphere of poetry :—

> " But you, whom every muse and grace adorn,
> Whom I foresee to better fortune born,
> Be kind to my remains ; and oh, defend
> Against your judgment, your departed friend !
> Let not the insulting foe my fame pursue,
> But shade those laurels which descend to you.
> And take for tribute what these lines express ;
> You merit more, nor could my love do less."

JOHN DRYDEN'S DRAMATIC WORKS.

The Wild Gallant. C. Acted at the King's Theatre,
February 5th, 1663. " The play so poor a thing as I
never saw in my life almost, and so little answering the
name that, from the beginning to the end, I could not,
nor can at this time, tell certainly which was *The Wild
Gallant.*"—Pepys.

The Rival Ladies. T. C. Acted 1664, at the King's
Theatre, Drury Lane. " A very innocent and most pretty,
witty play."—Pepys.

*The Indian Emperour ; or, the Conquest of Mexico by
the Spaniards.* T. This was the sequel to Sir Robert
Howard's tragedy, *The Indian Queen.* When Dryden's

play was performed handbills were distributed to the audience, explaining the connection of the story with Howard's play. *The Indian Emperour* had great success.

Secret Love; or, the Maiden Queen. T. C. Acted at the King's Theatre, 1667. This play was a great favourite with Charles II., and Nell Gwyn was greatly admired in the character of *Florimel.* Pepys, who was present at the first acting of the play, says, " The comical part done by Nell, who is *Florimel,* that I never can hope to see the like done again by man or woman. It makes me, I confess, admire her."

Sir Martin Mar-all; or, the Feign'd Innocence. C. Acted at the Duke of York's Theatre, Lincoln's Inn, 1667. This play was very successful; it is partly taken from Molière's *L'Etourdi.*

The Tempest; or, the Enchanted Island. Acted at the Duke of York's Theatre, 1667. This adaptation of Shakespeare's play was chiefly the work of Davenant; but Dryden composed the Prologue, which contains a brilliant account of the genius of Shakespeare.

An Evening's Love; or, the Mock Astrologer. C. Acted at the King's Theatre, 1668.

Tyrannick Love; or, the Royal Martyr. T. Acted at the King's Theatre, 1669. In this play Nell Gwyn acted the character of *Valeria,* and having stabbed herself, was about to be carried off dead, when suddenly arousing, she exclaimed :—

" Hold ! are you mad ? You damned confounded dog.
I am to rise, and speak the epilogue.

(*To the Audience*)

I come, kind gentlemen, strange news to tell ye ;
I am the ghost of poor departed Nelly.

> Sweet ladies, be not frighted ; I'll be civil ;
> I'm what I was, a little harmless devil.

> " O poet, damned dull poet, who could prove
> So senseless, to make Nelly die for love !
> Nay, what's yet worse, to kill me in the prime
> Of Easter term, in tart and cheesecake time !

> " As for my epitaph, when I am gone,
> I'll trust no poet, but will write my own :—
> Here Nelly lies, who, though she lived a slattern
> Yet died a princess, acting in St. Catherine."

Her delivery of this Epilogue is said to have delighted the king and audience beyond measure.

Almanzor and Almahide; or, the Conquest of Granada, by the Spaniards. T. In two parts, and written in heroic verse. Acted 1670.

Marriage-à-la-Mode. C. This successful comedy was produced in 1672, at Lincoln's Inn, by the King's Company, their old house having been burnt down. In 1674 they removed to the new theatre in Drury Lane, built from Sir C. Wren's design.

The Assignation ; or, Love in a Nunnery. C. Was produced in 1672, and was unsuccessful.

Amboyna. T. Acted 1673. Its object was to stir up popular feeling against the Dutch, with whom we were then at war.

The State of Innocence, and Fall of Man. Opera in Heroic verse. Altered from Milton's " Paradise Lost."

Aureng-Zebe ; or, the Great Mogul. Acted 1675. The last of Dryden's rhyming tragedies.

All for Love ; or, the World Well Lost. T. Acted at the King's Theatre in 1678. Dryden says, in his preface to the play, " In my style I have professed to imitate the divine Shakespeare, which, that I might perform more freely, I have disencumbered myself from rhyme." This tragedy treats of the loves of Antony and Cleopatra, and is considered the best of Dryden's plays.

The Kind Keeper; or, Mr. Limberham. C. Acted at the Duke's Theatre in 1678. Various reasons are assigned for its not having been produced at the King's Theatre; but it was only played three times, a failure which, from its coarseness, it deserved; but coarseness alone in those days would not have sufficed to damn it.

Œdipus. This tragedy was produced in 1678 at the Duke's Theatre. At this time Dryden was under an engagement with the King's Company to furnish them with three plays annually, which he neglected to do. They therefore complained to the Lord Chamberlain of the production of this play at the rival house as a breach of agreement; but it does not appear that they obtained any redress. In the " Vindication of the Duke of Guise," Dryden says he wrote the first and third acts, and drew the scenery of the play, the remainder was the work of Nathaniel Lee.

Troilus and Cressida; or, Truth Found Too Late. T. Adapted from Shakespeare. Acted 1679, at the Duke's Theatre.

The Spanish Friar; or, the Double Discovery. This tragi-comedy, produced at the Duke's Theatre in 1681, was a source of annoyance to Dryden when he became a Roman Catholic, for it contains a severe attack upon the priesthood; so that, although one of his best plays, he wished to suppress it. It was prohibited by James II.; but, after the Revolution, was the first play commanded by Queen Mary.

The Duke of Guise. T. 1682. Acted by the now united companies—the King's Servants, and the Duke's Company. It was the joint production of Lee and Dryden.

Albion and Albanius. An opera first acted publicly in 1685, when, after running six nights, the news of the landing of Monmouth and the ensuing panic stopped its career, and caused great loss to the theatre.

Don Sebastian. T. Brought out in 1690. This was his first appearance as dramatic author after the Revolution had deprived him of his pensions, to which he refers in his Prologue :—

> " The judge removed, though he's no more ' my lord,'
> May plead at bar, or at the council board ;
> So may cast poets write ; there's no pretension
> To argue loss of wit from loss of pension.
>
>   *   *   *   *   *   *   *   *
>
> And you well know a play's of no religion.
> Take good advice, and please yourselves this day ;
> No matter from what hands you have the play."

Amphitryon ; or, the Two Sosias. A very successful comedy. Acted 1690.

King Arthur; or, the British Worthy. A dramatic opera, acted at the Theatre Royal in 1691. The music was composed by Purcell, and the opera was a great success.

Cleomenes ; or, the Spartan Heroe. T. Acted in 1692. At the time when Dryden was engaged upon this play, he was suffering so severely from gout that he entrusted the completion of it to Southern.

Love Triumphant ; or, Nature Will Prevail. A tragicomedy, acted in 1693. It was a complete failure. Dryden had intended it for his last play, a resolution which its failure may probably have strengthened.

> " Now, in good manners, nothing shall be said
> Against this play, because the poet's dead."

It is said that he wrote one scene of a comedy called

The Mistaken Husband, which was acted at the Theatre Royal, 1675.

> "———————— What muse
> So flexible, so generous as thine,
> Immortal Dryden! From her copious fount
> Large draughts he took, and unbeseeming song
> Inebriated sang. Who does not grieve
> To hear the foul and insolent rebuke
> Of angry satire from a bard so rare,
> To trace the lubricous and oily course
> Of abject adulation, the lewd line
> Of shameless vice from page to page, and find
> The judgment bribed, the heart unprincipled,
> And only loyal at the expense of truth,
> Of justice, and of virtue?"
>
> HURDIS. "VILLAGE CURATE."

THOMAS SHADWELL.

(1688—1692.)

" Shadwell, the great support o' the comic stage,
Born to expose the follies of the age.
To whip prevailing vices, and unite
Mirth with Instruction, Profit with Delight.
For large ideas and a flowing pen,
First of our times, and second but to Ben.
Shadwell, who all his lines from Nature drew,
Cópied her out, and kept her still in view.
Who ne'er was bribed by title or estate,
To fawn and flatter with the rich and great.
To let a gilded vice or folly pass,
But always lashed the villain and the ass."

EPILOGUE TO " THE VOLUNTEERS."

THOMAS SHADWELL was born at Lanton Hall, in Norfolk, in 1640, and educated at Caius College, Cambridge. He was intended for the profession of the law, and studied for some time at the Inner Temple; but deserting its shady courts and dusty books, he went to travel on the Continent, whence he returned full of ambition to shine as a poet.

In that art he was also unsuccessful; but turning his attention to the drama, his really great talents won for him fame and reward, and perhaps a wife, for he married a lady connected with the theatre.

He produced seventeen comedies, all avowedly in imitation of Ben Jonson, whose memory he reverenced, and whose works he was never tired of eulogising as masterpieces of English dramatic literature.

In the dedication of *The Virtuoso,* he says of Ben Jonson:—

" He was incomparably the best dramatic poet that ever was, or I believe ever will be ; and I had rather be the author of one scene in his best comedies than of any play this age has produced."

" 'Twas he alone true humours understood,
And with great wit and judgment made them good."

In imitation of his master, Shadwell in his comedies represents the course of peculiar humours, or the train of events brought about by the eccentricities of certain individuals. This he does with great powers of observation and considerable wit, and the perusal of some of the comedies throws considerable light on the manners of his age. For the groundwork of some of his plots he was indebted to Molière, which author in some respects he more nearly resembles than he does Jonson.

" Of all our modern wits, none seem to me
Once to have touched upon true comedy,
But hasty Shadwell, and slow Wycherly.
Shadwell's unfinished works do yet impart
Great proofs of force of nature, none of art.
With just, bold strokes he dashes here and there,
Showing great mastery with little care,
Scorning to varnish his good touches o'er,
To make fools and women praise them more."

ROCHESTER.

Shadwell clearly explains what he considers to be the proper aim of comedy :—

" It does not consist in the representation of mere natural imperfections ; they are not fit subjects for comedy, since they are not to

I

be laughed at, but pitied. But the artificial folly of those, who are not coxcombs by nature, but with great art and industry make themselves so, is a proper object of comedy. Good comical humour ought to be such an affectation as misguides men in knowledge, arts, or science, or that causes defection in manners and morality, or perverts their minds in the main actions of their lives."

Granting this view of comedy to be the correct one, it must be allowed that Shadwell held a very high rank in its composition; but it is now the almost universal opinion that true comedy does not consist in the creation of intrigues caused by the entanglements of a variety of superficial and improbable "humours."

Shadwell lived on very friendly terms with Dryden for several years, and in 1674 they united with Crowne, in the composition of a spiteful attack on Elkanah Settle, the last City poet.

In 1676, Shadwell produced *The Virtuoso,* and in the epilogue he indulges in a sneer at Dryden's *Heroic Tragedies:*

" But of those ladies he despairs to-day,
Who love a dull, romantic, whining play :
Where poor frail woman's made a deity,
With senseless amorous idolatry,
And snivelling heroes sigh, and pine, and cry,
Though singly they beat armies and huff kings,
Rant at the gods and do impossible things ;
Though they can laugh at danger, blood and wounds,
Yet if the dame once chides, the milksop hero swoons."

This criticism was not beyond the bounds of courtesy; and in 1678 Dryden furnished Shadwell with a prologue for his comedy, *The True Widow.*

But in March, 1682, Dryden's *Medal* appeared, in which he espoused the views of the Court, in the much vexed question of the succession to the throne. Shadwell, a Whig, and staunch Protestant, befriended the popular party, and replied in :—

The Medal of John Bayes;

Or, a Satyr upon Folly and Knavery.

" How long shall I endure without reply,
    To hear this *Bayes*, this hackney-rayler lie?
    The fool uncudgell'd for one libel, swells,
    Where not his wit, but sauciness excells;
    Whilst with foul words and names which he lets flie,
    He quite defiles the *satyr's* dignity.
    For libel and true satyr different be,
    This must have *truth* and *salt*, with modesty.
    Sparing the persons, this does tax the crimes,
    Galls not great men, but vices of the times,
    With witty and sharp, not blunt and bitter rimes.
    Methinks the ghost of *Horace* there I see,
    Lashing this cherry-cheek'd Dunce of fifty-three;
    Who, at that age, so boldly durst profane,
    With base hir'd libel, the free satyr's vein.
    Thou stil'st it satyr, to call names, rogue, whore,
    Traytor and rebel, and a thousand more;
    An oyster wench is sure thy muse of late,
    And all thy *Helicon's* at *Billingsgate*.

      *   *   *   *   *   *   *

As far from satyr does thy talent lye,
    As from being cheerful, or good company;
    For thou art *Saturnine*, thou dost confess
    A civil word thy *dulness* to express.

      *   *   *   *   *   *   *

Now farewell wretched, mercenary *Bayes*,
    Who the King libell'd, and did *Cromwell* praise;
    Farewell, abandon'd rascal, only fit
    To be abus'd by thy own scurrilous wit."

Shadwell then traces the career of Dryden, in lines remarkable for their coarseness, accusing him of being obscene in his conversation, and servile in his muse.

The most noticeable passages have already been quoted, so far as modern ideas of propriety will allow; they contain a sufficient foundation of truth to render it a matter of great difficulty now to decide where fact ends and fiction begins.

Dryden was of course highly incensed at this attack, to which he replied in his great satire *Mac Flecknoe ; or, The Son of Flecknoe.* The plan of the poem required the mention of some author lately deceased, he therefore chose one Flecknoe, an obscure Irish poet, whom he pourtrays as the king of nonsense on his death-bed :—

> " And pondering which of all his sons was fit
> To reign and wage immortal war with wit,
> Cried, ' 'Tis resolved, for Nature pleads that he
> Should only rule who most resembles me.
> Shadwell alone my perfect image bears,
> Mature in dulness from his tender years,
> Shadwell alone of all my sons is he
> Who stands confirmed in full stupidity.
> The rest to some faint meaning make pretence,
> But Shadwell *never* deviates into sense.'
>
> *   *   *   *   *   *   *   *
>
> So Shadwell swore, nor should his vow be vain,
> That he till death true dulness would maintain ;
> And in his father's right and realm's defence,
> Ne'er to have peace with wit, nor truth with sense."

Then Shadwell receives the solemn paternal blessing from Flecknoe, who exclaims :—

> " Like mine thy gentle numbers feebly creep ;
> Thy tragic muse gives smiles, thy comic—sleep,"

and then disappears through a trap-door, leaving his mantle to Shadwell.

Dryden was not yet sufficiently revenged ; he had abused Shadwell's writings, it remained for him to ridicule his personal appearance. In the next month the second part of *Absalom and Achitophel* appeared, and for about

thirty lines poor Shadwell, as Og, is described in such
a grossly scurrilous and indecent manner that but little
can be quoted :—

> " Og, from a treason-tavern rolling home
> Round as a globe, and liquored every chink,
> Goodly and great he sails behind his link.
> With all this bulk there's nothing lost in Og,
> For every inch that is not fool is rogue :
> When wine has given him courage to blaspheme,
> He curses God, but God before cursed him ;
> And if man could have reason, none has more,
> That made his paunch so rich, and him so poor.
>
> *   *   *   *   *   *   *   *
>
> The midwife laid her hand on his thick skull,
> With this prophetic blessing—*Be thou dull !*
> Drink, swear, and roar, forbear no lewd delight,
> Fit for thy bulk, do anything but write."

However, the Revolution of 1688 brought the downfall
of Dryden, who was necessarily removed from the office of
Laureate.

He had identified himself with the most violent and
unpopular measures of King James's reign, and the
Protestant party would justly have complained if so
violent a Tory and Papist had been allowed to retain
a lucrative Court appointment.

Posterity has decided that Dryden was a great poet, but
at the time of the Revolution he was chiefly thought of as
a dramatist, sufficiently successful in bombastic tragedy,
but lamentably deficient in the province of comedy.
Those of his poems which had then appeared had, from
their controversial and party spirit, probably created for
him as many enemies as admirers; his great work, the
translation of *Virgil*, was not yet written, and as Eusden
says :—

" Great Dryden did not early great appear,
Faintly distinguished in his thirtieth year."

Shadwell, on the contrary, was very popular, he was
admiringly called the *True Blue Protestant Poet ;* his
manners and conversation were agreeable, his comedies
were immensely successful, and many eminent contemporaries considered him equal to Dryden, even as a poet.
There was, therefore, little cause to cavil at the appointment, for, although his odes have been severely criticised,
they were not, of course, written until after his promotion,
and the following poem is certainly no worse, bad as it is,
than many of the *official odes* composed by far more
celebrated Poets Laureate :—

ODE

On the Anniversary of the King's Birth.

By THOS. SHADWELL, Poet Laureat,

and Historiographer Royal.

Steriles transmissimus annos
Hac Ævi prima Dies.

Welcome, thrice welcome this auspicious morn
On which the great Nassau was born,
Sprung from a mighty race which was design'd
For the deliv'rers of mankind.
Illustrious heroes, whose prevailing Fates
Rais'd the distress'd to high and mighty states ;
And did by that possess more true renown,
Than their *Adolphus* gain'd by the Imperial crown.

They cooled the rage, humbled the pride of Spain,
But since the insolence of *France* no less,
Had brought the States into distress,
But that a precious scion did remain
From that great root, which did the shock sustain,
And made them high and mighty once again.

This Prince for us, was born to make us free
From the most abject slavery.
  Thou hast restor'd our laws their force again ;
We still shall conquer on the land by thee ;
  By thee shall triumph on the main.

But thee a Fate much more sublime attends,
Europe for freedom on thy sword depends ;
  And thy victorious arms shall tumble down
  The savage monster from the Gallick throne ;
To this important day, we all shall owe,
Oh glorious birth, from which such blest effects shall flow.

(*General chorus of voices and instruments.*)

On this glad day let every voice,
And instrument, proclaim our joys,
And let all EUROPE join in the triumphant noise.
  Io Triumphe let us sing,
  Io Triumphe let us sing,
And let the sound through all the spacious welkin ring.

Thus the prophetic muses say,
And all the wise and good will pray,
That they long, long, may celebrate this day.
  Soon haughty France shall bow, and coz'ning *Rome*,
  And *Britain* mistress of the world become ;
And from thy wise, thy God-like sway,
Kings learn to reign, and subjects to obey.

Shadwell's short tenure of the post of Laureate was chiefly remarkable from the fact that he it was who commenced the composition of regular Anniversary Odes, and for the extreme bitterness and virulence of the critical attacks to which these, and his other works, were subjected.

The contemptible spite of the turncoat Dryden vented itself in continual satires and epigrams, in which the personal appearance, religious convictions, and political opinions of Shadwell (who, with all his failings, was consistent and honourable) were unsparingly ridiculed

Shadwell was no match for Dryden, his wit was not so keen; and his inability to cope with his antagonist was so well known, that his somewhat sudden death gave rise to a rumour that he had committed suicide on reading a more than usually abusive lampoon.

Brady, who preached his funeral sermon in old Chelsea Church, denied this; and Shadwell's death (which happened at Chelsea, in November, 1692) is more generally ascribed to an accidental overdose of opium, a drug to the use of which he was greatly addicted.

He was only fifty-two years of age, and his loss was deeply lamented by that large portion of the public for whose amusement he had done so much, and though his dramatic works have now passed into unmerited oblivion, they were certainly highly valued by his contemporaries.

Brady said :—

" His natural and acquired abilities made him very amiable to all who conversed with him, a very few being equal in the becoming qualities which adorn and set off a complete gentleman ; his very enemies, if he has any now left, will give him this character, at least if they knew him so thoroughly as I did."

Shadwell's last play, *The Stock Jobbers*, was not performed until after his death, and the epilogue was spoken by an actor clad in deep mourning.

Of his literary powers, those only who read can judge ; but as his works are somewhat scarce, it is usual, as being more convenient, to adopt the opinions expressed by his enemy Dryden, as to their merits. Of his conversation and wit, the celebrated Earl of Rochester said :—" If Shadwell had burnt all he wrote, and printed all he spoke, he would have had more wit and humour than any other poet."

The Earl of Dorset, when using his influence to obtain

the office of Laureate for Shadwell, said to those who were advocating the claims of other poets, "Well, gentlemen, I will not pretend to determine how great a poet Shadwell may be, but I am sure he is an honest man."

Shadwell had studied music for many years, and he guided the composition of the melodies for the songs in his opera *Psyche*, to which Dryden refers :—

> " Or, if thou would'st thy different talents suit,
> Set thy own songs, and sing them to thy lute."

It is unfortunate that the coarseness of Shadwell's language banishes his plays from our modern stage, where loose expressions are only tolerated when veiled in poetical diction, or couched in *double entendre*, and no immorality is hinted at, except in the gestures and expressions of the actresses, which are not set down in the copy of the drama forwarded to the licenser of plays.

Notwithstanding the peculiarities of Shadwell's outspoken muse, there are many scenes in his comedies of great humour and originality; in *The Virtuoso*, for instance, the scene in the laboratory, where Sir Nicholas Gimcrack, the Virtuoso, is learning to swim upon a table, by imitating the movements of a frog in a bowl of water, has some exceedingly comical situations and dialogue, quite equal to the celebrated Undertaker's Scene in Steele's *Funeral*.

Lord Macaulay, in his History, praises these comedies for throwing a strong light upon life and society in Shadwell's times; and in the preface to *The Fortunes of Nigel*, Sir Walter Scott mentions that he was partly indebted to *The Squire of Alsatia* for the vivid account he gives of the disreputable sanctuary of Whitefriars.

In the dedication of the latter play to the Earl of Dorset, Shadwell observes that it was eminently successful :—

"No comedy these many years having filled the theatre so long together. And I had the great honour to find so many friends, that the house was never so full since it was built as upon the third day of this play, and vast numbers went away that could not be admitted."

Although Shadwell was buried in old Chelsea church, a handsome tablet was erected to his memory in Westminster Abbey, by his son, Dr. John Shadwell, with an inscription stating that he came of an ancient family and was poet laureate and historiographer to King William.

A bust surmounts the tablet, showing a clean shaven, very fat face, with a sharp prominent nose.

T. SHADWELL'S DRAMATIC WORKS.

The Sullen Lovers ; or, the Impertinents. A comedy acted by the Duke of York's servants, 1668. Partly taken from *Les Facheux,* of Molière.

The Royal Shepherdess.—Tragi-comedy, acted 1669.

The Humourists. Comedy acted by their Majesty's servants, 1671. This play gave offence, and was withdrawn for a time.

A comedy called *The Miser,* taken from *L'Avare,* and acted in 1672.

Epsom Wells. Comedy, acted in 1673.

Psyche. An unsuccessful operatic tragedy, acted 1675.

The Libertine. Tragedy, acted 1676, founded upon the old tale from whence springs the plot of Don Giovanni.

The Virtuoso. A successful and amusing comedy, acted in 1676.

The History of Timon of Athens, the Man Hater. Altered from Shakespeare, and played 1678.

The True Widow. A comedy, acted at the Duke's theatre in 1678.

The Woman Captain. Comedy, 1680.

The Lancashire Witches, and Teague O'Devilly, the Irish Priest. Comedy, 1682.

The Squire of Alsatia. Comedy, 1688.

Bury Fair. Comedy, 1689. Partly taken from Molière's *Précieuses Ridicules.*

The Amorous Bigot, with the second part of Teague O'Devilly. Comedy, 1690.

The Scourers. Comedy, 1691.

The Volunteers; or, the Stock Jobbers. Comedy, acted in 1693, and dedicated by Shadwell's widow to the Queen.

> " Who shall resume St. James's fife,
> And call ideal virtues into life ?
> On tip-toe gaping, lo, I stand,
> To see the future Laureate of the land ! "

PETER PINDAR.

NAHUM TATE.

(1692—1715.)

" Know, reader, that the Laureate's post sublime,
Is destined to record in tuneful rhyme,
The deeds of British monarchs, twice a year.
If great—how happy is the tuneful tongue,
If pitiful (as Shakespeare says) the song,
' Must suckle fools, and chronicle small beer.' "

PETER PINDAR.

BUT for two circumstances the name of Nahum Teat
would have been totally forgotten, and they are, that he
was part author of a new version of the Psalms, and was
Poet Laureate in the reigns of William III., Queen Anne,
and George I.

He was the son of Dr. Faithful Teat, a clergyman, was
born in Dublin in 1652, and educated at Trinity College,
in that City.

Determined to adopt the literary profession, he went to
London, where he became acquainted with Dryden, whom
he assisted in the composition of several plays, and for
whom he wrote most of the second part of *Absalom and
Achitophel*, which was published in November, 1682. In
the edition of this poem, published by Jacob Tonson in
1716 (when both Dryden and Tate were dead), the preface states that—

" In the year 1680, Mr. Dryden undertook the poem of *Absalom and Achitophel*, upon the desire of King Charles II. The performance was applauded by every one ; and several persons pressing him to write a second part, he, upon declining it himself, spoke to Mr. Tate to write one, and gave him his advice in the direction of it ; and that part beginning,

> ' Next these, a troop of busy spirits press,'

and ending

> ' To talk like Doeg, and to write like thee,'

containing near two hundred verses, were entirely Mr. Dryden's composition, besides some touches in other places."

Having a strong Tory tone, Tate's verses, though far inferior to Dryden's, brought him into notice at Court; and, encouraged by the patronage he received, he produced several plays, which, however, were only moderately successful. He had the temerity to alter *King Lear* for the stage, and, whatever may now be the opinion as to the merits of his version, it held possession of the boards for nearly a century.

On the death of Shadwell, Tate was appointed Poet Laureate; but the office of Historiographer Royal, which Shadwell and Dryden had previously also filled, was conferred upon Thomas Rymer.

The greatest merit of Tate's official odes is their brevity; they are characterised by more than the usual amount of fulsome adulation, and in the verses on the death of Queen Mary II., he stretches poetical license to the extent of asserting that queens have a special reception on their entry into Paradise.

Having borrowed metaphors and similes from Milton, he rearranges them in his own style, after the following fashion :—

> " With robes invested of celestial dies,
> She towr's, and treads the Empyrean Skies ;

Angelick choirs, skill'd in triumphant song,
Heaven's battlements and crystal turrets throng,
The signal's given, the eternal gates unfold
Burning with jasper, wreath'd in burnish'd gold ;
And myriads now of flaming minds I see—
Pow'rs, Potentates, Heaven's awful Hierarchy
In gradual orbs enthron'd, but all divine
Ineffably those sons of glory shine."

On the accession of Queen Anne, in 1702, the following new letters patent were issued :—

"These are to certify that I have sworn and admitted Nahum Tate into ye place and quality of Poet Laureate to Her Majesty in ordinary, to have, hold, and exercise and enjoy the said place, together with all rights, profits, privileges, and advantages thereunto belonging, in as full and ample manner as any Poet Laureate hath formerly held, and of right ought to have held and enjoyed the same.

"Given under my hand this 24th day of December, in the first year of her Majesty's reign.

"JERSEY."

During this reign, the appointment of Laureate was placed in the gift of the Lord Chamberlain; consequently, in 1714, Tate was again formally appointed. In these documents, the name is spelt *Tate,* although it is doubtful when and for what reason the poet abandoned the correct orthography of the family name of Teat.

Pope wittily summed up Tate's poetical talents, in lines of the utmost severity :—

"The Bard whom pilfer'd pastorals renown,
Who turns a Persian tale for half-a-crown
Just writes to make his barrenness appear,
And strains from hard-bound brains, eight lines a year ;
He, who still wanting, though he lives on theft,
Steals much, spends little, yet has nothing left :
And he, who now to sense, now nonsense leaning,
Means not, but blunders round a meaning ;

> And he, whose fustian's so sublimely bad,
> It is not poetry, but prose run mad.
> All these, my modest satire, bade translate,
> And own'd that nine such Poets made a *Tate*."

All this bitter satire might have been applied with justice to Tate, had he produced nothing better than his official odes; but such was certainly not the case; his translation of Ovid's *Remedy of Love*, included in Tonson's edition of "Miscellaneous Poems," is very gracefully written, and *Panacea*, a poem on the power and virtues of tea (then a highly-priced luxury), is excellent in its construction, although the subject lacks interest at the present time. Sir Walter Scott speaks indulgently of Tate, and admits him amongst the "second-rate bards, who by dint of expletive and pleonasm, can find smooth lines, if any one will supply ideas." Contemporary critics ranked him far higher; one says :—

> " The British laurel by old Chaucer worn,
> Still fresh and gay did Dryden's brow adorn,
> And that its lustre may not fade on thine,
> Wit, fancy, judgment, Tate in thee combine."

And another :—

> " Long may the laurel flourish on your brow,
> Since you so well a Laureate's duty know,
> For virtue's rescue daring to engage
> Against the tyrant vices of the age."

Swift, with the characteristic ill-nature which prompted him to sneer at every one whom he did not greatly fear, or who did not greatly fear him, taunts Tate for being too prolific :—

" Nahum Tate, who is ready to take oath that he has caused many reams of verse to be published, whereof both himself and his bookseller (if lawfully required) can still produce authentic copies, and therefore wonders why the world is pleased to make such a secret of it."

As an instance of Tate's happy knack of throwing off verses on the current topics of the day, a little epigram on *The Spectator* may be given; it appeared in No. 488, dated Friday, Sept. 19, 1712, accompanied by the following letter :—

" SIR,—Having heard the following epigram very much commended, I wonder that it has not yet had a place in any of your papers; I think the suffrage of our Poet Laureat should not be overlooked, which shows the opinion he entertains of your paper, whether the notion he proceeds upon be true or false.   I make bold to convey it to you, not knowing if it has yet come to your hands :—

ON THE SPECTATOR.

BY MR. TATE.

—————— ——Aliusque et idem
Nasceris.— HOR., Carm. Sæc. 10.

You rise another, and the same.

" When first the *Tatler* to a mute was turn'd,
  Great Britain for her censor's silence mourn'd ;
  Robb'd of his sprightly beams, she wept the night,
  Till the *Spectator* rose, and blaz'd as bright.
  So the first man the sun's first setting view'd,
  And sigh'd till circling day his joys renew'd.
  Yet, doubtful how that second sun to name,
  Whether a bright successor, or the same,
  So we ; but now from this suspense are freed,
  Since all agree, who both with judgment read,
  'Tis the same sun, and does himself succeed."

It must be remembered that Addison and Steele contributed to the *Tatler,* which ceased to appear in 1711, and were afterwards the chief writers for the *Spectator*.

In conjunction with Dr. Brady, Tate issued a version of twenty Psalms, and shortly afterwards the complete work, entitled, " A New Version of the Psalms of David," fitted to the tunes used in churches, by N. Brady, D.D., Chaplain in Ordinary to Her Majesty, and N. Tate, Esq., Poet Laureate. This work met with much hostile criticism, many ignorant and bigoted persons believing there was something sacred in the obsolete words, and quaint expressions in the old Sternhold and Hopkins' version, first published in 1562.

But the Bishop of London sent out letters to all the clergy of his diocese, recommending them to adopt the new arrangement, and the following order in Council officially sanctioned its use :—

" At the Court of Kensington, December 3, 1696. Present the King's most excellent Majesty in Council. Upon the humble petition of Nicholas Brady and Nahum Tate, this day read at the Board, setting forth that the petitioners have, with their utmost care and industry, completed a new version of the Psalms of David in English metre, fitted for public use ; and humbly praying His Majesty's Royal allowance that the said version may be used in such congregations as shall think fit to receive it ; His Majesty taking the same into his royal consideration is pleased to order in Council that the said new version of the Psalms in English metre be, and the same is hereby allowed, and permitted to be used in all churches and chapels and congregations as shall think fit to receive the same."

This Dr. Brady was, like Tate, an Irishman, a considerable versifier, and the author of at least one tragedy. He preached the sermon at the funeral of Shadwell; took an active part in the Revolution of 1688, for which he was well rewarded; and was a man of some talent, and considerable worldly wisdom.

Of Tate's poetical works, there is little more to be said ; he wrote about a dozen plays, and projected several prose

K

works. One of these, *The Monitor*, a dull, but well-meant, and very moral journal, which first appeared on March 2, 1713, had only a brief career, although published under royal and distinguished patronage; and this may be considered the last work of poor Tate, a Laureate inferior to many of the race, though very far from being the worst poet, and by no means a vicious one.

Dr. Johnson asserts that Tate was removed from the office of Laureate, on the accession of George I., to make way for Rowe. This has been denied; but the fact that Tate had to seek refuge from his creditors in the sanctuary of the Mint (some have stated that he was imprisoned), where he died in extreme poverty, on the 12th August, 1715, seems to corroborate the doctor's statement.

Tate was not a favourite in society; he was not a successful man; and when an almost entire redistribution of Court patronage took place, it was only to be expected that he should have to forfeit his office, in favour of a poet who (like Rowe) was of a courtly disposition, graceful manners, and who belonged to the dominant faction.

> " O ! pass more innocent, in infant state,
> To the mild limbo of our Father Tate ;
> Or peaceably forgot, at once be blest
> In Shadwell's bosom with eternal rest ! "

NAHUM TATE'S DRAMATIC WORKS.

Brutus of Alba ; or, the Enchanted Lovers. A tragedy, acted in 1678, with a prologue by Dryden.

The Loyal General. Tragedy. Acted 1680.

The History of King Lear. 1681.

The History of King Richard II.

The Ingratitude of a Commonwealth; or, the Fall of Caius Martius Coriolanus. Acted 1682.

Cuckold's Haven; or, An Alderman no Conjuror. A Duke, and No Duke. Farce. Acted 1685.

The Island Princess. Acted 1687.

Injured Love; or, the Cruel Husband. T. 1707.

Dido and Æneas. Opera. Performed at Mr. Joseph Priest's Boarding School, Chelsea.

Masque for Valentinian.

The Sicilian Usurper. This play was suppressed for political reasons.

During the reign of Nahum Tate there was a greater poet, and much more distinguished personage about the court, namely Matthew Prior, one of the lucky literary men of Queen Anne's reign. This gentleman, whom Thackeray tersely describes as a worldly philosopher of no small genius, good nature, and acumen, would probably have been appointed Laureate had the post become vacant during Anne's lifetime, as, according to Swift, he was very well at Court and with the ministry, was adviser to Lord Jersey, had distinguished himself in several diplomatic missions, and was for a time English ambassador to Louis XIV. Whether he sighed for the reversion of the laurels, or whether he thought Tate's muse was incapable of doing justice to the glorious events then transpiring, is doubtful; but he frequently supplemented the Laureate odes by courtly effusions far superior to those which were officially inspired by sack and pension.

The first of these, a long poem, entitled, "An English Ballad on the Taking of Namur by the King of Great

Britain," 1695, was a somewhat sarcastic imitation of an ode written by Boileau to congratulate Louis XIV. on his capture of the same city three years earlier.

There was also an ode to King William on his Majesty's arrival in Holland after Queen Mary's death, in 1695, and another on his arrival in Holland in 1696; and *Carmen Seculare*, for the year 1700, dedicated to the king.

Then, in 1704, a Prologue, which was spoken at Court before Queen Anne on her birthday, and in 1706 a longer and more ambitious poem, entitled, " An Ode Humbly Inscribed to the Queen on the Glorious Success of Her Majesty's Arms," written in imitation of Spenser's style, and containing some fine passages, although the poet's boastful prophecy—

> " And latest times shall in my number's read
> Anne's immortal fame, and Marlbro's hardy deed."

is capable of but limited application in the present day,

It will be seen that all these poems were of a semi-official character, and such as might have been expected from a Laureate, or a candidate for that title.

NICHOLAS ROWE.

(1715—1718.)

> " Enough for him that Congreve was his friend,
>   That Garth, and Steele, and Addison commend,
>   That Brunswick with the bays his temples bound,
>   And Parker with immortal honours crowned."
>
> AMHURST, on the death of Mr. Rowe.

NICHOLAS ROWE was born in 1673, at Little Beckford, in Bedfordshire, his father was a sergeant-at-law, and Nicholas studied for the same profession in the Middle Temple, after having achieved considerable distinction for his industry and abilities at Westminster School, under the celebrated Dr. Busby.

On the death of his father, in 1692, he inherited a fortune of about £300 a year—an ample competence in those days—and henceforth he deserted his dry legal studies for the more enticing pursuits of elegant literature. His first play, *The Ambitious Step-mother*, was so successful at the theatre in Lincoln's Inn Fields, that he was encouraged to continue dramatic composition.

His next tragedy was *Tamerlane*, produced in 1702, in which the hero was intended for a complimentary portrait of William III., whilst the villainous part of *Bajazet* was a caricature of Louis XIV. — suitable to the character popularly ascribed to him in England at that period.

Louis was the bugbear of the day, and the people were delighted thus to have an opportunity of beholding him—

> " Painted upon a pole, and underwrit
> ' Here you may see the tyrant! ' "

It became a custom to act this play annually on William's birthday, and the anniversary of his landing in England, the 4th and 5th of November.

Rowe's other tragedies are : *The Fair Penitent, Ulysses, The Royal Convert, Jane Shore,* and *Lady Jane Grey.* Although he was of an exceedingly cheerful disposition, and witty in conversation, Rowe's only attempt at comedy, *The Biter,* was a lamentable failure, and is not included in his works.

In 1709 he produced his well-known edition of Shakespeare's plays, with a carefully-compiled life of the great dramatist. In the collection of materials for this work he was assisted by the actor Betterton, who went to Stratford to glean any lingering traditions that might be found, but with small success.

For three years Rowe acted as under secretary to the Duke of Queensberry, on whose death, wishing to obtain further state employment, he applied to Lord Oxford, who strongly advised him to study the Spanish language. The sanguine poet naturally concluded that it was intended to confer upon him some post connected with Spanish affairs, and, elated by his good fortune, at once applied himself to the study of that noble language. Having attained considerable proficiency, he again appeared before Lord Oxford, and eagerly announced the fact. The minister complimented him upon his industry, calmly assured him that he was greatly to be envied the pleasure of reading Don Quixote in the original, and, without any mention of place or office, bowed the disappointed Rowe from the room.

During the latter part of Queen Anne's reign Rowe lived in retirement, but on the accession of George he at once received considerable signs of Court favour, being appointed Clerk of the Council to the Prince of Wales, Secretary of Presentations to the Lord Chancellor Parker, and one of the Land Surveyors of the Port of London.

In 1715 he succeeded Tate as Poet Laureate; but his connection with the post was unmarked by any circumstances of great interest, literary or political, and was of short duration, as he died in 1718. He wrote the usual odes, and the following extract shows that he could invest a threadbare theme with some grace, and a little life:—

ODE FOR THE NEW YEAR, 1717.

By Nicholas Rowe, Esq., Poet Laureate.

" WINTER! thou hoary venerable sire,
  All richly in thy furry mantle clad,
What thoughts of mirth can feeble age inspire,
  To make thy careful wrinkled brow so glad?

  " Now I see the reason plain,
  Now I see thy jolly train ;
  Snowy headed winter leads,
  Spring and summer next succeeds,
  Yellow autumn brings the rear,
  Thou art father of the year.
  While from the frosty mellow'd earth
  Abounding plenty takes her birth,
  The conscious sire exulting sees
  The seasons spread their rich increase ;
  So dusky night and chaos smil'd
  On beauteous form, their lovely child.
      O fair variety !
  What bliss thou dost supply !

> The foul brings forth the fair
> To deck the changing year.
> When our old pleasures die,
> Some new one still is nigh ;
> O fair variety !"

Rowe's disposition was particularly gay and vivacious, he had a charming voice, engaging manners, a graceful well-made person, and features of regular and manly beauty. These advantages, together with his witty and learned conversation, obtained for him the friendship of the greatest literary men of the day—Pope, Addison, Steele, and Swift, with many others of less celebrity.

Some one who had formed a judgment of Rowe's character solely from the perusal of his tragedies, remarked to Pope that he was far too grave a man to write any light pieces. "He grave," said Pope, "why he will laugh all day long : he will do nothing else than laugh."

Of his works, Dr. Johnson says,

"Rowe is chiefly to be considered as a tragic writer and a translator, for his version of Lucan's *Pharsalia* is one of the greatest productions of English poetry.

He also translated several portions of Ovid's "Metamorphoses."

His English verse may be taken to represent what Lord Macaulay calls the critical poetry of his age, the poetry by courtesy,—the poetry to which the memory, the judgment, and the wit contribute far more than the imagination. During the short time he held office as Laureate he appears to have escaped the fate of most of his predecessors; his amiability of temper preserved him from the dislike or envy of his contemporaries, whilst his cleverness protected him from ridicule.

Rowe died on the 6th December, 1718, and was buried in Westminster Abbey, where there is a handsome monument to his memory in Poet's Corner. On the front of the pedestal is the inscription :—

" To the memory of Nicholas Rowe, Esq., who died in 1718, aged forty-five; and of Charlotte, his only daughter, wife of Henry Fane, Esq., who, inheriting her father's spirit, and amiable in her own innocence and beauty, died in the twenty-second year of her age, 1739."

Then follows a poetical epitaph :—

> " Thy reliques, ROWE, to this sad shrine we trust,
> And near thy SHAKESPEARE place thy honour'd bust.
> Oh ! next him skilléd to draw the tender tear,
> For never heart felt passion more sincere ;
> To nobler sentiments to fire the brave,
> For never Briton more disdain'd a slave.
> Peace to thy gentle shade, and endless rest ;
> Blest in thy genius, in thy love too blest !
> And blest, that timely from our scene removed,
> Thy soul enjoys the liberty it loved."

> " To these so mourn'd in death, so loved in life,
> The childless parent, and the widow'd wife
> With tears inscribes this monumental stone
> That holds their ashes, and expects her own."

Pope's original lines were certainly superior :

> " Thy relics, Rowe, to this fair urn we trust,
> And, sacred, place by Dryden's awful dust.
> Beneath a rude and nameless stone he lies,
> To which thy tomb shall guide enquiring eyes.
> Peace to thy gentle shade, and endless rest !
> Blest in thy genius—in thy love too blest !
> One grateful woman to thy fame supplies
> What a whole thankless land to his denies."

LAURENCE EUSDEN.

(1718—1730.)

" While in their camp retir'd both armies lay,
   Some panting, others fearful, for the day,
   Eusden, a laurell'd Bard, by fortune rais'd,
   By very few been read, by fewer praised.
   From place to place, forlorn and breathless, flies
   And offers bribes immense for strong allies.
   In vain he spent the day, the night in vain,
   For all the laureate, and his bribes, disdain,
   With heart dejected he returned alone
   Upon the banks of Cham, to make his moan
   Resolv'd to spend his future days in ease,
   And only toil in verse himself to please,
   To fly the noisy candidates of Fame,
   Nor ever court again so coy a Dame."

THIS very small poet was born in Yorkshire, but at what date is not exactly known, for few biographers have taken much pains to discover the details of his early career. He was educated at Trinity College, Cambridge, and was afterwards for some time chaplain to Lord Willoughby de Broke, through whose interest probably he received the living of Coningsby, in Lincolnshire.

His poems (a few of which are preserved in Nicholls' collection) are now quite forgotten, and were held in little esteem during his lifetime. On the death of Rowe, his patrons exerted their influence, and with success, to obtain the office of Laureate for Eusden. The Duke of New-castle, then Lord Chamberlain, was chiefly to blame, for an appointment so ridiculous in itself, and reflecting such great dishonour on the office which had been held by Jonson, Davenant, and Dryden.

As *Figaro* says, "Il fallait un calculateur, ce fut un danseur qui l'obtint;" they wanted a poet king, they chose a drunken country parson.

Eusden, out of gratitude, composed several adulatory poems on his friends, and some odes to the king, in which excess of flattery, without the art to conceal it, is the most noticeable feature. It is true the Odes are very blasphemous, and to compare George I. or George II. to the Deity, although it might be an entirely novel idea which was never likely to occur to anyone else, is not altogether an agreeable one. This world offered him no comparison for the Georges, so he fearlessly chose one from the heavens; it would not have been courtier-like to have made a selection from any other place:

> " Praise undeserved, is scandal in disguise,
>   Well may he blush, who gives it, or receives ;
>   And when I flatter let my dirty leaves
>   (Like journals, odes, and such forgotten things
>   As Eusden, Philips, Settle, writ of Kings,)
>   Clothe spice, line trunks, or fluttering in a row,
>   Befringe the rails of Bedlam and Soho."—POPE.

Mr. Oldmixon, in his *Arts of Logic and Rhetoric*, remarks that:—

" The putting of the laurel on the head of one who writ such verses, will give futurity a very lively idea of the judgment and justice of those who bestowed it. For of all the galimatias I ever met with, none comes up to some verses of this poet, which have as much of the ridiculum and the fustian in them as can well be jumbled together; and are of that sort of nonsense, which so perfectly confounds all ideas, that there is no distinct one left in the mind."

As a sample of a style of composition, now happily extinct, the annexed fragment may be interesting, or even amusing; it is by no means an unfavourable specimen of Eusden's Odes:—

A POEM

On the Happy Succession and Coronation
of His present Majesty,
King George II.

By Laurence Eusden, 1727.

*   *   *   *   *   *   *   *

" So when Great Brunswick yielded to his fate
O'ercast and cheerless was Britannia's state,
Her cheeks to lose their bloomy hue begun,
And all her roses vanished with her sun.
Till a new Brunswick, with an equal ray,
Re-call'd at once her beauties, and the day,
Firm and un-changed, the spires and turrets stand,
Religion, joyn'd with Liberty's fair hand,
In triumph walk, and bless with wonted smiles, the land.
Hail, mighty monarch! whose desert alone
Would, without birth-right, raise thee to a throne.
    Thy virtues shine peculiarly nice,
    Un-gloom'd with a confinity to vice,
What strains shall equal to thy glories rise,
First of the world, and borderer on the skies?
How exquisitely great, who can'st inspire
Such joys, that Albion mourns no more thy sire;
Thy Sire! a Prince, she loved to that degree
She almost trespass'd to the Deity.
Imperial weight he bore with so much ease
Who, but thyself, would not despair to please?
A dull, fat, thoughtless heir, unheeded, springs
From a long, slothful line of restive kings

And thrones, inur'd to a tyrannic race,
Think a new tyrant not a new disgrace,
Tho' by the change the state no bliss receives,
And Nero dies in vain, if Otho lives.
But when a stem, with fruitful branches crowned,
Still ever seem (if they survive or fall,)
All heroes, and their country's fathers all.
His great forerunners when the last outshone,
Who could a brighter hope, or ev'n as bright a son ?
Old Rome, with tears the younger Scipio view'd,
Who not in fame her African renew'd.
Avant, degenerate grafts, or spurious breed,
'Tis a George only can a George succeed ;
The shafts of Death, the Pelian art have found,
They bring at once the balm that give the wound."

In another of these "gushing" effusions we find the lines ;—

" Such to Britannia is her king
As the softly murmuring spring.

CHORUS

" GENIUS ! now securely rest,
We shall ever now be blest.
Thou thy guardianship may spare
BRITANNIA is a BRUNSWICK'S care ! "

Such fustian could scarcely fail to evoke ridicule, and in the *Grub Street Journal*, August 27, 1730, there appeared a parody of Dryden's celebrated Epigram on Milton; Parson Eusden is the hero ;—

" Three Poets (grave divines) in England born,
The Prince's entry did with verse adorn.
The first in lowliness of thought surpass'd ;
The next in bombast ; and in both the last.
DULLNESS no more could for her Laureate do,
To perfect him, she joined the former two."

In the *Spectator* of June 7, 1711, there is a curious

letter on "Idols," contributed by Eusden, in which, although the humour is not very brilliant, there are some amusing illustrations of customs, which are not yet quite obsolete :—

"*Mr. Spectator.*

"Upon reading your late dissertation concerning idols, I cannot but complain to you that there are, in six or seven places of this city, coffeehouses kept by persons of that sisterhood. These idols sit and receive all day long the adoration of the youth within such and such districts. I know, in particular, goods are not entered as they ought to be at the Custom House, nor Law Reports perused at the Temple, by reason of one beauty who detains the young merchants too long near 'Change, and another fair one who keeps the students at her house when they should be at study.

"It would be worth your while to see how the idolators alternately offer incense to their idols, and what heartburnings arise in those who wait for their turn to receive kind aspects from those little thrones, which all the company but these lovers, call the bars. I saw a gentleman turn as pale as ashes, because an idol turned the sugar in a tea dish for his rival, and carelessly called the boy to serve him, with a 'Sirrah! why don't you give the gentleman the box to please himself ?' Certain it is, that a very hopeful young man was taken with leads in his pockets below bridge, where he intended to drown himself, because his idol would wash the dish in which she had but just drank tea, before she would let him use it.

"I am, Sir, a person past being amorous, and do not give this information out of envy or jealousy, but I am a real sufferer by it.

"These lovers take anything for tea and coffee. I saw one yester day surfeit to make his court, and all his rivals at the same time, loud in the commendation of liquors that went against everybody in the room that was not in love.

"While these young fellows resign their stomachs with their hearts, and drink at the idol in this manner, we who come to do business, or talk politics, are utterly poisoned.

"They have also drams for those who are more enamoured than ordinary ; and it is very common for such as are too low in constitution to ogle the idol upon the strength of tea, to fluster themselves with warmer liquors ; thus all pretenders advance as fast they can, to a fever or a diabetes.

" I must repeat to you, that I do not look with an evil eye upon the profit of the idols, or the diversions of the lovers ; what I hope from this remonstrance is only that we plain people may not be served as if we were idolators ; but that from the time of publishing this in your paper, the idols would mix ratsbane only for their admirers, and take more care of us who don't love them.

" I am, Sir,

" Yours T. T."

The appointment of Eusden as Laureate gave John Sheffield, Duke of Buckingham, the topic for his famous little satirical poem " The Election of a Poet Laureate," which he has treated in a similar style to Suckling's " Sessions of the Poets," previously alluded to.

> " A famous assembly was summoned of late,
> To crown a new laureat came Phœbus in state,
> With all that Montfaucon himself could desire,
> His bow, laurel, harp, and abundance of fire.
>
> *   *   *   *   *   *   *   *
>
> All came with full confidence, flushed with vain hope,
> From Cibber and Durfey, to Prior and Pope.
> Phœbus smiled on these last, but yet ne'ertheless,
> Said he hoped they had got enough by the press.
>
> *   *   *   *   *   *   *   *
>
> Lampooners and critics rush'd in like a tide,
> Stern Dennis and Gildon came first side by side,
> Apollo confess'd that their lashes had stings,
> But beadles and hangmen were never chose kings.
>
> *   *   *   *   *   *   *   *
>
> Steel long had so cunningly manag'd the town,
> He could not be blamed for expecting the crown,
> Apollo demurr'd as to granting his wish,
> But wish'd him good luck in his project of fish."*

---

* Steel had obtained a patent for bringing fish to the market alive.

Lame Congreve* unable such things to endure
Of Apollo begg'd either a crown or a cure ;
To refuse such a writer, Apollo was loth,
And almost inclin'd to have granted them both.

Buckingham next describes his own entry :—

" When Buckingham came he scarce car'd to be seen,
Till Phœbus desir'd his old friend to walk in,
But a laureat peer had never been known,
The commoners claimed that place as their own.

Yet if the kind God had been e'er so inclin'd
To break an old rule, yet he well knew his mind,
Who, of such preferment, would only make sport,
And laughed at all suitors for places at Court.

The god is bewildered by the clamour of the assembled candidates, eager for the crown, when—

" At last rush'd in Eusden, and cried, ' Who shall have it,
But I the true laureat, to whom the King gave it ?
Apollo begg'd pardon, and granted his claim,
But vow'd, that till then, he had ne'er heard his name."

The only poetical works composed by Eusden that have ever received attention or commendation, are his translations of parts of Ovid's "Metamorphoses ;" he commenced a translation of Tasso's poems, but before this work was ready for the press, his excesses in drink put an end to his life, on the 27th of September, 1730.

Gray laconically said of him,—

" That he was a person of great hopes in his youth, though at last he turned out a drunken parson."

The death of Eusden made way for the promotion of the well known actor, playwright, and hero of the *Dunciad*, Colley Cibber :—

---

* Congreve was at this time much afflicted with gout.

" She (Dulness) saw old Prynne in restless Daniel shine,
And Eusden eke out Blackmore's endless line;
She saw slow Phillips creep like Tate's poor page,
And all the mighty mad in Dennis rage.
In each she marks her image full exprest,
But chief in Bays's monster breeding breast;
Bays,* form'd by nature, stage and town to bless,
And act, and be, a coxcomb, with success."
Dulness with transport eyes the lively dunce,
Remembering she herself was Pertness once.
Now (shame to Fortune) an ill run at play
Blank'd his bold visage, and a thin third day:
Swearing and supperless the hero sate,
Blasphemed his gods, the dice, and damn'd his fate.
Then gnaw'd his pen, then dash'd it on the ground,
Sinking from thought to thought, a vast profound!
Plunged for his sense, but found no bottom there,
Yet wrote and flounder'd on, in mere despair.

A. POPE. " THE DUNCIAD."

* Colley Cibber.

L

POPE ON THE LAURELS.

THE following burlesque account of the office of Poet Laureate appeared in the *Memoirs of the Society of Grub Street,* No. 46, November 19, 1730. It was probably written by Pope; and is usually reprinted in the appendix to *The Dunciad :—*

"The time of the election of a Poet Laureate being now at hand, it may be proper to give some account of the *rites* and *ceremonies* anciently used at that solemnity, and only discontinued through the neglect and degeneracy of later times. These we have extracted from an historian of undoubted credit, a reverend bishop, the learned Paulus Jovius ; and are the same that were practised under the pontificate of Leo X., the great restorer of learning.

"As we now see an *age* and a *court,* that for the encouragement of poetry rivals, if not exceeds, that of this famous Pope, we cannot but wish a restoration of all its *honours* to *poesy ;* the rather, since there are so many parallel circumstances in the *person* who was then honoured with the laurel, and in *him,* who (in all probability) is now to wear it.

" I shall translate my author exactly as I find it in the eighty-second chapter of his *Elogia Vir. Doct.* He begins with the character of the poet himself, who was the original and father of all Laureates, and called Camillo.

" He was a plain country-man of Apulia, whether a *shepherd* or a *thresher,* is not material. 'This man (says Jovius), excited by the fame of the great encouragement given to poets at court, and the high honour in which they were held, came to the city, bringing with him a strange kind of lyre in his hand, and at least some *twenty thousand of verses.* All the wits and critics of the court flocked about him, delighted to see a *clown*, with a ruddy, hale complexion, and in his own long hair, so top full of poetry ; and at the first sight of him all agreed he was born to be *Poet Laureate.* He had a most hearty welcome in an *island* of the river Tiber (an agreeable place, not unlike our Richmond), where he was first made to *eat* and *drink plentifully*, and to *repeat his verses to everybody.* Then they adorned him with a new and elegant garland, composed of *vine-leaves, laurel* and *brassica* (a sort of cabbage), so composed,' says my author, ' emblematically, *ut tam sales, quam lepida ejus temulentia, Brassicæ remedeo cohibenda, notaretur.*' He was then saluted by common consent with the title of *archi-poeta* or *arch poet*, in the style of those days, in ours *Poet Laureate.*

" This honour the poor man received with the most sensible demonstrations of joy, his eyes drunk with tears and gladness. Next the public acclamation was expressed in a *canticle*, which is transmitted to us, as follows :—

> Salve, brassicea virens corona,
> Et lauro, archipoeta, pampinoque!
> Dignus principis auribus Leonis.

> All hail, arch-poet without peer !
> Vine, bay, or cabbage fit to wear,
> And worthy of the prince's ear.

" From hence he was conducted in pomp to the *capitol* of Rome, mounted on an *elephant*, through the shouts of the populace, where the ceremony ended.

" The historian tells us farther, 'That at his introduction to Leo, he not only poured forth verses innumerable, like a torrent, but also *sung* them with *open mouth.*'

" Nor was he only *once* introduced, or on *stated* days (like our Laureates), but made a *companion* to his *master*, and entertained as one of the instruments of his most *elegant pleasures.* When the prince was at table, the poet had his place at the window. When the prince had half eaten his meat, he gave with his own hands the rest to the *poet.* When the poet drank, it was out of the prince's own flaggon, insomuch (says the historian) that through so great good eating and drinking he contracted a most terrible gout.   Sorry I am to relate what follows, but that I cannot leave my readers' curiosity unsatisfied in the catastrophe of this extraordinary man. To use my author's words, which are remarkable, ' When Leo died, and poets were no more, this unhappy Laureate was forthwith reduced to return to his country, where oppressed with *old age* and *want,* he miserably perished in a *common hospital.'*

" We see from this sad conclusion (which may be of example to the poets of our time) that it were happier to meet with no encouragement at all, to remain at the plough, or other lawful occupation, than to be elevated above their condition, and taken out of the common means of life, without a surer support than the *temporary,* or, at best *mortal* favours of the great.   It was doubtless for this consideration, that when the Royal Bounty was lately extended to a *rural genius,** care was taken *to settle it upon him for life.*   And it hath been the practise of our Princes, never to remove from the station of Poet Laureate any man who hath once been chosen, though never so much greater geniuses might arise in his time.†   A noble instance, how much the *charity* of our monarchs hath exceeded their *love of fame.*

" To come now to the intent of this paper.   We have here the whole ancient ceremonial of the Laureate.   In the first place the crown is to be mixed with *vine-leaves,* as the vine is the plant of Bacchus, and full as essential to the honour, as the *butt of sack* to the salary.

" Secondly, the *brassica* must be made use of as a qualifier of the former.   It seems the *cabbage* was anciently accounted a remedy for drunkenness ; a power the French now ascribe to the onion, and style a soup made of it, *soupe d'yvrogne.*   I would recommend a large mixture of the *brassica* if Mr. Dennis be chosen ; but if Mr. Tibbald, it is not so necessary, unless the cabbage be supposed to signify the same thing with respect to *poets* as to *tailors,* viz., *stealing.*   I should judge it not amiss to add another plant to this garland, to wit, *ivy ;* not only as it anciently belonged to poets in

---

* Laurence Eusden.

† This is incorrect.   Dryden had been superseded to make way for Shadwell, and Tate gave way (as is supposed) that Rowe might take his post.

general; but as it is emblematical of the three vices of a court poet in particular ; it is *creeping*, *dirty*, and *dangling*.

" In the next place, a *canticle* must be composed and sung in laud and praise of the new poet. If Mr. CIBBER be laureated, it is my opinion no man can *write* this but himself ; and no man, I am sure, can *sing* it so affectingly. But what this canticle should be, either in his or the other candidates' case, I shall not pretend to determine.

"Thirdly, there ought to be a *public show*, or entry of the poet. To settle the order or procession of which, Mr. Anstis and Mr. DENNIS ought to have a conference.

" I apprehend here two difficulties : one, of procuring an *elephant;* the other of teaching the poet to ride him : therefore I should imagine the next animal in size or dignity would do best ; either a *mule* or a large *ass;* particularly if that noble one could be had, whose portraiture makes so great an ornament of *The Dunciad*, and which (unless I am misinformed) is yet in the park of a nobleman near this city.

" Unless Mr. CIBBER be the man ; who may, with great propriety and beauty, ride on a *dragon*, if he goes by land ; or if he chuse the water, upon one of his own *swans* from *Cæsar in Egypt.*

" We have spoken sufficiently of the *ceremony;* let us now speak of the *qualifications* and *privileges* of the Laureate. First, we see he must be able to make verses *extempore*, and to pour forth innumerable, if required. In this I doubt Mr. TIBBALD. Secondly, he ought to sing, and intrepidly, *patulo ore:* here, I confess the excellency of Mr. CIBBER. Thirdly, he ought to carry a *lyre* about with him : if a large one be thought too cumbersome, a small one may be contrived to hang about the neck like an order, and be very much a grace to the person. Fourthly, he ought to have a good *stomach*, to eat and drink whatever his betters think fit ; and therefore it is in this high office as in many others, no puny constitution can discharge it. I do not think CIBBER or TIBBALD here so happy : but rather a stanch, vigorous, seasoned and dry *old gentleman*, whom I have in my eye.

" I could also wish at this juncture, such a person as is truly jealous of the *honour* and *dignity* of *poetry;* no joker, or trifler ; but a bard in *good earnest;* nay, not amiss if a critic, and the better if a little *obstinate*.

" For when we consider what great privileges have been lost from this office (as we see from the forecited authentic record of Jovius), namely those of *feeding* from the *prince's table, drinking* out of his own *flaggon*, becoming even his domestic and companion ; it requires a man warm and resolute, to be able to claim and obtain the restoring of these high honours.

" I have cause to fear the most of the candidates would be liable, either through the influence of ministers, or for rewards or favours, to give up the glorious rights of the Laureate : yet I am not without hopes, there is *one*, from whom a *serious* and *steady* assertion of these privileges may be expected ; and, if there be such a one, I must do him the justice to say, it is Mr. DENNIS, the worthy president of our society."

Mr. Lewis Theobald (pronounced Tibbald) and Mr. John Dennis, were two writers of mean talents, whose criticisms of Mr. Pope's previous works were wanting in every attribute of sober judgment, or gentlemanly feeling ; in the place of which, the vilest personalities and most repulsive similes fill out their tedious paragraphs. *The Dunciad* has immortalised their names and many others, which had otherwise been long since forgotten :—

> " Who by my Muse to all succeeding times
> Shall live, in spite of their own doggrel rhymes."
> —DRYDEN.

COLLEY CIBBER.

(1730—1757.)

" Well, said Apollo, still 'tis mine
　　To give the real laurel,
For that my Pope, my son divine,
　　Of rivals ends the quarrel.
But guessing who would have the luck
　　To be the birth-day fibber,
I thought of Dennis, Tibbald, Duck,
　　But never dreamt of Cibber!"

　　　Memoirs of the Society of Grub Street.　No. 52.
　　　　　　December 31, 1730.

SATIRES, epigrams, and lampoons have at all times been plentifully written upon the Laureates and their works, and never have these been more amusing, or more plentiful, than when second-rate, dully respectable authors have held the post.

Such men as Eusden or Tate were almost too insignificant even to be lampooned, whilst distinguished authors, such as Dryden and Southey, gave little hold for ridicule in their writings, though both were severely satirised for their venality and political instability.

Cibber, an amiable man, and a man of genius, though certainly a very inferior poet, is an instance in point, for never has any man of so little public importance been so bitterly, so perseveringly, and so unjustly satirised.

Aware of the little foundation for many of these attacks, and content with the very fair share of success and approbation he received from the public in general, Cibber bore the envious and malicious stabs to which not only his works, and genius, but even his personal appearance and private character, were exposed, with imperturbable equanimity and good temper. He gaily laughed at Pope, whom any other man in his position would have most probably caned or challenged.

Although Pope pilloried Cibber as the hero of *The Dunciad*, he could not make him a dunce; epigrams abound to show that Cibber had no reputation as a poet— a title to which, by the way, he himself never laid claim— but no one ever denied that he was a splendid comedian; he has been unfairly taunted for his failure in the composition of tragedies, but Dr. Blair, in his admirable lectures on English literature, says of Cibber's *Provoked Husband :*—

"It is perhaps on the whole the best comedy in the English language; it is calculated to expose licentiousness and folly, and would do honour to any stage."

In one of the numerous and entertaining notes to *The Dunciad*, Pope quotes an account of Cibber's varied talents, adding satirically that, "Mr. Jacob omitted to remark that he is particularly admirable in tragedy."

To this sneer Cibber calmly replied :—

"Ay, sir, and your remark has omitted, too, that (with all his commendations) I can't dance upon the rope, or make a saddle, nor play upon the organ.

"My dear, dear Mr. Pope, how could a man of your stinging capacity let so tame, so low a reflection escape him? Why, this hardly rises above the petty malice of Miss Molly. 'Oh yes, you may think my sister as handsome as you please, but if you were to see her legs!' If I have made so many crowded theatres laugh, and in the right place, too, for above forty years together, am I to make up the number of your dunces, because I have not the equal talent of making them cry too? Make it your own case. Is what you have excelled in, at all the worse for your having so dismally dabbled in the farce of *Three Hours after Marriage?* What mighty reason will the world have to laugh at my weakness in tragedy, more than at yours in comedy?"

Unfortunately for Cibber's reputation *The Dunciad* lives, and will live so long as English is written or spoken, whilst few modern readers pause to remember the injustice of its satire, or to inquire into the origin of its bitter and unjustifiable malice.

Nothing is more simple than to give a sketch of the principal events of Colley Cibber's interesting career; for his autobiography, entitled *An Apology for the Life of Colley Cibber, Comedian,** written in a quaint, chatty style, contains all that is known of his early life, and very full accounts of his progress as actor, author, theatrical lessee and manager, and Poet Laureate.

The veracity of this work in all its main features has never been impugned; it contains interesting information about the stage in Cibber's time, very amusing anecdotes illustrative of the tone of society, and is generally accompanied by an excellent engraved likeness of the laureate, after a painting by Vanloo.

The account of his birth and parentage is as follows :—

"I was born in London, on the 6th of November, 1671, in Southampton-street, facing Southampton House. My father, *Caius Gabriel Cibber*, was a native of Holstein, who came into England some time before the Restoration of King Charles II., to follow his Profession, which was that of a statuary, etc. The Basso Relievo

---

* " There are some good things in thy Book, old Colley,
But all the rest is *self-sufficient folly*."
The Laureat, or the Right Side of C. C., Esq.

on the Pedestal of the great column in the City, and the two figures of the Lunaticks, the Raving and the Melancholy, over the gates of Bethlehem Hospital,* are no ill monuments of his Fame as an artist."

The Dunciad, of course, mentions these :—

> " Close to those walls where Folly holds her throne,
> And laughs to think Munroe would take her down,
> Where, o'er the gates, by his famed father's hand
> Great Cibber's brazen brainless brothers stand."

Cibber's mother was a descendant of Sir Antony Colley, who reduced his estate from three thousand pounds a year to about three hundred in the losing cause of Charles I. What little education Cibber had, was obtained at the free grammar school of Grantham in Lincolnshire; his friends attempted to obtain his election to Winchester College, but failed. So at the age of sixteen he left school, and set out to join his father, who was at that time employed by the Earl of Devonshire in embellishing the grounds and mansion of Chatsworth. But on reaching Nottingham, Colley met the force which the Earl of Devonshire was leading to the assistance of Prince William of Orange. He at once enlisted in the cause, replacing his father, who returned to his more congenial artistic duties at Chatsworth.

The Revolution was happily effected without bloodshed, so that, although the future Laureate was a witness of some great historical events, he had no opportunity to display his courage in the field, as his predecessors Ben Jonson and Davenant had done.

> " Go sheath that sword, thou valiant man,
> Not let thy passions loose,
> *That* cannot kill, but thy pen can
> Though stolen from a goose !

---

* These were removed in 1814, when the hospital was rebuilt.

" Upon the brink, of a pond of ink
   In bathos waddle and sigh ;
For like a goose, thy muse would sink
   Should it attempt to fly.''

He remained under the Earl of Devonshire's command until King William was firmly fixed on the throne, when the forces were disbanded, and Cibber obtained his discharge, with the promise of official patronage. He was of too active a mind to wait long for the promised preferment, and having a great passion for the stage, he viewed it as a favour to be allowed on the boards, and for nine months he performed small parts without any pay, at the end of which time he obtained a salary of ten shillings a week, which, with food and clothing at his father's house, made him, as he says, the happiest of mortals, although it is true the way in which he first obtained a salary was not of the most encouraging kind. He had to deliver a short message to Betterton, who was then playing. Cibber was very timid, stammered, broke down, and the whole scene was spoilt by his awkwardness. Betterton angrily said, "Fine Master Colley," to which the prompter replied, "Sir, he has no salary." "Then," said Betterton, " put him down at ten shillings, and forfeit five."

Cibber mentions, with pardonable pride, the first part in which he obtained applause; the character was but a slight one, it is true, being the chaplain in Otway's tragedy, *The Orphan.*

Having composed a prologue for the opening night, he offered it to the management gratis, in the consideration that he should be allowed to deliver it himself; this favour was refused him; he thereupon demanded and obtained two guineas for the poem. Powel spoke it, and it was well received.

Encouraged by this success, he wrote his first play, *Love's Last Shift* (literally translated by a French author into "La dernière Chemise de l'Amour"), which, after considerable trouble, he prevailed upon the managers to produce, and he quotes the judgment of the Lord Chamberlain (Lord Dorset) :—

" That it was the best First Play, that any author in his memory had produced ; and that for a young Fellow to show himself such an actor, and such a writer in one day, was something extraordinary."

In this play Cibber performed the part of Sir Novelty Fashion, a portrait of the fop of the day, and this line of business, to use a theatrical expression, was what he always excelled in; Lord Foppington, in Sir John Vanbrugh's *Relapse*, being considered his finest part.

Grisoni painted his portrait in this character, which gave rise to the following epigram :—

" To Kneller, Dryden writes, ' Some bear the rule
Thus thou sometimes art forced to draw a fool.
But so his follies in thy posture sink,
The senseless idiot seems at least to think !'
But thou GRISONI, with sincerer art,
Hast drawn the Laureat in his noblest part.
As in his *New Year's Ode*, in thy design
The thoughtless FOPLING shines in every line."

In the *Fool in Fashion*, Cibber wore a very remarkable large fair flaxen full-bottomed periwig, which attracted great attention. This wonderful wig made its entrance upon the boards every evening in a sedan chair, carried in by two pompous footmen, to the great delight of the audience.

After his successful *coup d'essai*, his comedies came out at tolerably regular intervals, and were received with con-

siderable favour. They certainly merited success for their
humour and originality, and the attribute of decency, then
very rare; for Cibber boasts that ladies would attend first
night representations of his pieces without the masks they
usually wore when listening to the grossly licentious plays
of his contemporaries. It was usual, at that time, for
ladies to hurry to the first performance of a play for fear
the general opinion might be formed that it was unfit for
ladies to witness; modest women, on the contrary, waited
for the verdict of the town; but if their curiosity overcame their patience, they took care to save appearances
by going to the theatre in masks, which were allowed in
the pit, side boxes, and gallery, a custom that encouraged
indecency amongst authors and actors, and immorality in
the audiences.

After a number of changes in the lesseeship of Drury
Lane, Cibber became a partner with Wilks and Doggett,
and the chapters devoted to the history of that theatre
during his management are the most interesting in his
biography.

In the early years of the reign of George I. party feeling
ran high, and political warfare was waged in the pulpit
and on the stage, between the High Church Tories or
Jacobites, and the Whigs, the adherents of the Hanoverian dynasty. Those who avoided taking the oaths of
allegiance to the new monarch were styled *Non Jurors*,
and to ridicule them, Cibber translated Molière's *Tartuffe*,
renaming it *The Non Juror*. It was produced at Drury
Lane in 1717, Cibber acting the part of Dr. Wolf, a
concealed Papist, who, by his intrigues and immorality,
nearly effects the ruin of a respectable family.

This comedy had great success, much to the annoyance
of the High Church party, whose rage was increased by

the facts that the prologue was written by the then
Laureate, Nicholas Rowe, and that the King and the
Prince both went to see the play, and heartily applauded
it. *Read's Weekly Journal,* of December 7, 1717, thus
reports it :—

" Last night the comedy called the ' Non Juror ' was acted at his
Majesty's theatre in Drury Lane, which, very naturally displaying
the *villany of that most wicked and abominable crew,* it gave great
satisfaction to all the spectators."

The king not only gave his permission for the printed
edition to be dedicated to himself, but rewarded the
author with a gratuity of two hundred pounds.

It is a somewhat remarkable fact that this play has
survived all Cibber's other writings, for, altered and re-
named *The Hypocrite,* it is sometimes played even now,
and was extremely popular in the days of Liston.

As the satire was chiefly directed against the enemies
of the Government, people did not dare openly to express
their disapprobation of the play, for fear of being considered disaffected to the king. " But," says Cibber,
" they knew it would not be long before they might with
more security give a loose to their spleen, and make up
accounts with me. And soon after the *Non Juror* had
received the favour of the town, I read in one of Mr. Mist,
his Weekly Journals, the following short paragraph, viz.,
' Yesterday died Mr. Colley Cibber, late Comedian of the
Theatre Royal, notorious for writing the *Non Juror.'*
The compliment in the latter part, I confess I did not
dislike, because it came from so impartial a judge ; and
really it so happened that the former part of it was very
near being true ; for I had that very day just crawled
out, after having been some weeks laid up by a fever.
The play *The Orphan* being to be acted that day, I

quietly stole myself into the part of the *Chaplain,* which I had not been seen in for many years before. The surprise of the audience at my unexpected appearance on the very day I had been dead in the News, and the paleness of my looks, seemed to make it a doubt whether I was not the ghost of my real self departed. But when I spoke, their wonder eased itself by an applause which convinced me, they were then satisfied, that my friend *Mist* had told a *Fib* of me."

Cibber's enemies also retorted in a pamphlet, entitled, *The Theatre Royal turned into a Mountebank's Stage.* This squib, purporting to be written by a *Non Juror,* has for its motto—

> " His crime was for being a Felon in Verse,
> And presenting the Theft to the King :
> Tho' the first was a trick not uncommon or scarce
> Yet the last was an Impudent Thing "—

and is devoted to a tedious examination of the plot and dialogue of the play, ridiculing Cibber for having borrowed from Molière, censuring him for his political views, and sneering at his talents in the following verses, more forcible than elegant :—

> " Thou Cur, half Dane, half English Breed,
> Thou Mongrel of *Parnassus,*
> To think lewd lines grown up to Seed,
> Can ever tamely pass us.

> " Thou write ' Non Jurors,' and be damn'd !
> Write anagrams for Cutlers ;
> None with thy Frippery will be shammed
> But Chamber Maids and Butlers.

> " In t'other World expect dry Blows,
> No tears can wash thy stains out,
> MOLIERE will pull thee by the Nose,
> And SHAKESPEARE dash thy brains out."

Amongst Cibber's numerous productions for the stage were acting versions of several of Shakespeare's tragedies; his alterations have been severely reprehended by Garrick and other dramatic critics, and it is evident that Cibber's genius was not cast for tragedy. His most ambitious attempt in that direction was *Cæsar in Egypt*, produced at Drury-lane in 1724; and, although mounted at very great expense, it was played to "a beggarly account of empty boxes," so that his brother lessees begged him to withdraw the piece.

Cibber struggled for another, and yet another night, but at length gave way with a good grace, making a pun at his own expense, which gave rise to the epigram :—

ON THE SIXTH NIGHT OF CIBBER'S
" CÆSAR IN EGYPT."

" When the pack'd audience from their posts retired,
   And Julius in a general hiss expired ;
   Sage Booth* to Cibber cried, ' Compute our gains !
   These dogs of Egypt, and their dowdy queans,
   But ill requite these habits and these scenes,
   To rob Corneille for such a motley piece ;
   His geese were swans ; but zounds ! thy swans are geese !'
   Rubbing his firm invulnerable brow,
   The bard replied, ' The critics must allow
   'Twas ne'er in Cæsar's destiny *to run !* '
   Wilks* bow'd, and bless'd the gay pacific pun."

This cheerfulness of disposition never deserted Cibber. So calmly did he bear the satires of his enemies, that he was called impenetrable and dull; but he knew that he robbed his satirists of half their success by showing that he held them in contempt. Cibber's failure in Tragedy

---

* Actors contemporary with Cibber, and partners in Drury-lane Theatre.

was the chief point upon which Pope chose to rally him; and ignoring for the time all Cibber's other works, he brands him at once as a fool and a plagiarist :—

> " High on a gorgeous seat, that far outshone
> Henley's gilt tub, or Fleckno's Irish throne,
> Or that where on her Curls the public pours,
> All-bounteous, fragrant grains and golden showers,
> Great Cibber sate : the proud Parnassian sneer,
> The conscious simper, and the jealous leer,
> Mix on his look : all eyes direct their rays
> On him, and crowds turn coxcomb as they gaze.
> Round him much embryo, much abortion lay,
> Much future ode, and abdicated play ;
> Nonsense precipitate, like running lead,
> That slipp'd through cracks and zigzags of the head ;
> All that on Folly Frenzy could beget,
> Fruits of dull heat, and sooterkins of wit.
> Next, o'er his books his eyes begin to roll,
> In pleasing memory of all he stole,
> How here he sipp'd, how there he plunder'd snug,
> And suck'd all o'er, like an industrious bug."

Even such lines as these he carelessly passed by ; and his biography contains many anecdotes which prove that he could enjoy a joke, even at his own cost, possessing the philosophical temperament which Hume happily describes " as preferable to ten thousand a year."

When the office of laureate became vacant by the death of Eusden, there was a good deal of speculation as to his probable successor. Pope, Dennis, Theobald, and even Stephen Duck, the Wiltshire thresher, were spoken of.

On the Candidates for the Laurel.

> " Shall royal praise be rhym'd by such a ribald,
> As fopling *Cibber*, or attorney *Tibbald ?*
> Let's rather wait one year for better luck ;
> One year may make a singing swan of Duck.

M

Great George, such servants since thou well canst lack,
Oh! save the salary, and drink the sack.''

Memoirs of Grub Street.

Such economy was not, however, to be effected; Cibber got the laurels and the sack, by appoinment, dated 3rd December, 1730, whilst the Queen consoled Duck by taking him under her especial care, and giving him a pension.

" Know, Eusden thirsts no more for sack or praise,
    He sleeps among the dull of ancient days ;
    Thou Cibber ! thou, his laurel shall support,
    Folly, my son, has still a friend at Court.
    Lift up your gates, ye princes !   See him come !
    Sound, sound ye viols, be the cat-call dumb !
    Bring, bring the madding bay, the drunken vine ;
    The creeping, dirty, courtly ivy join.

   *   *   *   *   *   *   *   *

    She ceased.   Then swells the chapel-royal throat :
    ' God save King Cibber !' mounts in every note,
    Familiar White's ' God save King Colley !' cries,
    ' God save King Colley !' Drury Lane replies :
    To Needham's quick the voice triumphal rode,
    But pious Needham dropt the name of God ;
    Back to the Devil * the last echoes roll,
    And ' Coll !' each butcher roars at Hockley-hole.
    So when Jove's block descended from on high
    (As sings thy great forefather Ogilby),
    Loud thunder to its bottom shook the bog,
    And the hoarse nation croak'd, ' God save King Log !' ''

The Dunciad.

---

* The Devil Tavern, in Fleet-street, where the Laureate's Birthday and New Year Odes were usually rehearsed before they were performed at Court, by the voices and instruments belonging to the choir of the Chapel Royal :—

   " When Laureates make odes, do you ask of what sort ?
       Do you ask if they're good, or are evil ?
     You may judge,—from the Devil they come to the Court,
       And go from the Court to the Devil !"

Of course the appointment did not please Cibber's rivals, who inquired—

"Tell me, if you can, which did the worse,
Caligula, or Grafton's Grace?
That made a consul of a horse
And this a Laureate of an ass."

The comparison was not a pleasant one; but Cibber certainly possessed one of the qualities of a donkey, namely, its patience under ill-treatment; and the following incident in connection with his tenure of the office of laureate is a good illustration of his ready wit and imperturbable good temper.

He tells us that in the year 1730 :—

"There were many authors whose merit wanted nothing but Interest to recommend them to the vacant *Laurel*, and who took it ill, to see it at last conferred upon a Comedian; insomuch, that they were resolved at least to show specimens of their various Pretensions, and accordingly enlivened the publick papers with ingenious Epigrams, and satyrical Flirts, at the unworthy Successor; these papers my friends, with a wicked smile, would often put into my hands, and desire me to read them fairly to the Company.

"This was a challenge which I never declined, and to do my doughty antagonists justice, I always read them with as much impartial spirit, as if I had writ them myself.

"While I was thus beset on all sides, there happened to step forth a poetical Knight Errant to my assistance, who was hardy enough to publish some compassionate Stanzas in my favour. These, you may be sure, the Raillery of my Friends could do no less than say, I had written to myself.

"To deny it, I knew, would but have confirmed their pretended suspicion; I therefore told them, since it gave them such joy to believe them my own, I would do my best to make the whole Town think so too. As the oddness of this Reply was, I knew, what would not be easily comprehended, I desired them to have a day's patience, and I would print an explanation to it.

"To conclude, in two days after I sent this letter, with some doggerel rhymes at the bottom, to the Author of *The Whitehall Evening Post :*—

" Sir.   The verses to the Laureat, in yours of Saturday last, have occasion'd the following reply, which I hope you'll give a place in your next, to show that we can be quick as well as smart, upon a proper occasion.   And, as I think it the lowest mark of a Scoundrel to make bold with any man's character in print, without subscribing the true name of the Author, I therefore desire, if the Laureat is concern'd enough to ask the question, that you will tell him my name, and where I live, till then I beg leave to be known by no other name than that of

" Your servant,

" FRANCIS FAIRPLAY.

" Monday, Jan. 11, 1730-31."

" These were the verses :—

> " Ah ! bah ! Sir Coll, is that thy way,
>   Thine own dull praise to write ?
> And would'st thou stand so sure a Lay ?
>   No, that's too stale a bite.

> " Nature, and Art, in thee combine,
>   Thy talents here excel :
> All shining Brass thou dost outshine
>   To play the cheat so well.

> " Who sees thee in *Iago's* part,
>   But thinks thee such a Rogue ?
> And is not glad, with all his heart,
>   To hang so sad a Dog ?

> " When *Bayes* * thou play'st, Thyself thou art ;
>   For that by Nature fit,
> No Blockhead better suits the part,
>   Than such a Coxcomb wit.

---

* In *The Rehearsal.*

" In *Wronghead* * too, thy Brains we see,
　　Who might do well at Plough ;
　As fit for Parliament was he,
　　As for the Laurel, Thou !

" Bring thy protected verse from Court,
　　And try it on the Stage ;
　Here it will make much better Sport,
　　And set the town in Rage.

" There Beaux, and Wits, and Cits, and Smarts,
　　Where Hissing's not uncivil,
　Will show their Parts to thy Deserts,
　　And send it to the Devil.

" But ah ! in vain, 'gainst Thee we write,
　　In vain thy verse we maul,
　Our sharpest Satyr's thy Delight,
　　For—*Blood ! thou'lt stand it all.*†

" Thunder, 'tis said, the Laurel spares ;
　　Nought but thy Brows could blast it ;
　And yet—O curst, provoking Stars !
　　Thy comfort is, *thou hast it.*

" This I offer as a proof that I was seven years ago the same cold candidate for Fame, which I would still be thought. You will not easily suppose I could have much concern about it, while to gratify the merry Pique of my Friends, I was capable of seeming to lead the poetical cry then against me, and at the same time of never letting the publick know till this Hour, that these verses were written by myself. Nor do I give them you as Entertainment, but merely to show you this particular Cast of my Temper."

This philosophy stood him in good stead on many occasions, when, as manager of Drury Lane, he was subjected to the attacks of disappointed dramatic authors, and the lampoons of every scribbler of rejected prologues

---

* In *The Provoked Husband.*
† A line in the Epilogue to *The Non Juror.*

and epilogues. Thus when Cibber was suspected (and most unjustly) of having influenced the Lord Chamberlain to suppress the second part of *The Beggar's Opera*, entitled, *Polly*, he was informed that a strong party would be formed against his next new play. This happened to be *Love in a Riddle*, of which the first scenes were inaudible from the prearranged clamour raised against the author.

Seeing that a portion of the audience had determined to damn the play, whatever its merits, Cibber stepped forward, and promised that it should be withdrawn, upon which a number of persons of the adverse clique retired from the house; the remainder of the comedy was played, and received far greater applause than had been anticipated. But it came too late: Cibber was a man of his word, the play was withdrawn, and another announced for the next day.

Amongst the numerous plays he altered or amended to suit the taste of the age, was an unfinished comedy by Sir John Vanbrugh, called *The Provoked Husband*.

On the death of Vanbrugh, Cibber completed and produced the comedy; his enemies, knowing that part of the work was Cibber's, and part from the pen of the renowned Vanbrugh, resolved to spare the dead man, but to have no mercy on the living one. But mistaking the *Wronghead* family for Cibber's creation, and giving credit to Vanbrugh for the house of *Lord Townly*, they applauded the very scenes they came to condemn, and hissed those they meant to applaud.

Cibber took the pardonable revenge of publishing the manuscript of Sir John as he left it, from which all the more elegant part of the drama was seen to be wanting, and the public learnt that it was indebted to

Cibber for the admirable scenes between Lord and Lady Townly.

Cibber's immediate predecessors had brought the laurels into contempt, and ridicule was heaped on Cibber simply because he accepted an office that others had degraded.

> " In merry old England it once was a rule,
> The king had his poet, and also his fool ;
> But now we're so frugal, I'd have you to know it,
> That Cibber can serve both for fool and for poet."

Even Dr. Johnson could not forbear from entering a protest against the appointment; his epigram is, however, nearly as severe to the king as to the poet :—

> " Augustus still survives in Maro's strain,
> And Spenser's verse prolongs Eliza's reign ;
> Great George's acts let tuneful Cibber sing,
> For Nature formed the Poet for that King."

Of all his enemies, Pope was the most bitter and the most witty ; and, to Pope's disgrace, it must be admitted that personal revenge animated him to attack the Laureate ; his malignant satires were not written in any fair, manly spirit of criticism. The following is the explanation given of the origin of the most celebrated, the most amusing, and the most unjust of all these attacks, viz., *The Dunciad*.

Pope published the first three books in 1728 to ridicule his antagonists, the hero then being one Lewis Theobald, a very inferior poet and dramatist. Shortly afterwards Cibber, whilst acting his favourite part of *Bayes*, in *The Rehearsal*, ridiculed, in a smart but not very malicious *impromptu*, a melancholy comedy, called *Three Hours after Marriage*, of which Pope was part author, with Gay and Arbuthnot.

Cibber thus relates the incident :—

" The play of *The Rehearsal,* which had laid for some years dormant, being by his present Majesty (then Prince of Wales) commanded to be revived, the part of *Bayes* fell to my share. To this character there had always been allowed such ludicrous liberties of observation upon anything new or remarkable in the state of the stage, as *Mr. Bayes* might think proper to take.

" Much about this time then, the *Three Hours after Marriage* had been acted without success, when *Mr. Bayes,* as usual, had a fling at it ; which in itself was no jest, unless the audience would please to make it one. But, however, flat as it was, Mr. Pope was mortally sore upon it. This was the offence ; in this play, two coxcombs being in love with a learned virtuoso's wife, to get unsuspected access to her, ingeniously send themselves as two presented rarities to her husband, the one curiously swathed up like an Egyptian mummy, and the other slily covered in the pasteboard skin of a crocodile ; upon which poetical expedient, I, *Mr. Bayes,* when the two Kings of Brentford came from the clouds onto the throne again, instead of what my part directed me to say, made use of the words, ' Now, Sir, this revolution I had some thought of introducing by a quite different contrivance ; but my designs taking air, some of your sharp wits, I found, had made use of it before me ; otherwise I intended to have stolen one of them in, in the shape of a mummy, and the other in that of a crocodile ! ' Upon which the audience, by their roar of applause, showed their contempt of the play this strata-gem belonged to."

This *jeu d'esprit* gave great offence to Pope, who after the play was over—

" Came behind the scenes to call me to account for the insult ; and accordingly fell upon me with all the foul language that a wit out of his senses would be capable of, choked with the foam of his passion."

Cibber insisted upon the privilege of the character, and said that he would repeat the same jest so long as the public approved of it. Thereupon Pope added a fourth book to *The Dunciad,* in which he placed the Laureate amongst the other victims of his envy, hatred, or contempt.

Cibber retorted in a pamphlet, which had the merits of truth and good nature, although the sarcasms were not so well pointed as those of his venomous little antagonist.*

This reply so incensed Pope, that he at once erased Theobald's name, and made Colley Cibber the hero of the entire *Dunciad.*

This change not only greatly damaged the unity of the satire, but Cibber reasonably insisted that the portrait did not resemble him, comparing the libel " to a purge with a wrong label," and Pope " to an apothecary who did not mind his business." It is certain that this contest of wit was more painful to Pope than to Cibber; but Pope's satire is immortal, whereas few now read Cibber's replies; Cibber therefore obtains less credit than he deserves, even if the readers of *The Dunciad* make liberal allowances for poetical exaggeration and personal spite. The singular happiness of his character, and the honest simplicity with which Cibber could admire the genius of his bitter foe, are both strikingly shown in his writings, which, by the way, contain the best excuse that has ever been offered for Pope's *Dunciad :*—

" When, therefore," Cibber says, " I find my name at length in the satyrical works of our most celebrated living author, I never look upon those lines as malice meant to me (for he knows I never provoked it), but profit to himself. One of his points must be to have many readers ; he considers that my face and name are more known

---

* " Quoth Cibber to Pope, though in verse you foreclose,
    I'll have the last word; for by God, I'll write prose.
    Poor Colley ! thy reasoning is none of the strongest,
    For know, the last word is the word that lasts longest."

than those of many thousands of more consequence in the kingdom : that, therefore, right or wrong, a *lick* at the *laureat* will always be a sure bait, *ad captandum vulgus*, to catch him little readers ; and that to gratify the unlearned, by now and then interspersing those merry sacrifices of an old acquaintance to their taste, is a piece of quite right poetical craft."

And he also gives very philosophical reasons for refraining from writing replies to his detractors :—

" If their censure is just, what answer can I make to it ? If it is unjust, why should I suppose that a sensible reader will not see it as well as myself ? Would not my bearing ill language from a chimney-sweeper, do me less harm, than it would be to box with him, though I were sure to beat him ? Then, as no criticism can possibly make me worse than I really am, so nothing I can say of myself can possibly make me better."

Of course *The Dunciad* gave rise to much enmity to Pope, and bitter lampoons and attacks issued every day from the press, to which Pope retorted; but although most of the wit was on his side, his sensitive nature made him writhe under the attacks of the numerous but clumsy foes his malignant satire had raised against him. It was even rumoured that he had been horsewhipped by two gentlemen, a pretended account with full particulars being sold in the streets. Pope condescended to deny this tale in an advertisement inserted in *The Daily Post* of June 14, 1728:—" Whereas, there has been a scandalous paper cried about the streets, under the title of, "A Popp upon Pope," insinuating that I was whipped in Ham Walks on Thursday last, this is to give notice that I did not stir out of my house at Twickenham all that day; and the same is a malicious and illgrounded report."— A. POPE.

The forged account appears to have been invented by Lady Mary W. Montague.

Pope had assumed the name of *Martinus Scriblerus:* one of his numerous enemies founded the title of *The Martiniad* upon this, and gave the following portrait of the deformed person of his adversary :—

> " At Twickenham, chronicles remark,
> There dwelt a little parish clerk,
> A peevish wight, full fond of fame,
> And Martin Scribbler was his name ;
> Meager and wan, and steeple-crown'd,
> His visage long and shoulders round,
> His crippled corse two spindle pegs
> Support, instead of human legs ;
> His shrivell'd skin, of dusky grain,—
> A cricket's voice, and monkey's brain."

Whilst another lampooner compared *The Dunciad* to the offspring of the celebrated Pope Joan.

TO THE AUTHOR OF " THE DUNCIAD."

> " With rueful eyes thou view'st thy wretched race,
> The child of guilt, and destined to disgrace.
> Thus when famed Joan usurped the Pontiff's chair,
> With terror, she beheld her new-born heir :
> Ill-starred, ill-favoured, into birth it came ;
> In vice begotten, and brought forth with shame !
> In vain it breathes, a lewd abandon'd hope !
> And calls in vain, the unhallow'd father—POPE ! "

This satire appeared in *The Daily Journal*, May 16, 1730, and derived considerable additional force from the fact that Pope was a Roman Catholic ; whilst from his well-known impatience of criticism, and extremely irritable temperament, it is probable that what Cibber exultingly said of all this controversy was true :—" Everybody tells me that I have made you as uneasy as a rat in a hot kettle, for a twelvemonth together."

Armstrong, a writer who was intimate with Cibber, gives his testimony to the Laureate's amiable disposition :—

" Besides his abilities as a writer of comedies, and the singular variety of his powers as an actor, he was, to the last, one of the most agreeable, cheerful, and best humoured men you would ever wish to converse with."

A more modern, and it may be a less partial writer, Mary Russell Mitford, sums up his character in a few brief but vivid lines, which do not err on the score of flattery :—

" He flourished in wig and embroidery, player, poet, and manager, during the Augustan age of Queen Anne, somewhat earlier, and somewhat later. A most egregious fop, according to all accounts, he was, but a very pleasant one notwithstanding, as your fop of parts is apt to be. Pope gained but little in the war he waged with him, for this plain reason, that the great poet accuses his adversary of dulness, which was not by any means one of his sins, instead of selecting one of the numerous faults, such as pertness, petulance, and presumption, of which he was really guilty."

Cibber desisted from writing for the stage many years before his death, which happened rather suddenly on the 12th December, 1757, when he had attained the good old age of 86. Although Cibber was not a great poet, he was persevering and consistent, and his integrity has never been questioned. As an actor and author he excelled in comedy; to say that he did not succeed in tragedy is no detraction from his other merits. Wanting all the higher attributes of a poet, his Laureate Odes were never collected, simply because they were not worthy of preservation. One specimen will suffice as an illustration of the quality of the compositions which Cibber produced twice or thrice a year for twenty-seven years, in his official capacity :—

An Ode to His Majesty,

For the New Year 17$\frac{30}{31}$.

By Colley Cibber.

" Once more the ever circling sun,
  Through the celestial signs has run ;
  Again old Time inverts his glass,
  And bids the annual seasons pass.

" The youthful spring shall call for birth,
  And glad with opening flowers the earth ;
  Fair summer load with sheaves the field,
  And golden fruits shall autumn yield :
  Each, to the winter's want, their stores shall bring,
  Till warmer genial suns recall the spring.

" Ye grateful Britons, bless the year
    That kindly yields increase,
  While plenty that might feed a war
    Enjoys the guard of peace.

" Your plenty to the skies you owe ;
    Peace is your monarch's care ;
  Thus bounteous Jove, and George below
    Divided empire share !

*   *   *   *   *   *   *   *

" Turn, happy Britons, to the throne your eyes,
    And in the royal offspring see
  How amply bounteous Providence supplies.
    The source of your felicity !

" Behold in every face,
    Imperial graces shine !
  All native to the race
    Of George and Caroline,"

————

" No, Sir, said Dr. Johnson, Colley Cibber was by no means a blockhead, but by arrogating to himself too much, he was in danger of losing that degree of estimation to which he was entitled. His friends gave out that he *intended* his Birthday Odes should be bad ; but that was not the case, Sir ; for he kept them many months by him, and a few years before he died he showed me one of them, with great solicitude to render it as perfect as might be, and I made some corrections, to which he was not very willing to submit.

" I remember the following couplet in allusion to the king himself :—

' Perched on the eagle's soaring wing,
The lowly linnet loves to sing.'

" Sir, he had heard something of the fabulous tale of the wren sitting upon the eagle's wing, and he had applied it to a linnet. Cibber's familiar style, however, was better than that which Whitehead has assumed. *Grand nonsense* is insupportable. Whitehead is but a little man to inscribe verses to players."

Two of Cibber's children, a son, Theophilus, and a daughter, Charlotte, obtained notoriety of a most unenviable description. The son became an actor, wrote a few plays long since forgotten, and gave his name to a poor vamped up work, entitled, *Cibber's Lives of the Poets;* he led the life of a worthless scamp, ill-treated his wife, the celebrated Susannah Cibber, from whom he was divorced, as the result of an ignoble plot which he formed to obtain a pecuniary recompense for her infidelity. This worthless son was drowned on his passage to Ireland in the same year in which old Colley Cibber died.

The life and surprising adventures of Charlotte Cibber were described by herself in a book, which, if it cannot be commended for its moral tone, has many features of interest, for she recounts her career in a free and apparently candid manner, careless of the opinion the world might form of her escapades.

Her confessions enter into the most minute detail of trivial events in which she figures, so that the story, like one of Defoe's novels, has a singular appearance of veracity.

She appears to have received a liberal education; but having no tastes for feminine duties or pastimes, exhibited unmaidenly eccentricities at an early age. Frequenting stables, curry-combing horses, and shooting, were her favourite amusements.

Once, when a mere child, she defended the house from an attack of thieves by firing pistols and blunderbusses out of the windows. When very young she was married to a celebrated violinist, but the match was a miserable one, and she went upon the stage, making her *début* in the small part of Mademoiselle in *The Provoked Wife* in 1730, being then twenty-seven years of age. She soon rose to such characters as Alicia, in *Jane Shore,* and became a very creditable actress, in receipt of a good salary. But by-and-by she quarrelled with the manager, abruptly quitted the stage, and opened a grocery and oil shop in Long Acre. In three months, finding she knew nothing of the trade, she relinquished the business and set up a puppet show in St. James-street, Haymarket. Here she lost everything, and had to sell for twenty pounds what, she says, had cost her five hundred guineas. She had so offended her father that he now utterly discarded her; then she wrote a piece called *The Battle of the Poets,* in which she scurrilously lampooned him. She was arrested for a small debt, and only released by a subscription of the most disreputable characters of Covent Garden. She then assumed male costume, and wandered about the country with strolling players until a young lady fell in love with her and proposed marriage; next she engaged herself as valet to a nobleman; not remaining long in this situation, she took to making and selling sausages; then became head

waiter at a tavern; after this she went back to strolling
for a time, until by the assistance of an uncle she was
enabled to open a tavern in Drury-lane; this, like all her
other undertakings, proved unsuccessful. For a short
time she joined her brother at the Haymarket, but soon
afterwards the theatre was shut by order of the Lord
Chamberlain. Back to strolling and puppet shows. In
1755 she published an autobiography, a very extraordinary
book, and upon the proceeds opened another public-house—
at Islington this time. In a few months she was again
reduced to beggary, and the closing days of her life were
spent in a wretched hovel, near the New River Head,
where she died in misery and destitution, only two years
after the death of her father.

COLLEY CIBBER'S DRAMATIC WORKS.

Love's Last Shift; or, the Fool in Fashion.   C.   Acted
1696.

Woman's Wit; or, the Lady in Fashion.   C.   Acted
1697.

Xerxes.   T.   Acted 1699.   A failure.

Love Makes a Man; or, the Fop's Fortune.   C.   Acted
1700.

The Tragical History of King Richard III.   Acted
1700.

*She Would and She Would Not; or, the Kind
Impostor.*   C.   Acted 1703,

The Careless Husband.   C.   Acted 1704.

Perolla and Izadora.   T.   Acted 1706.

The School Boy; or, Comical Rival.   C.   Acted 1707.

The Comical Lovers.   C.   1707.

The Double Gallant ; or, The Sick Lady's Cure. C.

The Lady's Last Stake ; or, The Wife's Resentment. C.

The Rival Fools. C. Acted 1709.

Venus and Adonis. Acted 1715.

Myrtillo.

The Non Juror. C. Acted 1717.

Ximena ; or, The Heroick Daughter. T. Acted 1719.

The Refusal ; or, The Ladies Philosophy. C. Acted 1720.

Cæsar in Egypt. T. Acted 1725.

The Provoked Husband; or, The Journey to London. C.

The Rival Queans, with the Humours of Alexander the Great. T. C. Acted 1729.

Love in a Riddle. Acted 1729.

Damon and Phillida. B. O. Acted 1729.

Papal Tyranny in the Reign of King John. T. Acted 1745.

And portions of several other plays.

RICHARD SAVAGE.

The Volunteer Laureate.

DR. JOHNSON, in his life of this wayward, unhappy genius (the illegitimate son of the Countess of Macclesfield and the Earl Rivers), gives the following account of his disappointment at not being appointed Eusden's successor, and the strange manner in which he showed his spleen :—

"Savage exerted all the interest which his wit, or his birth, or his misfortunes could procure, to obtain, upon the death of Eusden, the place of Poet Laureate, and prosecuted his application with so much diligence, that the king publicly declared it his intention to bestow it upon him ; but such was the fate of Savage, that even the king when he intended his advantage, was disappointed in his schemes ; for the Lord Chamberlain who has the disposal of the laurel, as one of the appendages of his office, either did not know the king's design, or did not approve it, or thought the nomination of the Laureat an encroachment upon his rights, and therefore bestowed the laurel upon Colley Cibber.

"Mr. Savage thus disappointed, took the resolution of applying to the queen, and therefore published a short poem on her birth-day, to which he gave the odd title of *The Volunteer Laureat.*

"The Queen sent him a present of fifty pounds, with a message to the effect 'that Her Majesty was highly pleased with the verses ; that she took particularly kind the lines there relating to the King ; that he had permission to write annually on the same subject ; and that he should yearly receive the like present, till something better (which was her Majesty's intention) could be done for him.' After this he was permitted to present one of his annual poems to her Majesty, had the honour of kissing her hand, and met with the most gracious reception.

"He therefore assumed the title of " *Volunteer Laureat*," not without some reprehensions from Cibber, who informed him that the title of *Laureat* was a mark of honour conferred by the King, from whom all honour is derived, and which therefore no man has a right to bestow upon himself; and added that he might with equal propriety style himself a Volunteer Lord, or Volunteer Baronet. It cannot be denied that the remark was just; but Savage did not think any title which was conferred upon Mr. Cibber, so honourable as that the usurpation of it could be imputed to him as an instance of very exorbitant vanity, and therefore continued to write under the same title, and received every year the same reward, until the Queen's death in 1737."

He wrote in all six odes, which are now forgotten; it is said that Savage bestowed but little care on their composition, and did not contemplate inserting them in the later editions of his works.

The Volunteer Laureat.

A Poem most Humbly Addressed to Her Majesty on Her Birth-day.

By Richard Savage.

1732.

" Twice twenty tedious moons have roll'd away
 Since Hope, kind flatt'rer! tun'd my pensive Lay
 Whisp'ring that you, who rais'd me from Despair,
 Meant by your smiles, to make life worth my care ;
 With pitying Hand an orphan's tears to screen,
 And o'er the *motherless* extend the QUEEN.
 'Twill be——the Prophet guides the Poet's strain !
 Grief never touch'd a heart like yours in vain ;
 Heav'n gave you power, because you love to bless,
 And Pity, when you feel it, is Redress.

" Two Fathers join'd to rob my claim of *one !*
My *Mother* too thought fit to have no *son!*
The Senate next, whose aid the helpless own
Forgot *my* Infant wrongs, and mine alone ;
Yet Parents pitiless, nor Peers unkind,
Nor titles lost, nor woes mysterious join'd,
Strip me of hope—— by Heav'n thus lowly laid,
To find a PHARAOH'S DAUGHTER in the Shade.

" You cannot hear unmov'd, when wrongs implore,
Your heart is woman, though your mind be *more ;*
Kind, like the Pow'r who gave you to our pray'rs,
You would not lengthen life to sharpen cares ;
They, who a *barren leave* to live bestow
Snatch but from death, to sacrifice to woe.

" Hated by her, from whom my life I drew,
Whence should I hope, if not from Heav'n and you ?
Nor dare I groan beneath affliction's rod,
My QUEEN my Mother, and my Father GOD.
The pitying MUSES saw me *wit pursue,*
A BASTARD SON, alas ! on that side too
Did not your eyes exalt the Poet's fire,
And what the *Muse* denies, the *Queen inspire,*
While rising thus your heav'nly soul to view,
I learn, how angels think, by copying YOU.

" Great Princess !—'tis decreed—once every year
I march uncall'd, your LAUREAT VOLUNTEER ;
Then shall your Poet his low genius raise
And charm the world with truths too vast for praise.
Nor need I dwell on *Glories* all your own
Since surer means to tempt your smiles are known,
Your poet shall allot your Lord his part,
And paint him in his noblest throne, your Heart.

" Is there a greatness that adorns him best,
A rising wish that ripens in his breast?
Has he foremeant some distant age to bless,
Disarm oppression, or expel distress ?

Plans he some scheme to reconcile mankind,
People the seas and busy ev'ry wind?
Would he by *Pity* the deceiv'd reclaim
And smile contending factions into shame?
Would his example lend the laws a weight
And breathe his own soft morals o'er his State?
The Muse shall find it all, shall make it seen,
And teach the World his praise, to charm his Queen.

" Such be the Annual truths my verse imparts,
Nor frown, fair FAV'RITE of a people's hearts!
Happy, if placed, perchance, beneath your eye,
My Muse *unpension'd* might her pinions try,
Fearless to fail, whilst you indulge her flame,
And bid me proudly boast *your Laureat's* name :
Renobled thus by wreaths my QUEEN bestows,
I lose all memory of wrongs and woes!"

WILLIAM WHITEHEAD.

(1757—1785.)

" Come, METHOD, come in all thy pride,
    DULLNESS and WHITEHEAD by thy side,
    DULLNESS and METHOD still are one,
    And WHITEHEAD is their darling son.

    *   *   *   *   *   *

" But HE, who in the Laureat chair,
    By Grace, not Merit, planted there ;
    In awkward pomp is seen to sit,
    And by his *Patent* prove his wit."

CHURCHILL. "THE GHOST."

WHEN the Duke of Devonshire (then Lord Chamberlain) offered the laureateship to Gray, he made the remarkable suggestion that the poet should hold the office as a sine-cure, and be excused from writing the usual odes.

In a letter to his friend and biographer, Mason, Gray explains his reasons for declining this very handsome offer :—

" I hope you couched my refusal to Lord John Cavendish in as respectful terms as possible, and with all due acknowledgments to the Duke. If you hear who it is to be given to, pray let me know, for I interest myself a little in the history of it, and rather wish somebody may accept it, that will retrieve the credit of the thing if it be retrievable, or ever had any credit. Rowe was, I think, the last man of character that had it ; Eusden was a person of great hopes in his youth, though at last he turned out a drunken parson ; Dryden was as disgraceful to the office from his character, as the poorest scribbler could have been from his verses.

"The office itself has always humbled the possessor hitherto ; if he were a poor writer, by making him more conspicuous ; and if he were a good one, by setting him at war with the little fry of his own profession ; for there are poets little enough even to envy a poet laureat."

Mason was also proposed for it; but he says that Lord John Cavendish made the apology to him, "that being in orders, he was thought less eligible than a layman." This could scarcely have been the true motive for not selecting Mason, as clergymen had held the office previously; it was then conferred upon Whitehead, and unsolicited, if, as Whitehead says :—

> "The following fact is true
> From nobler names, and great in each degree,
> The pension'd laurel has devolv'd to me,
> To me, ye bards ; and what you'll scarce conceive,
> Or, at the best, unwillingly believe,
> Howe'er unworthily I wear the crown,
> Unask'd it came, and from a hand unknown."
>
> A CHARGE TO THE POETS.

That Mr. Mason was a little nettled at being passed over may be judged from the sarcastic remark he inserted on the subject in his life of Whitehead, that

"He wonders the privilege offered to Gray, of holding the office as a sinecure, was not also offered to Mr. Whitehead ; as the King (George II.) would readily have dispensed with hearing poetry, for which he had no taste, and music for which he had no ear."

It was not until the appointment of Robert Southey, that the Duke of Devonshire's suggestion of ceasing to write official odes was adopted.

To return to Whitehead, of whose uneventful life there

is little to be said, and of whose literary merits a contemporary author remarked :—

> " Next Whitehead came, his worth a pinch of snuff,
> But for a Laureat,—he was good enough."

He was born at Cambridge in 1715, and was the son of a respectable baker. He was educated at Winchester school, and showed a taste for poetry at an early age; on one occasion this taste brought him under the notice of Pope, who paid a visit to the school in 1733, with the Earl of Peterborough.

The Earl offered a guinea each to those six youths who should compose the best poems on a subject to be chosen by Mr. Pope. The selected topic was the Earl's warlike career, and Whitehead was one of the six successful competitors. Having obtained a scholarship, he entered at Clare Hall, Cambridge, in the humble capacity of a sizar, and was made Master of Arts in 1742. He then became tutor to the son of the Earl of Jersey, in whose house he passed the greater part of his quiet and inoffensive life.

Whitehead's poems present few remarkable features, the style is formed upon that of Pope, lacking however the brilliant wit and polished versification of his master.

When he obtained the laureatship (through the interest of his patron, the Earl of Jersey), Mason, it is said, advised him to employ a deputy to write the necessary annual odes, in order to reserve his own powers, unaffected by this tedious monotony of song; that then on rare occasions, with a more interesting topic, as a royal marriage, or declaration of peace, the merit of his own verses would strike the public with surprise.

Whitehead disregarded this advice; he wrote the usual official poems, which had the negative merit of being considered superior to those of his predecessor; and he was engaged in the composition of a birthday ode when he died.

One of the most interesting of Whitehead's odes is the one for the New Year 1761, in which, after deploring the horrors of war, and rejoicing over the victories in Canada, he thus celebrates the accession of George III.

> " ———— And who is he, of regal mien,
>   Reclin'd on Albion's golden fleece,
>   Whose polish'd brow, and eye serene
>   Proclaim him elder born of Peace ?
>   Another GEORGE !—ye winds, convey
>   Th' auspicious name from pole to pole !
> Thames, catch the sound, and tell the subject sea
>   Beneath whose sway its waters roll.
>   The hoary Monarch of the deep,
>   Who sooth'd its murmurs with a father's care,
>   Doth now eternal sabbath keep,
>   And leaves His trident to his blooming Heir.
>   O, if the Muse aright divine,
>   Fair Peace shall bless his opening reign,
>   And through its splendid progress shine,
>   With every art to grace her train.
>   The wreaths, so late by Glory won,
>   Shall weave their foliage round his throne,
>   Till kings, abash'd, shall tremble to be foes,
> And Albion's dreaded strength secure the world's repose."

These poetical aspirations for peace were not destined to be realised in the long and turbulent reign that ensued, when " Albion's dreaded strength " was wasted on a hundred bloody battle-fields, and costly, useless, and unsuccessful wars impoverished the nation, and drove the starving people to the verge of a revolution.

Whitehead was more successful as a dramatist than as a poet. He wrote two tragedies, *The Roman Father* (an

imitation of *Les Horaces,* of Corneille) and *Creusa, Queen
of Athens,* which he dedicated to the Earl of Jersey. A
comedy, called *The School for Lovers,* in which Garrick
and Mrs. Cibber played the leading characters; and the
farce entitled *A Trip to Scotland.* This had considerable
success, and, when printed, was dedicated to David
Garrick.

As Laureate, Whitehead did not escape the usual fate
of being lampooned by the envious wits, and small poets
of his day. Foremost amongst his antagonists was the
witty, but unprincipled Churchill, to whose biting sarcasms Whitehead was unable to reply effectively in verse,
he therefore treated them with mild contempt, contenting
himself with the remark :—

> " Hence I, though older far, have lived to see,
> Churchill forgot, an empty shade like me."

In his *Charge to the Poets,* a harmless, somewhat heavy
poem, Whitehead presumed to dictate to his brother
bards :—

> " Then since my King and Patron have thought fit
> To place me on the throne of modern wit,
> My grave advice, my brethren, hear at large,
> As Bishops to their Clergy give their charge."

Churchill would not acknowledge his supremacy, and
replied :—

> " Thee, WHITEHEAD, Thee I now invoke,
> Sworn foe to Satyr's gen'rous stroke,
> Which makes unwilling conscience feel,
> And wounds, but only wounds to heal.
> Good natur'd, easy creature, mild,
> And gentle as a new-born child,
> Thy *heart* would never once admit
> E'en *wholesome* rigour to thy wit,

> Thy head, if Conscience should comply,
> Its kind assistance would deny,
> And lend thee neither force, nor art,
> To drive it onward to the heart.
> O may thy sacred power controul
> Each fiercer working of my soul,
> Damp every spark of genuine fire,
> And languors, like thine own, inspire;
> Trite be each Thought, and ev'ry Line
> As *moral*, and as *Dull* as THINE."

Some of Whitehead's shorter poems have an agreeable tone of gaiety and sprightliness; *The Song for Ranelagh* is one of the most pleasant in its style :—

> " Ye belles, and ye flirts, and ye pert little things,
>   Who trip in this frollicksome round,
> Pray tell me from whence this impertinence springs,
>   The sexes at once to confound ?
> What means the cocked hat and the masculine air,
>   With each motion design'd to perplex ?
> Bright eyes were intended to languish, not stare,
>   And softness the test of your sex.

> " The girl who on beauty depends for support,
>   May call every art to her aid ;
> The bosom display'd and the petticoat short,
>   Are samples she gives of her trade.
> But you on whom fortune indulgently smiles,
>   And whom pride has preserv'd from the snare,
> Should slyly attack us with coyness, and wiles,
>   Not with open, and insolent war.

> " The VENUS, whose statue delights all mankind,
>   Shrinks modestly back from the view,
> And kindly should seem by the artist design'd
>   To serve as a model for you.
> Then learn, with her beauty, to copy her air,
>   Nor venture too much too reveal ;
> Our fancies will paint what you cover with care,
>   And double each charm you conceal.

> " The blushes of morn, and the freshness of May,
> Are charms that no art can procure ;
> O be but yourselves, and our homage we pay,
> And your empire is solid and sure.
> But if, Amazon like, you attack your gallants,
> And put us in fear of our lives,
> You may do very well for sisters and aunts,
> But, believe me, you'll never be wives."

He is here alluding to the very reprehensible practice of ladies appearing in male costume at the Ranelagh masquerades, which, although only attended by fashionable society, were conducted in such a lax manner, that the guards placed in the rooms were found of little service in maintaining order and decorum.

Whitehead's last poetical work, except indeed the official odes, was a fable called *The Goat's Beard*, published in 1777. This peculiarly feeble poem is founded on some lines of *Phœdrus*, which relate that when the she goats had, by their entreaties, obtained from Jupiter the privilege of having beards, as well as the males, the he goats grew angry, and complained that the god had degraded their dignity, by admitting females to equal honours with themselves.

To which Jove replied :—

" That if they would take care to preserve the real and essential advantages which their sex gave them over the other, they would have no reason to be dissatisfied with letting them participate in what was merely ornamental."

This slender plot Whitehead treated as an allegory, changing the goats into men and women, for whose benefit he enlarges the eight pithy lines of *Phœdrus* into about 800 dull ones of his own.

The Goat's Beard was answered by an attack entitled,

Asses' Ears, a Fable, in which the office of laureat is denied to men of genius, and judged worthy to be held only by such men as the present possessor, a Cibber, or a Shadwell.

Whitehead, in addition to the laureatship, held the office of Registrar and Secretary to the Most Honourable Order of the Bath. He died April 14, 1785, at the age of seventy, and was buried in South Audley Street chapel.

AN EPITAPH ON W. WHITEHEAD, ESQ.

Intended for His Monument in Westminster Abbey.

" BENEATH this stone a Poet Laureat lies,
　Nor great, nor good, nor foolish, nor yet wise ;
　Not meanly humble, nor yet swell'd with pride.
　He simply liv'd—and just as simply died :
　Each year his Muse produced a Birth Day Ode,
　Compos'd with flattery in the usual mode :
　For this, and but for this, to George's praise,
　The Bard was pension'd, and receiv'd the Bays."

THE LAUREAT.

An Ode.

" THAT Laurel, once by Dryden worn,
　But since by many dunces borne,
　　Each rival dunce cry'd fie on !
　The boasted laurel was, they said,
　No more than a poor —————,
　　At Court call'd Dann-de-Lion.

" For scenes of comedy renown'd,
　And justly for his acting crown'd,
　　The prince of fops and folly ;
　For kings, nor poetry regarding,
　And writing odes not worth one farthing,
　　Long liv'd the Laureat Colly.

" Him, Pope assail'd by legions backed
And often to his couplets tack'd
 The name of idle Cibber ;
Yet Coll, unskill'd in long and short,
Made in plain prose a smart retort
 To Pope a damn'd Grim Gribber.*

" Will. Whitehead bade the reign commence
Of Birth-day odes and common sense ;
 And there his efforts rested ;
True poetry, by genius fir'd,
Billy's cold bosom ne'er inspir'd ;
 For Bill was chicken-breasted.

" Warton, on Greek and Roman base,
Rescued the laurels from disgrace,
 With fame no foes shall hinder.
Blest with the gift of ev'ry tongue,
Themes Royal royally he sung,
 A HORACE, and a PINDAR !''

" Warton, I know you'll ne'er repine
That witlings carp at ev'ry line,
 And with your lyricks quarrel.
Alas ! from party, spite, or whim,
Such ever is the fate of him
 Who boasts the Royal laurel.

---

* See Sir R. Steele's *Conscious Lovers.* (*Tom.*) I pinched him to the
quick about *Grim Grimmer.* ACT 3.

THOMAS WARTON.

(1785—1790.)

" WILL WHITEHEAD, Sire, hath wish'd the world *good night*,
　　Pray who shall fabricate your *next year's Ode?*
　As I most laudably can *read* and *write*,
　　Let me the line with GEORGE'S *virtues* load !
" Sire, if you'll make me LAUREAT, I declare
　I'll chaunt you, if you do but take the air ;
　And if it should your Royal humour suit,
　I'll sing your *horse to boot.*

" But *Sire*, perchance you've been *be-rhym'd so long*,
　Your *Royal Ear* is sick of BIRTH-DAY SONG !
　In this case, you'll be better serv'd by NONE ;
　　For, order me the SALARY and WINE,
　　I'll whisper to APOLLO and the NINE,
　And so contrive to let the ODE ALONE."
　　　　　　PINDAR'S ODE ON THE DEATH OF WHITEHEAD.

THE father of Thomas Warton was vicar of Basingstoke,
in which town the future laureate was born in 1728.　It
has been said that he was educated at Winchester school,
probably because his brother afterwards became head
master of that establishment.　This was not however the
case ; he remained under his father's tuition until he was

admitted a commoner of Trinity College, Oxford, on the 16th March, 1743.

He early displayed a great attachment to poetry, and when only seventeen years of age wrote *The Pleasures of Melancholy*, which was published anonymously in 1747. The following year he published *The Triumph of Isis*, a poem in defence of Oxford, as an answer to Mason's attack upon that seat of learning in his *Isis, an Elegy*. About the time of the 1745 Rebellion, Oxford men were suspected of favouring the Stuart party; it is doubtful how far the suspicion was well founded; but some drunken brawls occurred, and after an inquiry into the circumstances, considerable blame was thrown upon the Vice-Chancellor, and the heads of several of the Colleges.

The following epigram, said to have been written by the father of Thomas Warton, was current at the time :—

> " The King observing with judicious eyes
>   The state of his two universities ;
>   To Oxford sent a troop of horse ; for why ?
>   That learned body wanted loyalty.
>   To Cambridge he sent books, as well discerning
>   How much that loyal body wanted learning."

Mason seized the opportunity to sing the praises of Cambridge, adverting in his poem to the above circumstances, and decrying the university of Oxford. Warton replied in his *Triumph*, by enumerating the distinguished men who had studied at Oxford, and, in a tone of mild expostulation, accuses Cambridge of venality and servility :—

> " Still sing, O CAM, your fav'rite Freedom's cause ;
>   Still boast of Freedom, while you break her laws."

The finest passage in this poem is that descriptive of

Oxford, which is indeed well worthy of a place with the best of our descriptive poetry:—

> " Ye fretted pinnacles, ye fanes sublime,
> Ye towers that wear the mossy vest of time ;
> Ye massy piles of old munificence,
> At once the pride of learning and defence ;
> Ye cloisters pale, that lengthening to the sight,
> To contemplation, step by step, invite ;
> Ye high-arch'd walks, where oft the whispers clear,
> Of harps unseen have swept the poet's ear ;
> Ye temples dim, where pious duty pays
> Her holy hymns of ever-echoing praise ;
> Lo ! your lov'd Isis, from the bordering vale,
> With all a mother's fondness bids you hail !
> Hail, Oxford, hail ! of all that's good and great,
> Of all that's fair, the guardian and the seat :
> Nurse of each brave pursuit, each generous aim,
> By truth exalted to the throne of fame !
> Like Greece in science and in liberty,
> As Athens learn'd, as Lacedemon free ! ''

Dr. Johnson so greatly admired this poem, that when he first heard it read, it is said, he clapped his hands with delight until they were sore. Some of his admiration may have been the result of party feeling, for he was no enemy to the Jacobites; and Warton, whilst zealously defending the cause of freedom in his poem, does not boast of the loyalty of Oxford to the Hanoverian king, or even assert his own.

In the common room belonging to the bachelors and gentlemen commoners of Trinity College, it was formerly the practice to elect annually certain officers, and amongst others a *poet laureate*, whose duty it was to celebrate in English verses the lady patroness, who was also annually elected. On an appointed day the members of the room assembled, and the poet laureate, crowned with a wreath of laurel, recited his verses. Warton was elected to this post in 1747, and again in 1748; his verses, which are still preserved in the common room, are written in an elegant and flowing style, and have that kind of merit which doubtless insured them applause when they were read, with the advantages of local and personal interest.

On the 1st of December, 1750, he became M.A., and in 1751 he succeeded to a Fellowship, and was thus placed in easy and independent circumstances, favourable to his habits of meditation and study.

In 1754 he published his *Observations on the Faerie Queene of Spenser*, in one volume octavo; this he afterwards corrected and enlarged, and republished in two volumes in 1762. The fame which this great critical work brought him, doubtless led to his election to the Professorship of Poetry, in 1757,—the duties of which office he fulfilled with great credit for the usual term of ten years.

In 1782 Warton was presented by his College to the small living of Hill Farrance, in Somersetshire; he also held another small clerical appointment, and was elected a member of the celebrated Literary Club.

His greatest and most important work, *The History of English Poetry*, still a standard book, containing most valuable information, was issued, the first volume in 1774, the second in 1778, and the third in 1781; unfortunately it was never completed. It concludes with " a general view and character of the poetry of Queen Elizabeth's age," a period which Warton styles the most poetical of our annals.

Warton's pen was seldom idle, for in addition to these grave historical and critical books, he wrote many lively odes and sonnets, and some amusing satirical and humorous poems. Of the latter the most admired is his *Panegyric on Oxford Ale,* which, like Philip's *Splendid Shilling,* is a parody of Milton's blank verse.

A PANEGYRIC ON OXFORD ALE.

" Balm of my cares, sweet solace of my toils,
 Hail, JUICE benignant! O'er the costly cups
 Of riot-stirring wine, unwholesome draught,
 Let Pride's loose sons prolong the wasteful night ;
 My sober evening let the Tankard bless,
 With toast embrown'd, and fragrant nutmeg fraught,
 While the rich draught with oft-repeated whiffs
 Tobacco mild improves. Divine repast !
 Where no crude surfeit, or intemperate joys
 Of lawless Bacchus reign ; but o'er my soul
 A calm Lethean creeps ; in drowsy trance
 Each thought subsides, and sweet oblivion wraps
 My peaceful brain, as if the leaden rod
 Of magic Morpheus o'er mine eyes had shed
 Its opiate influence. What tho' sore ills
 Oppress, dire want of chill-dispelling coals
 Or cheerful candle (save the makeweight's gleam
 Haply remaining) heart-rejoicing ALE
 Cheers the sad scene, and every want supplies.''

* * * * * * * *

Deeply imbued as Warton was with the beauties of the earlier English poets, such as Chaucer, Drayton, Fairfax, and Spenser, it is not surprising that quaint words, such as *aye, eld, watchet, murky,* and antiquated phrases should be found in his own poems.

This peculiarity of style was, in the judgment of Dr. Johnson, a serious fault, and was ridiculed by him in the lines:—

" Wheresoe'er I turn my view,
 All is strange, yet nothing new.
 Endless labour all along,
 Endless labour to be wrong ;

Phrase that time has flung away,
Uncouth words in disarray,
Trick'd in antique ruff and bonnet
Ode, and elegy, and sonnet."

Much friendship existed between these celebrated men at the time of Dr. Johnson's visit to Oxford, but it seems to have been followed by a coolness; for whilst the lexicographer contemptuously criticised Warton's poetry, Warton remarked that he did not entertain a very high opinion of Johnson as a man of taste, or as a classical scholar.

In 1785 Warton was elected Camden Professor of History, and in the month of May of that year he succeeded Whitehead as Laureate. His first official ode was for the King's birthday, June 4, 1785; it was neither happy in its conception, nor its execution, and gave rise to one of the most exquisite of literary jokes, namely,—*The Probationary Odes for the Laureatship.*

This collection of satires and parodies purported to be the competitive essays of Warton's rivals; amongst them the King's ministers send in characteristic compositions; those by Sir Cecil Wray, Lord Chancellor Thurlow, Dundas the Treasurer of the Navy, and the Attorney-General, are very comical, and abound in humorous allusions, which were greatly appreciated at the time, although now a key is required to their meaning. Amongst all this burlesque was placed the Laureate's *real* Birthday Ode, and the Editor of the *Probationary Odes* sent Warton a copy of the book, thanking him " for the inimitable effort of *genuine humour* which proceeded from him on that occasion, without which the world would have been deprived of the most astonishing exhibition of genuine joke that ever graced the annals of literature."

But as the Laureate was one of the most amiable of

men, he could afford to laugh at a good joke, even if it happened to be levelled at himself, and not only took no offence at the sarcasms aimed at him, but admitted their cleverness. It is greatly to be regretted that time has rendered obscure many of the allusions contained in the *Probationary Odes*, and Horace Walpole, writing in their praise at the time, says :—

"I would send them, but you would want too many keys ; and indeed, I want some myself : for, as there are continually allusions to parliamentary speeches and events, they are often obscure to me till I get them explained."

Clever personalities abound in the work, such as imitations of Lord Thurlow's outrageous habit of swearing, and there are some parodies of *Ossian*, which will be appreciated by any one who has endeavoured to learn anything of Fingal. A great part of the book now reads like mere boisterous fun and bathos, thus differing from *The Rejected Addresses*, which, though founded on a somewhat similar basis, were built of more durable material, and do not depend for vitality upon mere personalities. Whilst the great works of the language (which they parody) remain, *Rejected Addresses* will be read with delight, and the greater number of them will be as keenly appreciated, as when they first made their modest appearance before the public.

In future Warton was more fortunate with his official odes, although his fame as a scholar and commentator could scarcely be increased by compositions on such trite subjects as New Year's Day and the King's Birthday; nevertheless he imparted unwonted interest to some of these poems, the following, which is the best of these official odes, contains some valuable criticisms on the works of his predecessors :—

ODE ON HIS MAJESTY'S BIRTHDAY,

June 4, 1787.

I.

" The noblest bards of Albion's choir
        Have struck of old this festal lyre,
        Ere Science, struggling oft in vain,
        Had dared to break her Gothic chain.
Victorious Edward gave the vernal bough
Of Britain's bay to bloom on Chaucer's brow ;
Fir'd with the gift, he chang'd to sounds sublime
His Norman minstrelsy's discordant chime :
        In tones majestic hence he told
        The banquet of Cambuscan bold ;
        And oft he sung (howe'er, the rhyme
        Has moulder'd to the touch of time)
        His martial master's knightly board,
        And Arthur's ancient rites restor'd ;
The prince in sable steel that sternly frown'd,
And Gallia's captive king, and Cressy's wreath renown'd.

II.

" Won from the shepherd's simple meed,
        The whispers wild of Mulla's reed,
        Sage Spenser wak'd his lofty lay
        To grace Eliza's golden sway.
O'er the proud theme new lustre to diffuse,
He chose the gorgeous allegoric muse ;
And call'd to life old Uther's elfin tale,
And rov'd thro' many a necromantic vale,
        Pourtraying chiefs that knew to tame
        The goblin's ire, the dragon's flame ;
        To pierce the dark enchanted hall,
        Where Virtue sate in lonely thrall.
        From fabling fancy's inmost store
        A rich romantic robe he bore ;
A veil with visionary trappings hung,
And o'er his virgin queen the fairy texture flung.

III.

" At length the matchless Dryden came,
　　To light the Muses' clearer flame ;
　　To lofty numbers grace to lend,
　　And strength with melody to blend ;
To triumph in the bold career of song
And roll th' unwearied energy along.
Does the mean incense of promiscuous praise,—
Does servile fear, disgrace his regal bays ?
　　　I spurn his panegyric strings,
　　　His partial homage, tun'd to kings !
　　　Be mine to catch his manlier chord,
　　　That paints th' impassioned Persian lord,
　　　By glory fir'd, to pity sued,
　　　Rous'd to revenge, by love subdued ;
And still, with transport new, the strains to trace
That chant the Theban pair, and Tancred's deadly vase.

IV.

" Had these blest bards been call'd to pay
　　The vows of this auspicious day,
　　Each had confessed a fairer throne,
　　A mightier sovereign than his own !
Chaucer had bade his hero-monarch yield
The martial fame of Cressy's well-fought field
To peaceful prowess, and the conquests calm,
That braid the sceptre with the patriot's palm :
　　　His chaplets of fantastic bloom,
　　　His colourings warm from Fiction's loom,
　　　Spenser had cast in scorn away,
　　　And deck'd with truth alone the lay ;
　　　All real here, the bard had seen
　　　The glories of his pictur'd Queen !
The tuneful Dryden had not flatter'd here,
His lyre had blameless been, his tribute all sincere ! ''

It will be seen from this poem that Warton did not
indulge in the usual hyperbolical flattery of everything

Royal, as was usually the practice of Laureates, and the satirist, Peter Pindar, praises him for his honesty:—

> " Tom proved unequal to the laureat's place,
>   He warbled with an Attic grace :
>   The language was not understood at court,
>   Where bow and courtesy, grin and shrug resort ;
>   Sorrow for sickness, joy for health, so civil,
>   And love, that wished each other to the devil !
>
> " Tom was a scholar—luckless wight !
>   Lodged with old manners in a musty college ;
>   He knew not, that a palace hated knowledge,
>   And deemed it pedantry to spell and write,
>   Tom heard of royal libraries, indeed,
>   And weakly fancied that the books were read."

The little eccentricities of Warton's private life are related with wonder by his serious biographers, as though far beneath the dignity of such a grave and thoughtful scholar, nevertheless they appear to have been harmless enough.

We are told that he was an early riser, took regular exercise, and was fond of drinking ale and smoking his pipe with persons of mean rank and education; that he believed in preternatural apparitions ; that he was a great punster, gay and witty in his conversation, although it is true Dr. Johnson compared his mode of speaking to the gobbling of a turkey cock.

He was fond of military spectacles, or any public exhibition to which music and show usually attract a crowd; on one occasion he dressed himself as a carter in order to be able to view an execution unrecognised, fearing perhaps that it might be thought a college dignitary was showing an evil example to his juniors by assisting at such a debasing public ceremony.

All the anecdotes related of him do credit to his heart,

although, perhaps, they do not tend to prove that he affected the solemnity and decorum one might have looked for in such a man.

His brother, Dr. Joseph Warton, head master at Winchester School, was frequently visited by the Laureate, who entered somewhat too heartily into the scholars' sports and mischief, and would frequently perform their exercises to save them from punishment, his only preliminary question being, "How many faults?" in order to adapt the style to the student's capacity. Once it happened that the theme was obviously too well performed, and the head master, guessing the real author, called his brother to listen to the successful lad. "Is it not a good exercise?" said the doctor; "worth half-a-crown, is it not?" "Yes, certainly it is," replied the unsuspecting poet. "Well, then," replied his brother, "you shall give the boy one."

This truly good and amiable man enjoyed his full honours but a brief space; his somewhat sudden death, from gout, occurred on the 21st May, 1790. He was buried in Trinity College Chapel with the highest academical honours, which he well deserved, both on account of his valuable services to literature, and his worth as a man. The following inscription is placed over his remains :—

THOMAS WARTON.
S. T. B. et S. A. S.
Hujus Collegii Socius,
Ecclesiæ de Cuddington
In Com. Oxon. Rector,
Poetices iterum Prælector,
Historices Prælector Camden,
Poeta Laureatus.
Obiit 21 Die Maii,
Anno Domini 1790.
Ætat 63.

Hazlitt, in his *Lectures on the English Poets,* says :—

" Warton was a poet and a scholar, studious with ease, learned without affectation.   He had a happiness which some have been prouder of than he, who deserved it less ; he was Poet Laureate,—

> " ' And that green wreath which decks the bard when dead,
> That laurel garland crown'd his living head.'

" But he bore his honours meekly, performed his half-yearly task regularly, and was the author of some of the finest sonnets in the language."

Thomas Warton was succeeded by Henry James Pye. Pybus and Sir James Bland Burgess were also mentioned as candidates for the appointment, a report which gave rise to an epigram, in which the name of a fourth, and very unlikely candidate, namely, Peter Pindar (Dr. Wolcott), was introduced :—

> " Nos Pœtœ sumus tribus,
> Peter Pindar, Pye et Pybus ;
> Si ulterius vie pergis,
> Nobis add, Sir James Bland Burgess."

HENRY JAMES PYE.

(1790—1813.)

" The monarch, mute till then, exclaimed, What, what?
  Pye come again ! No more—no more of that ! "
" THE VISION OF JUDGMENT."

PYE succeeded Warton as Laureate; but for that fact his
name would be forgotten. He wrote several second-rate
books on uninteresting topics, composed a quantity of
tedious rhyme which he meant for poetry, was Member
for Berks, and spoke in the House of Commons on three
several occasions.

" ' But hold ! ' exclaims a friend, ' here's some neglect ;
  This, that, and t'other line seem incorrect,'
  What then ? the selfsame blunder Pope has got,
  And careless Dryden. Aye, but Pye has not.
  Indeed, 'tis granted, faith ! but what care I ?
  Better to err with Pope, than shine with Pye."

Byron said of him that he was eminently respectable in
everything but his poetry. This, indeed, appears to have
been the case, but certainly affords no reasonable explanation of his appointment to the office of Laureate.

Pye was descended from an ancient family, and one of
his ancestors, Sir Robert Pye, was immortalised by Ben
Jonson. He was auditor of the Exchequer in 1618, and

in that capacity should have paid Ben his salary as
Laureate. This duty was very irregularly performed ;
and at a time when poor Jonson was more than usually
pressed by his creditors, he wrote a long petition, or, as he
called it,—

> " My woful cry
>   To Sir Robert Pye ;
>   And that he will venture
>   To send my debenture.
>   Tell him his Ben
>   Knew the time when
>   He loved the Muses ;
>   Though now he refuses
>   To take apprehension
>   Of a year's pension,
>   And more, is behind ;
>   Put him in mind
>   Christmas is near."

The son of this Sir Robert Pye married a daughter of
the patriot, Hampden, from which union was descended
the subject of this notice, who was born in London, on the
10th July, 1745, and was educated at Magdalen College,
Oxford. He was made a D.C.L. in 1772.

On succeeding to his paternal estates, he found them
overwhelmed with debts, which he was, however, under no
legal obligation to discharge, but he honourably sold much
of the property to satisfy his father's creditors, and shortly
afterwards suffered a still further loss from a fire. He
held a commission in the Berks-Militia, and in 1784
engaged in a contested election for the representation of
that county in the House of Commons.

He was made Laureate in 1790, and two years afterwards was appointed one of the police magistrates of
London. He was the author of *The Democrat, The*

Aristocrat, The Progress of Refinement, an epic poem entitled *Alfred,* and some translations from Homer, Aristotle, and Pindar; but his most interesting book is doubtless the *Comments on the Commentators on Shakespeare.* This work is dated from Queen Square, Westminster, and is dedicated to John Penn, Esq., of Stoke Park.

In this he deals somewhat severely with the Editors of Shakespeare, more especially with Malone and Steevens. The rage for everything Shakespearean was at its height about this time, partly from Garrick's intelligent efforts to make him popular on the stage, and partly no doubt from the rapidly increasing class of readers who could obtain access to good editions of his works.

Since Nicholas Rowe had first edited Shakespeare in 1709, numerous other editions had appeared, and Pope, Dr. Johnson, Warburton, Steevens, Malone, and others had given the world the benefit of their opinions and notes on the great dramatist, whose text frequently suffered from the over zeal of the editors.

In the *Westminster Magazine* for October, 1773, appeared an amusing list of the Shakespeare restorers who had succeeded each other up to that period, and it gives a tolerably correct idea of the manner in which each author had dealt with the subject:—

SHAKESPEARE'S BEDSIDE.

" Old Shakespeare was sick ; for a doctor he sent ;
But 'twas long before any one came ;
Yet at length, his assistance Nic Rowe did present :
Sure all men have heard of *his* name.

" As he found that the poet had tumbled the bed,
He smooth'd it as well as he could ;
He gave him an anodyne, comb'd out his head,
But did his complaint little good.

" Dr. Pope to incision at once did proceed,
 And the bard for the simples he cut ;
For his regular practice was always to bleed,
 Ere the fees in his pocket he put.

" Next Tibbald advanced, who at best was a quack,
 And dealt but in old woman's stuff ;
Yet he caused the physician of Twick'nham to pack,
 And the patient grew cheerful enough.

" One Warburton then, though allied to the Church,
 Produced his alterative stores ;
But his med'cines so oft left the case in the lurch,
 That Edwards kicked him out of doors.

" Next Johnson arrived to the patient's relief,
 And ten years he had him in hand ;
But, tired of his task, 'tis the general belief
 He left him before he could stand.

" Now Steevens came loaded with black-letter books,
 Of fame more desirous than pelf ;
Such reading, observers might read in his looks,
 As no one e'er read but himself.

" Then Warner, by Plautus and Glossary known,
 And Hawkins, historian of sound ;
Then Warton and Collins together came on,
 For Greek and potations renown'd.

" The cooks the more numerous, the worse is the broth,
 Says a proverb I well can believe ;
And yet to condemn them untried I am loth,
 So at present shall laugh in my sleeve."

The Shakespeare mania culminated in Ireland's impudent but clever forgeries, which deceived many learned
and acute critics of the day; and when Ireland prevailed
upon Sheridan to produce *Vortigern* at Drury Lane, in
1796, Mr. Pye wrote a prologue to the tragedy, but as it
expressed a doubt about the authenticity, it was laid aside

to make place for one written by Sir James Bland
Burgess. This commenced with a bold assertion that the
piece about to be performed was the work of Shakespeare,
and demanded the respectful attention of the audience
to it on that account.

The piece utterly broke down the first night, and when
the imposition was discovered, there were some bitter
caricatures and satires published at Ireland's expense;
one of these was a portrait of the forger, grasping a
volume of Shakespeare, with a motto, taken from the *Maid
of the Mill*:—

> " Such cursed assurance
> Is past all endurance,"

and the following parody of Dryden's *Epigram on Milton,*
supposed to have been written by William Mason :—

> " Four forgers, born in one prolific age,
> Much critical acumen did engage ;
> The first* was soon by Doughty Douglas scar'd,
> Tho' Johnson would have screen'd him had he dar'd.
> " The next† had all the cunning of a Scot
> The third,‡ invention, genius—nay, what not ?
> Fraud now exhausted, only could dispense
> To her fourth son,§ their threefold impudence."

It is said that Ireland was so enraged at the publication
of this caricature, that he broke the shop windows where
it was exposed for sale.

After *Vortigern and Rowena* had been once played,
and the audience had shown in the most unmistakable
manner their disbelief in its authenticity, and contempt
for its merits, Ireland yet had the audacity to urge
Sheridan and Kemble to have a second performance, but

---

* Lauder.   † Macpherson.   ‡ Chatterton.   § Ireland.

Sheridan dismissed him with a very emphatic negative. After Ireland had left the room, Kemble said, "Well, sir, you cannot now doubt that the play is a forgery." "Damn the fellow," replied Sheridan, " *I believe his face is a forgery;* he is the most specious man I ever saw !"

Ireland afterwards wrote a book, admitting that he was the author of *Vortigern* and other imitations of Shakespeare with which he had deceived many literary men, and describing in a bold, almost exulting tone, the numerous ingenious devices he adopted to carry out the deception, particularly in the selection of ink, paper, writing, and orthography, to resemble old manuscripts.

Pye laboured diligently to produce the required official odes ; they are "full of sound and fury, signifying nothing;" patriotism and loyalty are dimly shadowed forth in such lines as—

> " To arms ! your ensigns straight display !
> Now set the battle in array,
> The oracle for war declares,
> Success depends upon our hearts and spears !"

Indeed, he made a virtue of necessity by claiming more credit for his patriotism than for his poetry :—

> " I am glad to have it observed that there appears throughout my verses a zeal for the honour of my country ; and I had rather be thought a good Englishman than the best poet, or the greatest scholar that ever wrote."

But his contemporaries looked for something beyond amiable platitudes, patriotic aspirations, and loyal flattery. Pye's muse was, however, a very small bird, whose feeble crow was imitated by a rival in the following :—

BIRTHDAY ODE.

> " Hail, all hail, thou natal day,
> Hail the very half hour I say,

On which great GEORGE was born !
Tho' scarcely fledg'd, I'll try my wing,—
And tho' alas, I cannot sing,
I'll *crow* on this illustrious morn !

" Sweet bird, that chirp'st the note of folly,
So pleasantly, so drolly !—
Thee oft, the stable yards among,
I woo, and emulate thy song !
Thee, for my emblem still I choose !
Oh ! with thy voice inspire a *Chicken of the Muse !* "

The odes, as composed by the Laureate, were set to music by the Court composer, and performed at the State Drawing Rooms, when the words were happily drowned by the instruments. At one time the public were admitted to the antechamber on these occasions, but an abuse of the privilege led to its abolition. Gibbon refers to this custom in *The Decline and Fall of the Roman Empire :*—

" The title of Poet Laureate, which custom rather than vanity perpetuates in the English Court, was first invented by the Cæsars of Germany. From Augustus to Louis the muse has been too often false and venal, but I much doubt whether any age or court can produce a similar establishment of a stipendiary poet, who in every reign, and at all events is bound to furnish twice a year, a measure of praise and verse, such as I believe may be sung in the chapel, and in the presence of the Sovereign."

Indeed the odes were becoming more and more the butt of every humorous writer, and it was pretty evident their end was approaching. Pye's mediocrity as a poet hastened their fate, and at the same time drew down ridicule upon the ancient office he held.

P

EPISTLE TO THE POET LAUREATE.

1790.

" Of all the Poets of our Isle
    Who rhyme for fame or fee,
Methinks our gracious Sovereign's smile
    Was wisely fixed on thee.

" Thou, who of poetry or Pitt
    The merits canst rehearse,
Prepared alike to show thy wit
    By venal vote or verse.

" Or he, the Patron of thy lays,
    To trumpet right or wrong,
On vice itself to lavish praise
    The triumph of thy song.

" I see the mercenary fit
    Of tuneful madness rise,
The caitiff wretch for earth unfit
    Exalted to the skies.

" Methinks with rage at every line
    A British Breast should glow,
And British hands disdain to twine
    The laurel round thy brow."

This satire is too long to quote entire, it concludes :—

" So shalt thou wade through thick and thin
    To pour a mortal lay,
And plunge in falsehood to the chin
    Thy Dullness to display.

" So shall thy unpoetic eye
    In a vile phrenzy roll ;
So shall the names of *George* and *Pye*
    BE BLESSED from Pole to Pole."

But Pye was the last Laureate who regularly wrote official odes, and, as literary curiosities, a New Year's Day Ode, and a Birthday Ode are inserted :—

ODE FOR THE NEW YEAR, 1791.

BY HENRY JAMES PYE, ESQ.,

POET LAUREAT.

I.

" When from the bosom of the mine
    The magnet first to light was thrown,
Fair commerce hail'd the gift divine,
    And, smiling, claim'd it for her own.
' My bark (she said) this gem shall guide
Thro' paths of ocean yet untry'd,
While as my daring sons explore
Each rude inhospitable shore,
    'Mid desert lands and ruthless skies,
    New seats of industry shall rise.
And culture wide extend its genial reign,
Free as the ambient gale, and boundless as the main.'

II

" But Tyranny soon learn'd to seize,
    The art improving Science taught,
The white sail courts the distant breeze,
    With horror and destruction fraught ;
From the tall mast fell War unfurl'd
His banners to a new-found world ;
Oppression, arm'd with giant pride,
And bigot Fury by her side ;
    Dire Desolation bath'd in blood,
    Pale Av'rice, and her harpy brood,
To each affrighted shore in thunder spoke,
And bow'd the wretched race to Slav'ry's iron yoke.

III.

" Not such the gentler views that urge
 Britannia's sons to dare the surge ;
 Not such the gifts her Drake, her Raleigh bore
 To the wild inmates of th' Atlantic shore,
 Teaching each drear wood's pathless scene
 The glories of their virgin queen.
 Nor such her later chiefs who try,
 Impell'd by soft humanity,
 The boist'rous wave, the rugged coast,
 The burning zone, the polar frost,
That climes remote, and regions yet unknown,
May share a GEORGE'S sway, and bless his patriot throne.

IV.

" Warm Fancy, kindling with delight,
 Anticipates the lapse of age,
And as she throws her eagle's flight
 O'er Time's yet undiscovered page,
Vast continents, now dark with shade,
She sees in verdure's robe array'd,
Sees o'er each island's fertile steep
That frequent studs the southern deep,
His fleecy charge the shepherd lead,
The harvest wave, the vintage bleed :
See Commerce springs of guiltless wealth explore,
Where frowns the western world on Asia's neighbouring shore.

V.

" But, lo ! across the blackening skies,
 What swarthy dæmon wings his flight ?
At once the transient landscape flies,
 The splendid vision sets in night.——
And see Britannia's awful form,
With breast undaunted, brave the storm :
Awful, as when her angry tide
O'erwhelm'd the wreck'd Armada's pride.

Awful, as when the avenging blow
Suspending o'er a prostrate foe,
She snatch'd in vict'ry's moment, prompt to save,
Iberia's sinking sons from Calpe's glowing wave.

VI.

" Ere yet the tempest's mingled sound
Burst dreadful o'er the nations round,
What angel shape, in beaming radiance dight,
Pours through the severing clouds celestial light!
'Tis Peace—before her seraph eye
The fiends of Devastation fly.
Auspicious, round our monarch's brow
She twines her olive's sacred bough ;
This victory, she cries, is mine,
Not torn from War's terrific shrine ;
Mine the pure trophies of the wise and good,
Unstained of woe, and undefil'd with blood,

BIRTHDAY ODE FOR THE YEAR 1800.

" God of our fathers rise,
And through the thund'ring skies
Thy vengeance urge
In awful justice red,
Be thy dread arrows sped,
But guard our Monarch's head,
God save great George.

" Still on our Albion smile,
Still o'er this favor'd isle,
O, spread thy wing !
To make each blessing sure,
To make our fame endure,
To make our rights secure,
God save our King !

" To the loud trumpet's throat,
  To the shrill clarion's note,
      Now jocund sing.
From every open foe,
From every traitor's blow,
Virtue defend his brow,
    God guard our King ! "

As Pye was a pleasant, convivial man, it was somewhat peculiar that the Laureate's annual perquisite of a tierce of canary from the Royal cellar, should, during his tenure of the office, have been commuted for an annual payment of £27.

Mr. Pye died at Pinner, on August 13, 1813, when the title of Laureate was conferred upon Robert Southey.

ROBERT SOUTHEY,

(1813—1843.)

" BOB SOUTHEY ! You're a poet—Poet Laureate,
　　And representative of all the race ;
　　Although 'tis true that you turn'd out a Tory at
　　Last,—yours has lately been a common case,
　　And now, my Epic Renegade ! what are ye at ?
　　　With all the Lakers, in and out of place ?
　　A nest of tuneful persons, to my eye
　　　Like ' four-and-twenty Blackbirds in a pie.'

" You, Bob ! are rather insolent, you know,
　　At being disappointed in your wish
　To supersede all warblers here below,
　　And be the only blackbird in the dish ;
　And then you overstrain yourself, or so,
　　And tumble downwards like the flying fish
　Gasping on deck, because you soar too high, Bob !
　And fall, for lack of moisture, quite a-dry, Bob ! "

DON JUAN.

THIS learned man and voluminous author, who in his
private capacity was one of the most amiable, moral, and
conscientious of men, has been severely criticised for his
political backslidings, his advocacy of the most intolerant
measures, and his bigoted adherence to views he adopted,

from supposed interested motives, diametrically opposed
to those he had advocated in his early works.

It certainly appears that he merited much of the
obloquy he was subjected to, and in recording the events
of his literary career it will be necessary to show that he
was occasionally the aggressor, that he generally treated
his opponents with scant courtesy, and replied to their
arguments by bare assertions; time has shown that he
was on the then losing side, but whether that side deserved
to win, or to lose, will ever be a moot point so long as party
politics exist in this country.

Commencing his public career with the most advanced
and theoretical Republican notions, he closed it as a
pensioner of the Tories, the apologist of despotism, the
advocate of religious persecution, and the bitter foe of
liberty of the Press, that Press to which alone he owed his
advancement in life.

Robert Southey was born on the 12th August, 1774, in
Bristol. His boyhood was almost entirely passed in the
house of an eccentric maiden aunt, from whom he received
the rudiments of his education; he afterwards attended
several schools in the neighbourhood of Bristol, displaying
at an early age that intense love of study which was
destined to make him the best read man in Europe.

At fourteen years of age he was sent up to Westminster
School, whence he was expelled for writing an article
which appeared in the fifth number of *The Flagellant*, a
small critical magazine, started by himself, and a few of
the other scholars.

This article was upon the subject of Corporal Punishment, and was written in the most dangerous of all styles
for a novice to attempt—namely, the ironical; it gave
great offence to the authorities, who commenced a pro-

secution against the publisher. Southey boldly avowed the authorship, and Dr. Vincent, the then Head Master, insisted upon his expulsion, a severe and degrading punishment, considerably in excess of the fault.

His uncle, the Rev. Herbert Hill, now offered to defray his expenses at college, and Southey proceeded to Oxford, but the affair of *The Flagellant* had made him notorious, and he was refused admission to Christchurch College; the authorities at Balliol, however, proved more liberal, and he entered there early in 1793.

Here again he came into collision with the authorities, originating from a somewhat undignified struggle with the university barber. It was then the custom for all the students, without distinction, to have their hair dressed, covered with pomatum and powdered. Southey refused to submit to this operation, preferring to wear his brown, curly locks in their natural state. In vain the barber pleaded immemorial usage, the refinements of taste and civilisation, and the absolute impossibility of useful study with the hair unpowdered. Southey persisted, and several other young men followed his example, discarding the dirty, absurd, and unwholesome use of pomatum and powder.

Coleridge, whilst on a visit to Oxford, was introduced to Southey, and they shortly became firm friends; Coleridge started an Utopian idea of forming a colony in the backwoods of America, where no tax collector, no aristocrat, no monarch should disturb the felicity of their new world.

Enthusiastic in his desire for liberty and equality, Southey became a convert to Pantisocracy, and persuaded several others to join the cause, but want of sufficient funds to pay even for the outward passage first showed Southey into what an impracticable scheme he had entered; several disagreements arose amongst the intending emigrants, Southey withdrew his support, and the whole idea was shortly afterwards abandoned.

Southey's father desired him to enter the Church; to this profession his peculiar religious views were a bar: he commenced the study of medicine, but relinquished that in great disgust; and having no settled employment, or prospects in life, he was yet so imprudent as to make preparations for marriage when only nineteen years of age. He communicated his rash intention to his aunt, Miss Tyler, who had hitherto been his best friend; she was naturally indignant, and ordered Southey out of the house at once, and, as it proved, for ever. The lovesick boy had a twelve-mile walk home to Bath, on a cold, wet night, during which he meditated on the opposition of all his friends to his marriage, and his entire dependence on them for even bare subsistence.

He now determined to turn his attention to literature, and, in conjunction with his friend, Robert Lovell, he published a small volume of poems, and about the same time joined Coleridge in giving some public lectures at Bristol.

Southey selected historical topics, Coleridge spoke on politics and morals; the lectures were well attended, and Southey having received fifty pounds for his epic poem, *Joan of Arc*, was, for a time, relieved from pecuniary embarrassment.

Mr. Hill having been appointed chaplain to the British Factory at Lisbon, offered to take his nephew with him, so that he might have an opportunity of studying the Spanish and Portuguese languages and literature, in which he considered there was a wide field for research.

The offer was accepted, and Southey's visit to the Peninsula resulted in his acquirement of a profound knowledge of its history and literature, which was afterwards of great service to him.

But there can be little doubt that Southey's uncle had other motives for proposing this tour; time and absence he hoped might have the effect of weakening the love of the young author for a lady whose beauty and virtue were her only possessions; and he vainly imagined that he might, by calm reasoning, overcome Southey's objections to enter the Church, which it was thought he might find a fairly remunerative vocation.

Indeed, Mr. Hill hints at these ideas in a letter he wrote to a friend :—

" My nephew is a very good scholar, of great reading, of an astonishing memory; when he speaks he does it with fluency, with a great choice of words. He is perfectly correct in his behaviour, of the most exemplary morals, and the best of hearts. Were his character different, or his abilities not so extraordinary, I should be less concerned about him; but to see a young man of such talents as he possesses, by the misapplication of them, lost to himself and to his family, is what hurts me very sensibly indeed. In short he has everything you could wish a young man to have, excepting common sense and prudence."

The Unitarian views held by Southey proved too firmly rooted to be overcome by his uncle's persuasions, and with regard to the marriage question, he decided that in a very summary manner, conceiving that as he was the most interested person, he could act in opposition to the wishes of all his friends, with impunity. On the day he was to sail from England, the 14th November, 1795, he was privately married to Miss Edith Fricker, in Redcliffe Church; a step which he probably took as much to quiet the apprehensions of the young lady (who was no stranger to the objections his friends felt to their union), as from his own desire to avoid the contingencies of time and absence.

As soon as the marriage ceremony was concluded, Southey parted from his young wife, who returned to her friends, whilst he set sail for Lisbon, whence he did not return until May, 1796.

Coleridge and Lovell were married each to one of his wife's sisters, and she was left therefore with good and true friends until the return of her husband. It is only necessary to add that the sequel of this romantic match was most happy, and when, after a long wedded life, his wife's mind gave way, Southey wrote, " I am parted from my wife by something worse than death; forty years she has been the life of my life." Happily she did not linger long in that melancholy state, her death occurred in 1837.

Although Southey had made arrangements with Mr. Cottle, a Bristol publisher, for the sale of *Joan of Arc*, the first edition did not appear until after his return to England.

To this poem Coleridge had made large contributions, for although a temporary coolness existed between them when Southey at first withdrew from the colonisation scheme, yet the breach was soon healed, and they resumed reading and working together. Their friendship gained strength with age, although Coleridge never scrupled to criticise Southey's writings frankly, and at times most severely.

On his return from the Peninsula, Southey still found himself without any regular employment; the sale of his writings brought him in but a small and uncertain income; he therefore entered at Gray's Inn as a law student in 1797. He soon discovered that the study of law was as distasteful to him as medicine had previously been;

he scarcely knew whether to persevere in his irksome task, or to return to his beloved history and poetry; his decision in favour of the latter course was assisted by the kind offer from an old schoolfellow, Mr. Wynn, of £160 a year. On what account this handsome annuity was offered it is difficult to detemine, but Southey accepted it, forsook the law, and commenced two of his most important poems, *Madoc* and *Thalaba*, besides writing numerous articles and reviews for the periodical press.

In 1800 he again visited Portugal, accompanied by his wife, partly to recruit his health, and partly to gather materials for the history he contemplated writing of that country.

He now commenced to throw off his early ideas, seeing how *inexpedient* it was to speak the truth too plainly and too forcibly about the Government of the time, bad as it then undoubtedly was; and at length he changed sides so completely as to praise the acts of an administration which was abhorred by nearly all patriotic, and disinterested men. One of the first signs that his conversion was appreciated, was his appointment as secretary to Mr. Corry, Chancellor of the Exchequer for Ireland, with a salary of £350 a year, and very light duties.

Southey did not long retain this comfortable situation; for Mr. Corry having proposed that he should undertake the education of his sons, Southey not only indignantly declined to do so, but also resigned his secretaryship, and again trusted himself to the fickle favour of the public, and the chances of the press.

He settled at Keswick, and adopted a course of life and study better adapted for a hermit than an observant man of letters, from which he never afterwards greatly departed :—

" My actions," he wrote, " are as methodical as St. Dunstan's quarter-boys. Three pages of history after breakfast (equivalent to five in small quarto printing) ; then to transcribe and copy for the press, or to make my selections and biographies, or what else suits my humour, till dinner time ; from dinner to tea I read, write letters, see the newspapers, and very often indulge in a *siesta;* after tea I go to poetry, and correct and re-write, and copy till I am tired, and then turn to anything else till supper. And this is my life, which if it be not a very merry one, is yet as happy as heart could wish."

The proprietors of the *Edinburgh Review* invited Southey to contribute to it; he declined the offer, not wishing his articles to be associated with those of other writers to whose political views he objected; but when, in 1809, the *Quarterly Review* was started, he at once enlisted on its staff, and constantly wrote for it. All his early aspirations for freedom and equality had now departed, and he wrote in favour of the most violent and despotic measures, calling, with all the energy of a pervert, for the suspension of the *habeas corpus,* and the punishment of all those who dared to print the speeches of opposition members in the House of Commons; recommending exclusion, persecution, and the repression of all attempts at reform, by the aid of martial law; and generally preferring civil war, or a revolution, to the slightest concession to the Whigs, or the most trifling modification of the constitution.

These miserably mistaken notions are now of little importance, except as explaining the curious contrasts and inconsistencies to be found in his writings at different periods of his career, and as being the text upon which his opponents—notably Byron, Moore, Hunt, and Macaulay—fix their attention when criticising his works.

In July, 1814, Coleridge wrote :—

" I looked over the first five books of the first quarto edition of *Joan of Arc* yesterday, at Hood's request, in order to mark the lines written by me. I was really astonished, first, at the schoolboy wretched allegoric machinery,—second, at the transmogrification of the fanatic virago, into a modern novel-pawing proselyte of *The Age of Reason*, a Tom Paine in Petticoats, but so lovely ?—

' On her ruby cheek hung pity's crystal gem,'

third, at the utter want of all rhythm in the verse, the monotony and deadplumb down of the pauses, and of the absence of all bone, muscle, and sinew, in the single lines."

Coleridge then wrote in the volume the following list of abbreviations he intended to use in his marginal notes :—

S. E. means Southey's English—*i.e.*, no English at all.

N. means nonsense.

J. means discordant jingle of sound, one word rhyming or half-rhyming to another, proving either utter want of ear, or else very long ones.

L. M. Ludicrous metaphor.

I. M. Incongruous metaphor.

S. = pseudo-poetic slang, generally, too, not English.

And, with a red pencil, he proceeded pretty freely to annotate the poem, remarking at length, with humorous impatience, " Mercy on us, if I go on thus I shall make the book what I suppose it never was before, *red all thro'*."

The greater part of Book 2, and many other detached speeches written by Coleridge, were left out by Southey when he printed a second edition of *Joan of Arc*. Another of his early poems, *Wat Tyler*, was written during the early days of the French Revolution, into the spirit of which Southey entered with all the enthusiasm of youth, and the fire of genius. *Wat Tyler* therefore contained sentiments which self-interest afterwards taught him to deplore, and very shame prompted him to conceal;

it rails against kings, and princes, taxation, and state wars. The finest character in the poem, John Ball, a priest, indulges in speeches such as the following :—

> " My brethren, these are truths, and weighty ones.
> Ye are all equal : Nature made ye so,
> Equality is your birth-right ;—when I gaze
> On the proud palace, and behold one man
> In the blood-purpled robes of royalty,
> Feasting at ease, and lording over millions ;
> Then turn me to the hut of poverty,
> And see the wretched labourer, worn with toil,
> Divide his scanty morsel with his infants ;
> I sicken, and, indignant at the sight,
> Blush for the patience of humanity."

Many years after this was written, and, as Southey fondly hoped, forgotten, he being at the time a pensioned supporter of the Government, he was startled by reading an advertisement of "WAT TYLER," by Robert Southey, "a Dramatic Poem, with a preface suitable to recent circumstances. London, W. Hone," and shortly afterwards he received a copy of the drama, addressed to *Robert Southey, Poet Laureate, and Renegade.* By the advice of his friends, Southey applied for an injunction to restrain the publication; Lord Eldon refused to grant this protection, on the plea that "a person cannot recover damages upon a work which in its nature is calculated to do injury to the public." This decision was not only extremely annoying to Southey, but greatly increased the notoriety of the reprint of the drama, of which no less than 60,000 copies were sold in a very short time, and it is even now much more frequently met with than any of his other poems. Southey's political opponents did not let the matter rest here, for both Lord Brougham and Mr. William Smith, member for Norwich, drew attention in the House to Southey's inconsistent writings, contrasting *Wat Tyler* with his later Conservative articles in *The Quarterly Review*, and inquiring why the Government had taken no steps to prosecute the author of that treasonable play.

These proceedings reflected little credit on either party. Southey was doubtless a turncoat; but his opponents, in the bitterness of party spite, made no allowances for the merits of his later works, or for his great services to literature; nor do they seem to have reflected that, though he held different opinions from theirs on public questions, he was in private life one of the most blameless of men.

As early as 1807, the Government had conferred a pension of £200 a year upon him, and when Pye died Southey was named Poet Laureate, Sir Walter Scott having previously declined the post, upon which his noble name would have thrown a new lustre.

In the preface to the third edition of his poems, Southey gives the following account of his obtaining the office :—

" It was stated in some of the newspapers that Walter Scott and myself became competitors for the Poet Laureateship upon the death of Mr. Pye; and that we met accidentally at the Prince Regent's levee, each in pursuit of his pretensions, and that some words, which were not over courteous on either side, passed between us on the occasion ; to such impudent fabrications will those persons resort who make it their business to pander for public curiosity.

"The circumstances relating to that appointment have been made known in Mr. Lockhart's life of Sir Walter. His conduct was, as it always was, characteristically generous, and in the highest degree friendly. Upon his declining the office, and using his influence without my knowledge to obtain it for me, his biographer says (Vol. iii. p. 88) :—

" ' Mr. Southey was invited to accept the vacant laurel ; and, to the honour of the Prince Regent, when he signified that his acceptance

Q

must depend on the office being thenceforward so modified as to demand none of the old formal odes, leaving it to the Poet Laureate to choose his own time for celebrating any great public event that might occur, his Royal Highness had the good sense and good taste at once to acquiesce in the propriety of this alteration. The office was thus relieved from the burden of ridicule, which had, in spite of so many illustrious names, adhered to it.'

" The alteration, however, was not brought about exactly in this manner. I was on the way to London when the correspondence upon this subject between Sir Walter Scott and Mr. Croker took place. No wish for the laureateship had passed across my mind, nor had I ever dreamt that it would be proposed to me. My first impulse was to decline it ; not from any fear of ridicule, still less of obloquy ; but because I had ceased for several years to write occasional verses ; and though willing as a bee to work from morn till night in collecting honey, I had a great dislike to spinning like a spider. Other considerations overcame this reluctance, and made it my duty to accept this appointment. I then expressed a wish to Mr. Croker that it might be placed on a footing which would exact from the holder nothing like a schoolboy's task, but leave him at liberty to write when, and in what manner he thought best, and thus render the office as honourable as it was originally designed to be.

" Upon this Mr. Croker observed that it was not for us to make terms with the Prince Regent. ' Go you,' said he, ' and write your Ode for the New Year. You can never have a better subject than the present state of the war affords you.' He added that some fit time might be found for representing the matter to the Prince in its proper light.

" My appointment had no sooner been made known, than I received a note with Sir William Parson's compliments requesting that I would let him have the ode as soon as possible, Mr. Pye having always provided him with it six weeks before New Year's Day.

" I was not wanting in punctuality ; nevertheless it was a great trouble to Sir William that the office should have been conferred upon a poet who did not walk in the ways of his predecessor, and do according to all things that he had done ; for Mr. Pye had written his odes always in regular stanzas and in rhyme. The labour which the chief musician bestowed upon the verses of the chief poet was so much labour lost. The performance of the annual odes had been suspended from the time of the King's illness in 1810. Under the circumstances of his malady, any festal celebration of the birthday would have been a violation of natural feeling and public propriety. On those occasions it was certain that nothing would be expected from me during the life of George III. But the New Year's performance might perhaps be called for, and for that therefore I always prepared.

" Upon the accession of George IV., I made ready an Ode for St. George's Day, which Mr. Shield, who was much better satisfied with his yoke-fellow than Sir William had been, thought happily suited for his purpose. All my other odes related to the circumstances of the passing times, and could have been appropriately performed only when they were composed ; but this was a standing subject, and till this should be called for, it was needless to provide anything else.

" The annual performance had however by this time fallen completely into disuse ; and thus terminated a custom which may truly be said to have been more honoured in the breach than in the observance.

" KESWICK, *Dec.* 12, 1837."

Southey also held the title of Historiographer Royal, to which he was certainly well entitled, but there was no salary attached to this office. After his appointment as Laureate he commenced writing a series of adulatory poems, such as *The Carmen Triumphale,* and, upon the death of George III., *The Vision of Judgment,* celebrating the ascension into heaven of that obstinate and misguided monarch.

In this most impious work, he fearlessly condemns or rewards political personages at the day of judgment, according as their opinions coincide or not with his own, in a manner so little short of blasphemy, as to disgust his best friends and create greater activity amongst his foes.

Q 2

He never once appears to have realised the expediency of
Pope's prayer,

> " Let not this weak, unknowing hand
> Presume Thy bolts to throw,
> And deal damnation round the land
> On each I judge Thy foe,"

for in poetry or prose, history or politics, it was only
necessary to differ with Southey's views to be proclaimed
by him a fool or a knave, and very commonly both.

In the Preface to his *Vision of Judgment* Byron explains his reasons for writing it: "It hath been wisely
said, that 'One fool makes many,' and it hath been
poetically observed

> " ' That fools rush in where angels fear to tread.'

"If Mr. Southey had not rushed in where he had no
business, and where he never was before, and never will
be again, the following poem would not have been written.
It is not impossible that it may be as good as his own,
seeing that it cannot, by any species of stupidity, natural
or acquired, be *worse*. The gross flattery, the dull im-
pudence, the renegade intolerance, and impious cant, of
the poem by the author of *Wat Tyler*, are something so
stupendous as to form the sublime of himself—containing
the quintessence of his own attributes. So much for his
poem—a word on his Preface. In this Preface it has
pleased the magnanimous Laureate to draw the picture of a
supposed 'Satanic school,' the which he doth recommend
to the notice of the Legislature; thereby adding to his
other laurels the ambition for those of an informer. If
there exists anywhere, except in his imagination, such a
school, is he not sufficiently armed against it by his own
intense vanity ? The truth is, that there are certain

writers whom Mr. Southey imagines, like Scrub, to have
'talked of *him*,' for they laughed consumedly!

"But I have a few questions to ask—

"Firstly—Is Mr. Southey the author of *Wat Tyler?*

"Secondly—Was he not refused a remedy at law by the
highest judge of his beloved England, because it was a
blasphemous and seditious publication?

"Thirdly—Was he not entitled by William Smith, in
full parliament, 'a rancorous renegade?'

"Fourthly—Is he not poet laureate, with his own lines
on Martin, the regicide, staring him in the face?

"And fifthly—Putting the four preceding items together,
with what conscience dare *he* call the attention of the
laws to the publications of others, be they what they may?

"I say nothing of the cowardice of such a proceeding,
its meanness speaks for itself; but I wish to touch upon
the *motive*, which is neither more nor less than that Mr.
Southey has been laughed at a little in some recent publications, as he was of yore in the *Anti-Jacobin* by his
present patrons. Hence all this 'skimble-scamble stuff'
about 'Satanic' and so forth. However, it is worthy of
him—*qualis ab incepto.*

"If there is anything obnoxious to the political opinions
of a portion of the public in the following poem, they may
thank Mr. Southey. He might have written hexameters,
as he has written everything else, for aught that the
writer cared, had they been upon another subject. But
to attempt to canonise a monarch, who, whatever were his
household virtues, was neither a successful nor a patriot
king, inasmuch as several years of his reign passed in war
with America and Ireland, to say nothing of the aggression
upon France, like all other exaggeration necessarily begets
opposition.

"In whatever manner he may be spoken of in this new *Vision* his *public* career will not be more favourably transmitted by history. Of his private virtues (although a little expensive to the nation) there can be no doubt.

"With regard to the supernatural personages treated of, I can only say that I know as much about them, and (as an honest man) have a better right to talk of them than Robert Southey. I have also treated them more tolerantly. The way in which that poor, insane creature, the Laureate, deals about his judgments in the next world is like his own judgment in this. If it was not completely ludicrous it would be something worse.

"I don't think there is much more to say at present."

Southey replied to this parody in terms so intemperate and so personal that Byron, then residing at Pisa, sent him a challenge; fortunately Mr. Kinnaird, to whom it was entrusted, did not deliver it to the Laureate.

Undeterred by ridicule, and unfortunately for his reputation, Southey continued to compose poems for various Court celebrations, but only at irregular intervals.

These odes, of which the following are the titles, are entombed in the complete editions of his works :

"An Ode written during the Negotiations with Bonaparte in January, 1814."

"Ode written during the War with America."

"Carmina Aulica," written in 1814, on the arrival of the Allied Sovereigns in England, "being Odes to the Prince Regent of Great Britain, to Alexander I. of Russia, and to William IV. of Prussia."

"Ode on the Battle of Algiers."

"Ode on the Death of Queen Charlotte."

"Ode for St. George's Day."

"Ode written after the King's Visit to Ireland."

"Ode written after the King's Visit to Scotland."

"Carmen Triumphale for the commencement of the year 1814."

"Carmen Nuptiale. The Lay of the Laureate, on the marriage of the Princess Charlotte." This concludes with the verse, made famous by Byron's satire,

L'ENVOY.

"Go, little book, from this my solitude,
 I cast thee on the waters : go thy ways,
And if, as I believe, thy vein be good,
 The world will find thee after many days.
Be it with thee according to thy worth,
Go, little book! in faith I send thee forth."

The Princess Charlotte had been betrothed to the Prince of Orange, and to celebrate the event Southey had written the chief part of a poem, when the match was suddenly broken off. The Princess was shortly afterwards married to the Prince Leopold of Saxe-Coburg, and then (not to lose his labours) out came the *Carmen ;* the flattery intended for one prince was most impartially applied to another, as has been characteristic of the Court muse since Dryden's time. Such stanzas as could only truthfully apply to really good and great men were written in favour of a Charles II. or a George IV.; not until after the death of a monarch do the people know anything of his real character; then it is no longer considered necessary, being no longer profitable, to invent virtues, hide faults, or deny crimes.

When Waller was taunted with having written better verses in praise of Cromwell than those he composed in honour of Charles II., he replied that poets were always more successful in fiction than reality. If this axiom were correct, it would seem a paradox that most of Southey's

Courtly odes were so poor, for they certainly belonged more to the realm of fiction than to that of reality.

In 1816, Southey was considerately advised to rest satisfied with the sherry, salary, and safe obscurity of his predecessors. The same writer remarks that "a poet laureate is naturally a ridiculous personage, and has scarcely any safe course to follow in times like the present, but to bear his faculties with exceeding meekness, and keep as much as possible in the shade. The laurel which the monarch gives has nothing at all in common with that bestowed by the Muses, and the warrant is of no authority in the court of Apollo."

Southey's other works issued from the press in rapid succession, but they did not command a large sale, probably because he seldom chose very attractive or popular topics. His histories are ponderous compilations evolved from the stores of his vast reading, without any other effort than to make them the receptacles for dry undigested facts, and unconnected incidents. There were ten volumes of poetry, although but few people know even the titles of them now; the topics on which they are written are indeed "caviare to the general," whilst his style of composition is far from alluring—

> "Oh Southey! Southey! cease thy varied song,
> A Bard may chant too often and too long :
> As thou art strong in verse, in mercy, spare !
> A fourth, alas! were more than we could bear.
> But if, in spite of all the world can say,
> Thou still wilt verseward plod thy weary way ;
> If still in Berkley ballads most uncivil,
> Thou wilt still devote old women to the devil,
> The babe unborn thy dread intent may rue ;
> 'God help thee,' Southey, and thy readers too."

His most celebrated prose works are *The History of the*

Peninsular War, a *History of Portugal* (which was never completed), and another of *Brazil*, the translation of *The Chronicles of the Cid*, *The Book of the Church*, and the sequel to it, contained in letters addressed to Charles Butler, Esq., entitled, *Vindiciæ Ecclesiæ Anglicanæ; or, the Book of the Church vindicated and amplified.*

He also wrote a number of works on special, and oftentimes peculiar subjects, such as *The Doctor;* and *Sir Thomas More; or, Colloquies on the Progress and Prospects of Society*—a work better known from Lord Macaulay's Essay on it, than from any merit of its own.

Numerous articles for the *Quarterly* and other periodicals flowed from his active pen, touching upon nearly every branch of literature, history, and political economy, essays, moral and political, and translations of Spanish and Portuguese classical works.

But of all his writings the most generally admired are his biographies, such as *The Life of John Wesley, with a View of the Rise and Progress of Methodism; The Life of Admiral Lord Nelson; The Life of the Rev. Andrew Bell, comprising the Rise and Progress of the system of Mutual Tuition.*

Speaking of his *Life of Wesley*, Southey said "that he thought it was written in too fair a spirit to satisfy any set of men;" it is, nevertheless, considered one of the masterpieces of English biography.

The Life of Nelson originally appeared as an article in the *Quarterly*, and Mr. Murray urged Southey to enlarge it into book form, although the subject might well have been considered out of Southey's range of art. However he afterwards said, "I have satisfied myself in the execution far more than I could have expected to do;" admitting at the same time that he had to pick his way amongst the sea terms as carefully as a cat walking over crockery-ware.

In it the narrative is continuous and clear; and the materials being so full of character, the adventures so thrilling, picturesque, and sublime, the work was deservedly successful, and is now perhaps the most often read, and the best known of all his writings.

Henry Kirke White, Cowper the poet, and John Bunyan each found a biographer in Southey; whilst the *Lives of the English Divines, Essays on the Lives and Works of the Uneducated Poets,* and *Specimens of the later British Poets, who died from* 1685 *to* 1800, partake partly of the natures of history, criticism, and biography.

Southey's prose works are broad and clear in style, the language elegant, and the flow of the narrative easy and regular. But in theological and historical works he allowed party feelings to interfere with the impartiality of the historian, and to so great an extent that the bias is almost always painfully evident to the reader.

Once when Southey had been ridiculed for his change of political views, he wrote that he was "no more ashamed of having been a Republican, than of having been a boy before he was a man."

There is certainly no cause for shame in either case. A conscientious religious or political belief is not a subject of which any honest man need be ashamed; but for a man to desert his principles at the precise moment when he will most benefit himself in a pecuniary way by so doing, and to adopt ever afterwards the most violent tone, and cry loudly for the harshest and most intolerant measures to be put in force against those who hold the opinions he once advocated, these are indeed actions for which one ought to feel ashamed, although it does not appear that Southey ever explained or apologised for his early indiscretions, or justified his later conduct. Macaulay, when alluding to this unpleasant side of Southey's character, says that he possessed two faculties to an inordinate extent—the faculty of believing without a reason, and that of hating without a provocation.

A Republican in his youth, an Ultra-Tory in after life, recommending severe punishment for demagogues, proscriptions, massacres, or civil war, rather than any concession to a discontented people, George IV. should have revived the Holy Office, appointing Southey—Grand Inquisitor, with a choice magazine of racks, thumb-screws, iron boots, slow fires, and red-hot pincers.

His conversion may have arisen from honest conviction; it is to be hoped that it did; yet without referring to the change his opinions underwent, it would be impossible to believe that the man who wrote *Joan of Arc* and *Wat Tyler* could have been the author of *The Vision of Judgment, The Book of the Church,* or the official odes. In one of the latter, *The Lay of the Laureate,* dedicated to the Princess Charlotte, in 1816, he says:—

> " That wreath which in Eliza's golden days
> My master dear, divinest Spenser, wore,
> That which rewarded Drayton's learned lays,
> Which thoughtful Ben, and gentle Daniel bore,
> Grin, Envy, through thy rugged mask of scorn!
> In honour it was given, with honour it is worn."

" With honour it is worn," Southey might fearlessly assert of the poetical crown, for not even his bitterest enemy could assert that it lost dignity in his keeping, although it has been truthfully said of his official odes that they are for the most part worse than Pye's, and as bad as Cibber's; his longer poems, however, though full of faults, are very extraordinary productions.

Not the least peculiar feature in Southey's poetry is the original style of versification he adopted, frequently most irregular, and without rhyme, yet not destitute of a certain rhythmical harmony which lends itself well to declamation, although the extracts require to be carefully selected.

This new style met with severe treatment from the critics, and but little favour from the public, at a time when so many bright stars were in the poetical firmament to attract attention and chain the imagination.

The small sale of his poems was a constant source of regret to Southey, who saw that Byron, Scott, or Moore could obtain £3,000 for poems no longer than those of his which realised but £300.

He consoled himself with the mistaken idea that he was writing for posterity, and obstinately adhered not only to the style he had adopted, which with all its faults has many charms, but continued to select topics such as could interest but few in the reading world, and the general public not at all. In *Rejected Addresses* there is an admirable and most amusing imitation of one of his finest epics, *The Curse of Kehama*, in which both the language and metre are cleverly parodied.

Nearly the whole of Southey's time was devoted to reading and writing; he seldom gave himself time for meditation, working as methodically at his poetry as he did with history, regularly composing so many lines a day, and building epics, as other men build houses, on a regular system of work against time, or contract for quantity. His secluded country residence, and aversion to general society, made him almost a stranger to the broad stage of life, caused him to judge unfavourably of many

men and opinions with which he was only acquainted by
repute, and ofttimes led him to express the most unjust
and mistaken views about the characters and works of his
opponents.

An opportunity was afforded him to emerge from his
retirement and enter the House of Commons, in which a
seat was offered him, together with an annuity of £300, on
the sole condition of supporting in the House the views
he had expressed in his *Book of the Church* and other
Tory writings.

Southey declined these offers, and others even more
suitable to his tastes and learning, one of them being the
post of Librarian to the Advocate's Library, at Edinburgh,
with light and most congenial duties, and a salary of £400
per annum ; a still more tempting proposal came from
Mr. Walter, of *The Times*, who promised him £2,000
a year to generally superintend the literary work, and
furnish a leading article for that journal.

Southey was too much attached to his residence at
Greta Hall, and to his own solemn regularity of life, to
enter upon new duties in a strange locality amidst unknown people. It was generally (but erroneously) supposed that he had made a large fortune by the sale of his
works, his periodical writings, and his pensions ; the truth
being that his most abstruse books had but a small sale.
As a rule he drew on account from his publishers, and was
often in their debt ; his house expenses were heavy, and
in the purchase of books he was extremely lavish ; he
accumulated a library of 14,000 volumes, which at his
death sold for £2,900, probably about one-third of what
they cost Southey. When therefore Sir Robert Peel
offered the Laureate a baronetcy, his means would not
permit him to support the dignity of the title, and he

frankly informed Sir Robert of his reason for declining the honour.

The almost immediate result of this correspondence was the grant of a further pension of £300 a year; this addition to his income was all the more welcome as his later writings were unsuccessful—some of them indeed gave unmistakable signs of the fading in the powers of his mind.

The death of his wife in 1837 caused him intense grief, and thenceforward both his bodily and mental faculties rapidly declined. In 1839 he contracted a second marriage with Miss Caroline Bowles, the poetess, an act for which it seems difficult to account, considering his advanced age, and the then bad state of his health.

In the following year he had a paralytic stroke from which he never recovered; he lingered in a state of melancholy dotage for some time, until death happily released him on the 21st March, 1843.

He was buried at the western end of Crosthwaite Churchyard, by the side of his first wife; Wordsworth attended his funeral, and wrote the verses which are inscribed on the base of the recumbent statue erected in Crosthwaite Church by public subscription.

> " Ye vales and hills, whose beauty hither drew
> The poet's steps, and fixed him here; on you
> His eyes have closed; and ye, loved books, no more
> Shall Southey feed upon your precious lore:
> To works that ne'er shall forfeit their renown,
> Adding immortal labours of his own,
> Whether he traced historic truths with zeal,
> For the State's guidance or the public weal;
> Or Fancy, disciplined by curious art,
> Informed his pen; or wisdom of the heart,
> Or judgments, sanctioned in the patriot's mind
> By reverence for the rights of all mankind:

> Wide were his aims, yet in no human breast
> Could private feelings meet in holier rest.
> His joys, his griefs, have vanished like a cloud
> From Skiddaw's top, but he to heaven was vowed
> Through a long life, and pure and steadfast faith
> Calmed in his soul the fear of change and death."

There is also a fine bust to his memory in Poet's Corner, standing close to the Shakespeare monument.

The general testimony to Southey's private relations, as husband, father, and friend, was most favourable; it was only in his writings that he was vain, egotistical, and intolerant; he entertained the most exalted opinions of his own poems, especially the epics, and fondly imagined that posterity would recognise their superlative beauties. His singularly constituted mind led him to utter the harshest criticisms against his political and literary opponents, as for instance when he characterised Byron's poetry as of the "Satanic" school. But Byron, in his vigorous and witty satire, *The Vision of Judgment*, reviewed Southey's public career in a simple recapitulation of facts, which carries far more force with it than all the harsh names Southey could invent :—

> " He had written praises of a regicide;
>   He had written praises of all kings whatever;
>   He had written for republics far and wide,
>   And then against them bitterer than ever;
>   For Pantisocracy he once had cried
>   Aloud, a scheme less moral than 'twas clever;
>   Then grew a hearty anti-jacobin—
>   Had turn'd his coat, and would have turn'd his skin.

> " He had sung against all battles, and again
>   In their high praise and glory; he had call'd
>   Reviewing ' the ungentle craft,' and then
>   Become as base a critic as e'er crawl'd—

> Fed, paid, and pamper'd by the very men
> By whom his muse and morals had been maul'd :
> He had written much blank verse, and blanker prose,
> And more of both than anybody knows."

And yet Byron was not insensible to some of Southey's merits, nor ashamed to record his admiration of them :—

"Yesterday," he wrote, "at Holland House, I was introduced to Southey—the best-looking bard I have seen for some time. To have that poet's head and shoulders, I would almost have written his *Sapphics*. He is certainly a prepossessing person to look on, and a man of talent, and all that—and—there is his eulogy. His appearance is epic ; and he is the only existing entire man of letters. His manners are mild, but not those of a man of the world, and his talents are of the first order. His prose is perfect. Of his poetry there are various opinions : there is, perhaps, too much of it for the present generation—posterity will probably select. He has passages equal to anything. At present he has a party, but no public—except for his prose writings. *The Life of Nelson* is beautiful."

"He's dead, he's dead, the Laureate's dead! 'Twas thus the cry began,
  And straightway every garret-roof gave up its minstrel man ;
  From Grub Street, and from Houndsditch, and from Farringdon Within,
  The poets all towards Whitehall poured on with eldritch din.''

So say the Bon Gaultier Ballads, in which are half a dozen burlesque poems, supposed to have been written by competitors for the office of Laureate on the death of Southey. The idea was far from novel, but Messrs. Aytoun and Theodore Martin have admirably hit off the prominent features of style in their imitations of Lord

Macaulay and Tom Moore; Lord Lytton (then Sir Edward
Bulwer Lytton) steps forward to justify his bewildering
admixture of sentiment and crime, remarking with
charming candour:—

> " For in my nether heart convinced I am,
>   Philosophy's as good as any other *bam*.
> But these remarks are neither here nor there.
>   Where was I? Oh, I see—old Southey's dead!
> They'll want some bard to fill the vacant chair,
>   And drain the annual butt—and oh! what head
>   More fit with laurel to be garlanded
> Than this, which, curled in many a fragrant coil,
> Breathes of Castalia's streams, and best Macassar oil?
>
> *   *   *   *   *   *   *
>
> " Yes, I am he who sung how Aram won
>   The gentle ear of pensive Madeline!
> How love and murder hand in hand may run,
>   Cemented by philosophy serene,
>   And kisses bless the spot where gore has been!
> Who breathed the melting sentiment of crime,
> And for the assassin waked a sympathy divine!"

But Robert Montgomery (the author of *Satan* and
other long forgotten poems) put in his claim:—

> " I fear no rival for the vacant throne;
>   No mortal thunder shall eclipse my own!
>   Let dark Macaulay chant his Roman lays,
>   Let Monckton Milnes go maunder for the bays,
>   Let Simmons call on great Napoleon's shade,
>   Let Lytton Bulwer seek his Aram's aid,
>   Let Wordsworth ask for help from Peter Bell,
>   Let Campbell carol Copenhagen's knell,
>   Let Delta warble through his Delphic groves,
>   Let Elliott shout for pork and penny loaves,—
>   I care not, I! resolved to stand or fall;
>   One down another on, I'll smash them all!

R

" Back, ye profane ! this hand alone hath power
 To pluck the laurel from its sacred bower ;
 This brow alone is privileged to wear
 The ancient wreath o'er hyacinthine hair ;
 These lips alone may quaff the sparkling wine,
 And make its mortal juice once more divine."

There is also a parody of Tennyson's *The Merman*, entitled *The Laureate,* this was rather premature, for Wordsworth first received the laurels, as Bon Gaultier says :—

" They led our Wordsworth to the Queen, she crowned him with
 the bays,
 And wished him many happy years, and many quarter days ;
 And if you'd have the story told by abler lips than mine,
 You've but to call at Rydal Mount, and taste the Laureate's
 wine !"

WILLIAM WORDSWORTH.

(1843—1850.)

" We learn from Horace ' Homer sometimes sleeps ;'
   We feel without him, Wordsworth sometimes wakes ;
To show with what complacency he creeps
   With his dear ' waggoners ' around the lakes.
He wishes for a ' boat ' to sail the deeps—
   Of Ocean ?—no of air ; and then he makes
Another outcry for a ' little boat,'
And drivels seas to set it well afloat.

" If he must fain sweep o'er th' ethereal plain,
   And Pegasus runs restive in his ' waggon,'
Could he not beg the loan of Charles's wain ?
   Or pray Medea for a single dragon ?
Or if too classic for his vulgar brain,
   He fear'd his neck to venture such a nag on,
And he must needs mount nearer to the moon,
Could not the blockhead ask for a balloon ?

" ' Pedlars ' and ' Boats ' and ' Waggons !' Oh, ye shades
   Of Pope and Dryden has it come to this ?
That trash of such sort not alone evades
   Contempt, but from the bathos' vast abyss
Floats scum-like uppermost, and these Jack Cades
   Of sense and song above your graves may hiss—
The ' little boatman ' and his ' Peter Bell '
Can sneer at him who drew Achitophel !"—BYRON.

WORDSWORTH held the title, and drew the pension of
Poet Laureate, but whether he was worthy of either will

probably remain undecided as long as any other debatable questions in Literature or Art; it is purely a matter of taste, and the admirers of Wordsworth, though energetic in his praise, are but few in number.

His apologists are usually so extreme in their views, that they injure the cause they fight for; it is not an easy task to persuade people that mere commonplace remarks, and trite simple reflections, conveyed in very blank verse, contain the highest attributes of poetry, and that grandeur of language and dignity of sentiment are, or ought to be, obsolete. Yet this is, to a certain extent, an epitome of their arguments, and Sir John Coleridge, in a lecture he delivered at Exeter not long since, having commenced by stating that Wordsworth was not so popular a poet as many others he considered less worthy, proceeded to sum up the total of Wordsworth's power in a passage full of bare assertion, and most inconsequential reasoning :—

" Wordsworth, it is true, is probably now, by most cultivated and intellectual men, admitted to be a great and original writer ; a writer whose compositions it is right to be acquainted with as a part of literary history and literary education. Few men would now venture to deny him genius, or to treat his poetry with contempt. No one probably would dare to echo or even to defend the ribald abuse of the *Edinburgh Review*. But he is not generally appreciated ; even now he is far too little read ; and, as I think, for the idlest and weakest of all reasons. He suffers still from the impression produced by attacks made upon him by men who, I should suppose, if they had tried, were incapable of feeling his beauty and his grandeur, but who seem to me never to have had the common honesty to try. Fastening upon a few obvious defects, seizing upon a few poems (poems admitting of complete defence, and, viewed rightly, full of beauty, yet capable no doubt of being presented in a ridiculous aspect), the critics of the *Edinburgh Review* poured out on Wordsworth abuse, invective, malignant personality, which deterred the unreflecting mass of men from reading for themselves and finding out, as they must have found out, the worthlessness of the criticism. They destroyed his popularity and blighted his reputation, though they have had no power whatever over his fame. Lord Jeffrey was the chief offender in this matter. . . . But the sentence of the critic either suspended men's judgments or overbore them, and the poems were unread. The power of *The Edinburgh Review* of those days, written as it was by a set of men of splendid and popular abilities, was indeed prodigious. It stopped for years the sale of Wordsworth's poems ; and though he outlived its calumnies, and found at length a general and reverent acceptance, yet prejudices were created which impeded his popularity ; and even now the echoes of Lord Jeffrey's mocking laughter fill the ears of many men, and deafen them to the lovely and majestic melody of Wordsworth's song.''

The simple fact is that Wordsworth's poetry did not attract the public, and probably never will. Articles which appeared in *The Edinburgh Review* forty years ago are not now very easy to obtain, and cannot, at the present time, influence public opinion to any appreciable extent. Hostile criticism often has a very decided effect at the time it is written, but that effect is, as a rule, only temporary if the criticism is unjust. Were ever men more bitterly, savagely, and unjustly treated by the reviewers than Byron, Shelley, and Keats, upon whom ridicule, personal abuse, and political spite were unsparingly showered ? Yet can it be supposed that their works are now any the less read and admired than if they had not been so abused.

Wordsworth's poems are easy of access. Whatever *beauties* they ever possessed can still be found in them, all the adverse criticism in the world cannot have altered one syllable of what was written, and yet the public refuses to be enthusiastic, notwithstanding all that Sir John Coleridge asserts about the power and genius of Wordsworth, and the terrible results of Jeffrey's mocking laughter.

Besides, Wordsworth was the pet of a powerful literary *clique*, by whom he was certainly as much overpraised, as he was perhaps underrated by the *Edinburgh* Reviewers.

Those who do not admire Wordsworth's style have at least one stronghold; it is impossible for any reader of Byron, Shelley, or Pope to fail to perceive that what he is reading is certainly poetry, and that of a high class; whilst many sensible men find little of what they consider poetry in Wordsworth. Coleridge admits that some of his poems are capable of being presented in a ridiculous aspect, and it seems pretty evident that such writings must be wanting in true poetic dignity; and whether the reader is an admirer of the so-called *Lake School* of poetry, or of what Southey contemptuously styled the *Cockney-Satanic* school, he must admit that there are hundreds of lines written by Wordsworth which it would have been well for his fame had he never printed.

As for the term, the Lake School, in itself it conveys but little meaning; the three "Lakers," Coleridge, Wordsworth, and Southey, were very dissimilar men in their genius, their pursuits, and their works. Coleridge, metaphysical and contemplative, with an analytical turn of mind, the greatest thinker of the three; Southey, industrious as a bee, ever reading or compiling, reflecting but seldom; Wordsworth, not a great reader, and indolent by disposition, went sauntering to and fro, mentally stringing his ideas together, repeating the composition on his return home to his sister, or an amanuensis, to avoid the mechanical part of writing, which he hated.

As Wordsworth's poems are more particularly localised in the Lake District, and abound in descriptions of the scenery and natural phenomena of that lovely country, the term Lake poet may be taken to apply *par excellence* to him. Charles Lamb once shocked his susceptibilities by jocularly taking hold of his large nose, instead of his hand, saying, "Well, old Laker, how are you?" thus showing a dreadful want of reverence for the solemn and austere bard.

As to the revolution which Wordsworth desired to bring about in poetry, he explains in the preface to his *Lyrical Ballads* that his purpose was to imitate, and, as far as was possible, to adopt the very language of men. Hitherto the great aim of the poet had been to express the noblest sentiments in the choicest language: all this is wrong, says Wordsworth; conversation is poetry; let us have the every-day talk of rustics cut up into lines—it makes splendid poetry. "*Par ma foi*," as M. Jourdain says, "il y a plus de quarante ans que je dis des vers sans que j'en susse rien, et je vous suis le plus obligé du monde de m'avoir appris cela."

As he found poetry in the most commonplace events of life, and described them in familiar language, he naturally contended that there was little real difference between poetry and prose, a theory on which Byron gaily rallies him :—

> " The simple Wordsworth framer of a lay
> As soft as evening in his favourite May,
> Who warns his friend ' to shake off toil and trouble,
> And quit his books, for fear of growing double ;'
> Who, both by precept and example, shows
> That prose is verse, and verse is merely prose ;
> Convincing all, by demonstration plain,
> Poetic souls delight in prose insane."

When, however, the reader turns to his short occasional poems, his ballads, and his sonnets, great is the relief, for it is in these that he shows his genius; few ballads in the language are finer or more pathetic, for instance, than *Hart-Leap Well*, with its kindly advice :—

> " Never to blend our pleasure or our pride
> With sorrow of the meanest thing that feels."

But Wordsworth vainly imagined that his fame was assured by his longer poems, and in his prolix prefaces endeavours to instruct his reader as to the manner and order in which they are to be perused ; the time has not yet arrived when people study poetry by a slow and steady progress, as they would Euclid, from problem to problem, consequently his prefaces are not often read, and the systematic arrangement of the poems into periods is unheeded.

He cautions the reader against one mode of criticism which had been applied to poetry in which the language closely resembles life and nature.   Such verses, he remarks, have been parodied, and Dr. Johnson's stanza is a fair specimen of the manner :—

> " I put my hat upon my head
> And walked into the Strand,
> And there I met another man
> Whose hat was in his hand."

In this verse, he says, the matter is contemptible ; it wants sense, it is neither interesting in itself, nor can lead to anything interesting.

After reading the above ludicrous lines and Wordsworth's sensible remarks upon them, it is astonishing in how many places in his own writings one finds " contemptible matter," long passages of wordy triviality, and minute details of what is neither interesting in itself nor leading to anything interesting.   He who has the patience to read *The*

Idiot Boy will find some examples in this style of writing.

> " Thy lisping prattle and thy mincing gait,
>   All thy false mimic fooleries I hate ;
>   For thou art Folly's counterfeit, and she
>   Who is right foolish hath the better plea ;
>   Nature's true Idiot I prefer to thee."
>
>   CUMBERLAND.

Wordsworth's life was singularly uneventful, and attended with more success than usually falls to the lot of authors whose works have not acquired popularity.

He was born on the 7th April, 1770, at Cockermouth, and was educated at Hawkshead, in Lancashire, whence he proceeded to St. John's College, Cambridge. There he displayed a great impatience of control, and that intense belief in the correctness of his own opinions and actions which increased with his age, and only ceased on his death. He was not distinguished for his industry, especially showing a distaste for mathematics; he however took his degree of B.A. in January, 1791, and then left Cambridge.

He made several visits to France at the time when ideal Republican notions were first being discussed, which he at once adopted, and declared himself an enemy of hereditary monarchy and the peerage. In imitation of his friend, Southey, he afterwards judged it expedient to change these opinions, or to smother them in his own breast.

He planned a monthly literary magazine, which he proposed to call *The Philanthropist;* it was to preach Republicanism to the British public, but it was *not* to be revolutionary. The distinction is rather hard to define, as it is tolerably certain that before the monarchy could be abolished the privileged classes, the holders of sinecure offices, and a rich and numerous aristocracy would make a desperate, because interested, struggle against the popular cause, which could only triumph, in fact, through, and by a revolution.

Whether Wordsworth had reasoned out his scheme now matters little, as he could not inspire any publisher with sufficient confidence to start the project.

His friends wished him to enter the church, but he did not think himself fitted for that vocation, and was doubtful what means to adopt to earn a livelihood. This uncertainty was increased by his inheriting a legacy of £900, upon the interest of which sum he lived in a dreamy, indolent manner for several years, only occasionally earning a trifling amount by his pen.

In October, 1802, he set out in company with his sister on a journey to Penrith to seek Miss Mary Hutchinson, the school companion of his boyish days, who was now to be his wife. After several changes of residence he finally settled at Rydal Mount, in Westmoreland, and there in comparative seclusion passed the remainder of his life, relieved only in its calm monotony by occasional tours to Scotland and the Continent.

These annual wanderings were Wordsworth's greatest delight, and his friend, Sir George Beaumont, bequeathed him an annuity of £100, with the somewhat whimsical stipulation that the money should be expended in an *annual excursion;* in addition to this legacy, Wordsworth's circumstances were much ameliorated by the payment of a debt long due to his family from the Earl of Lonsdale; £1,800 each thus came to the poet and his sister.

In 1814 he published *The Excursion*,* the most ambitious work that had yet come before the public from his pen. A quarto volume of 447 pages, it was yet announced as only forming a portion of *The Recluse*, which Wordsworth designed to write, and which was to contain a continuous record of his poetical opinions, and critical self-examination.

The Prelude was to lead, followed by *The Excursion*, and a third poem entitled *The Recluse*, consisting " of the sensations and opinions of a poet living in retirement," was to complete the series, but the latter part of the design was never completed.

It was the publication of *The Excursion* which gave rise to Jeffrey's celebrated article in *The Edinburgh Review*, November, 1814. This article combines at once the keenest criticism of Wordsworth's style, with the kindliest advice and most hearty commendation that had as yet been bestowed upon his works by any critic of eminence.

The temptation to quote from it is irresistible. It will be seen that although it condemns strongly it also praises judiciously and with no niggard hand, a fact which Wordsworth's admirers are apt to forget in their angry denunciations of the critic who would not worship their idol. It opens thus :—

" This will never do. It bears no doubt the stamp of the author's

---

* " And Wordsworth in a rather long ' Excursion '
   (I think the quarto holds five hundred pages)
Has given a sample from the vasty version
   Of his new system to perplex the sages ;
'Tis poetry—at least by his assertion,
   And may appear so when the dog-star rages—
And he who understands it would be able
To add a story to the Tower of Babel."—*Don Juan.*

heart and fancy; but unfortunately not half so visibly as that of his peculiar system.

" His former poems were intended to recommend that system, and to bespeak favour for it by their individual merit; but this, we suspect, must be recommended by the system—and can only expect to succeed where it has been previously established. It is longer, weaker, and tamer than any of Mr. Wordsworth's other productions ; with less boldness of originality, and less even of that extreme simplicity and lowliness of tone which wavered so prettily, in the lyrical ballads, between silliness and pathos.

" We have imitations of Cowper, and even of Milton here, engrafted on the natural drawl of the Lakers—and all diluted into harmony by that profuse and irrepressible wordiness which deluges all the blank verse of this school of poetry, and lubricates and weakens the whole structure of their style. The case of Mr. Wordsworth, we perceive, is now manifestly hopeless ; and we give him up as altogether incurable, and beyond the power of criticism.

" Whilst making up our mind, though with the most sincere pain and reluctance, to consider him as finally lost to the good cause of poetry, we shall endeavour to be thankful for the occasional gleams of tenderness and beauty which the natural force of his imagination and affections must still shed over all his productions, and to which we shall ever turn with delight, in spite of the affectation and mysticism and prolixity with which they are so abundantly contrasted.

" Long habits of seclusion, and an excessive ambition of originality, can alone account for the disproportion which seems to exist between this author's taste and his genius ; or for the devotion with which he has sacrificed so many precious gifts at the shrine of those paltry idols which he has set up for himself among his lakes and his mountains. If Mr. Wordsworth, instead of confining himself almost entirely to the society of the dalesmen, and cottagers, and little children, who form the subjects of his book, had condescended to mingle a little more with the people that were to read and judge of it, we cannot help thinking that its texture would have been considerably improved.

" The volume before us, if we were to describe it very shortly, we should characterise as a tissue of moral and devotional ravings, in which innumerable changes are rung upon a few very simple and familiar ideas :—but with such an accompaniment of long words, long sentences, and unwieldy phrases—and such a hubbub of strained raptures and fantastical sublimities, that it is often extremely difficult for the most skilful and attentive student to obtain a glimpse of the author's meaning—and altogether impossible for an ordinary reader to conjecture what he is about.

" He has thought fit to make his chief prolocutor, in this poetical dialogue, and chief advocate of Providence and Virtue, *an old Scotch Pedlar*, who rambles about in his former haunts, and gossips among his old customers. The character of the work is decidedly didactic ; and more than nine-tenths of it are occupied with a species of dialogue, or rather a series of long sermons or harangues which pass between the pedlar, the author, an old chaplain, and a worthy vicar who entertains the whole party at dinner on the last day of their excursion.

" Why should Mr. Wordsworth have made his hero a superannuated pedlar ? Did Mr. Wordsworth really imagine that his favourite doctrines were likely to gain anything in point of effect or authority by being put into the mouth of a person accustomed to higgle about tape or brass sleeve-buttons ?

" Is there anything in his learned, abstracted, and logical harangues, that savours of the calling that is ascribed to him ? Are any of their materials such as a pedlar could possibly have dealt in ?

" A man who went about selling flannel and pocket handkerchiefs in this lofty diction, would soon frighten away all his customers ; and would infallibly pass either for a madman, or for some learned and affected gentleman, who, in a frolic, had taken up a character which he was peculiarly ill qualified for supporting.

" But the truth is, that Mr. Wordsworth, with all his perversities, is a person of great powers ; and has frequently a force in his moral declamations, and a tenderness in his pathetic narratives, which neither his prolixity nor his affectation can altogether deprive of their effect.

" Besides those more extended passages of interest or beauty, which we have quoted, there are scattered up and down the book, and in the midst of its most repulsive portions, a very great number of single lines and images, that sparkle like gems in the desert, and startle us with an intimation of the great poetic powers that lie buried in the rubbish that has been heaped around them.

" Nobody can be more disposed to do justice to the great powers of Mr. Wordsworth than we are ; and from the first time that he came before us, down to the present moment, we have uniformly testified in their favour, and assigned indeed our high sense of their value as the chief ground of the bitterness with which we resented their perversion."

The latter half of the article is devoted to extracts and comments intended to display the beauties to be found in the work, and both in their selection, and the remarks made about them, the critic is often generous and scarcely ever unjust.

And now that more than sixty years have passed we know how good was the advice he gave; few poets who have printed so much as Wordsworth are so little known. A few of his shorter poems are to be found in books of extracts, and children's school gifts, yet amongst the ordinary readers of poetry it is as rare to meet with one who has waded through *The Excursion,* as with one who has read *Jerusalem Delivered* from beginning to end.

Shortly before the publication of *The Excursion* Wordsworth adopted profitable Tory opinions, and, like Southey, reaped his reward in place and pension, being appointed in 1813 to the well-paid sinecure office of distributor of stamps for the counties of Westmoreland and Cumberland, value £500 per annum, which post he retained until 1842, when he resigned it in favour of his son, receiving himself a Government pension of £300 a year in its stead. Thus munificently were literary men then rewarded by the Government, if they held cōrrect views about the King, Church and State; what, however, became of less pliant, but equally great writers (Burns, for example), was of little consequence to those in power. The Literary Fund pensions of the present day do not appear to be biassed by party motives to so great an extent as in the days of the Georges, but some strange and unaccountable gifts are even now bestowed; when there are so many poor deserving authors whose services to literature have been valuable and important, it seems unjust to bestow £150 a year on a rich man, whose works are never mentioned but to be ridiculed for their imbecility and their author's vanity. Had it not been for the grants Wordsworth received from the State, it is not improbable that he would have endeavoured to adopt a mode of composition more generally attractive, so that his works might have had a larger and more immediate sale; as it was, he affirmed, when he was about fifty years of age, that the whole of the money he had received for his writings had not then amounted to seven score pounds.

This statement would seem to require some qualification; he had published much poetry, and it is most improbable that he *gave* it to the publishers, although it is undoubtedly true that his books had a slow sale, and are not even now in great demand.

The systematic arrangement of his poems has been referred to; his latest disposal of them was as follows:—

Poems written in Youth; Poems referring to the Period of Childhood; The Borderers; Poems founded on the Affections; Poems on the Naming of Places; Poems of the Fancy (including The Waggoner); Poems of the Imagination, including Peter Bell; Miscellaneous Sonnets; Memorials of Tours in Scotland in 1803 and in 1814; Poems dedicated to National Independence and Liberty; Memorials of a Tour on the Continent in 1820; Memorials of a Tour in Italy in 1837; The River Duddon; The White Doe of Rhylstone; Ecclesiastical Sonnets, in three Parts; Yarrow Revisited, and other Poems; Evening Voluntaries; Poems composed during a Tour in 1833;

Poems of Sentiment and Reflection; Sonnets dedicated to Liberty and Order; Sonnets upon the Punishment of Death; Miscellaneous Poems; Inscriptions; Selections from Chaucer; Poems referring to the Period of Old Age; Epitaphs and Elegiac Pieces; The Prelude, or Growth of a Poet's Mind; and The Excursion.

It would indeed be a difficult task to enumerate the titles of so many distinct poems of any other modern English writer, so generally ignored as most of the above.

His only dramatic attempt, *The Borderers*, was offered to the manager of Covent Garden Theatre and rejected; the plot has neither probability, ingenuity, nor adaptability to stage purposes. *The Quarterly* said, "As to the diction of the piece, a mawkish monotony pervades it, and a beggar woman is the single character who utters a line or two of worthy verse."

Criticising *The White Doe of Rhylstone*, Jeffrey wrote in *The Edinburgh Review :*—

"This, we think, has the merit of being the very worst poem we ever saw imprinted in a quarto volume. It consists of a happy union of all the faults without any of the beauties which belong to its author's school of poetry."

Hartley Coleridge refers to the ill-success of *The White Doe* in a happy little parody :—

> " He lived amidst th' untrodden ways
>   To Rydal Lake* that lead ;
>   A Bard whom there were none to praise,
>   And very few to read.
>
> " Behind a cloud his mystic sense,
>   Deep hidden who can spy ?
>   Bright as the night when not a star
>   Is shining in the sky.

---

* The Poet's residence.

> " Unread his works—his ' Milk-white Doe'
>   With dust is dark and dim ;
> It's still in Longman's shop, and oh !
>   The difference to him." *

On the death of Southey, the Lord Chamberlain offered Wordsworth the post of Laureate, which he declined on the plea that he was too far advanced in life to undertake the duties of the office; thereupon Sir Robert Peel wrote : " Do not be deterred by the fear of any obligations which the appointment may be supposed to imply. I will undertake that you shall have *nothing required* from you." Thus pressed, Wordsworth consented to accept the title and the pension; but being already in receipt of a large Government allowance the latter fact is immaterial.

The warrant of his appointment, preserved in the Lord Chamberlain's Office, is dated April 6, 1843, and specifies that he is " to have, hold, exercise, and enjoy all the *rights, profits,* and privileges appertaining to the office."

The warrant is signed by the then Lord Chamberlain, Earl De La Warr.

---

* The above lines are founded upon Wordsworth's " Lucy ": —

> " She dwelt among the untrodden ways,
>   Beside the springs of Dove,
> A maid whom there were none to praise,
>   And very few to love.

> " A violet by a mossy stone
>   Half hidden from the eye !
> Fair as a star, when only one
>   Is shining in the sky.

> " She lived unknown, and few could know
>   When Lucy ceased to be ;
> But she is in her grave, and, oh,
>   The difference to me ! "

S

He wrote a sonnet on the occasion, which for its vanity and egotism is, perhaps, unparalleled :—

> " Bays ! which in former days have graced the brow
> Of some, who lived and loved, and sang and died ;
> Leaves that were gathered on the pleasant side
> Of old Parnassus from Apollo's bough ;
> With palpitating hand I take ye now,
> Since worthier minstrel there is none beside,
> And with a thrill of song half deified,
> I bind them proudly on my locks of snow.
> There shall they bide, till he who follows next,
> Of whom I cannot even guess the name,
> Shall by Court favour, or some vain pretext
> Of fancied merit, desecrate the same,
> And think perchance, he wears them quite as well
> As the sole bard who sang of Peter Bell ! "

In an essay on *People with One Idea*, Hazlitt gives another instance of Wordsworth's almost insufferable self-conceit. He happened to drop into a small party, where they had in hand Scott's *Rob Roy*, then just published. Some one read the motto on the title-page, which happened to be a quotation from Wordsworth :—

> " For why ?   Because the good old rule
> Sufficeth them ; the simple plan,
> That they should take who have the power,
> And they should keep who can."

This was a hint sufficient, a word to the wise. He instantly went to a bookshelf in the next room, took down the volume of his own poems, read the whole of that in question aloud with manifest complacency, replaced it on the shelf, and walked away, taking no more notice of Walter Scott than if there had been no such person, nor of the new novel than if it had never been written.

How differently Sir Walter Scott would have behaved

in such circumstances, it is easy to imagine; but, as Hazlitt remarks, Wordsworth considered himself not only without an equal but above and beyond comparison.

There was little of the courtier in Wordsworth's character; he kissed hands on his appointment, it is true, and there his connection with royalty appears to have begun and ended,—if we except a sonnet he wrote on the death of George III. in 1820 :—

> " Ward of the law! dread shadow of a king!
>   Whose realm has dwindled to one stately room ;
>   Whose universe was gloom immersed in gloom,
>   Darkness as thick as life o'er life could fling,
>   Save haply, for some feeble glimmering
>   Of faith and hope ; if thou, by nature's doom,
>   Gently has sunk into the quiet tomb,
>   Why should we bend in grief, to sorrow cling,
>   When thankfulness were best!   Fresh flowing tears,
>   Or, where tears flow not, sigh succeeding sigh ;
>   Yield to such after-thought the sole reply
>   Which justly it can claim.   The nation hears
>   In this deep knell—silent for threescore years,
>   An unexampled voice of awful memory."

During the seven years he was Laureate he wrote no poems relating to the office; in fact he had almost desisted from every kind of composition for some time before his death.   He had always disliked writing, and as he grew older it became even more distasteful to him, whilst his sister, who had hitherto acted as his copyist, was now a confirmed invalid, and could render him no assistance.

He therefore spent most of his time rambling about, contemplating the scenery of the beautiful district in which he lived; nature had always been more attractive to him than books :

> " Up! up! my friend, and quit your books ;
>   Or surely you'll grow double :

> Up! up! my friend, and clear your looks,
>   Why all this toil and trouble?

> " Books! 'tis a dull and endless strife;
>   Come hear the woodland linnet,
> How sweet his music; on my life
>   There's more of wisdom in it.

> " And hark! how blithe the throstle sings!
>   He too, is no mean preacher;
> Come forth into the light things,
>   Let Nature be your teacher."

These lines were addressed to Southey, who probably did not consider that the native wood notes wild of the linnet, or the throstle, would materially assist him in his historical or critical labours; and he retaliated by comparing Wordsworth in a library, to a bear in a tulip garden, so little care or thought did he give to the perusal of other men's writings.

It appears that Wordsworth rather prided himself upon this independence of book lore.

" My reading powers," he says, " were never very good, and now they are much diminished, especially by candle light; and as to *buying* books, I can affirm that in new books I have not spent five shillings for the last five years. And as to old books, my dealings in that way, for want of means, have been very trifling. Nevertheless, small and paltry as my collection is, I have not read a fifth part of it."

Wordsworth died on the 23rd April, 1850, and was buried in Grasmere churchyard.

His moral character was, according to Southey, "truly exemplary and admirable;" but in public he betrayed an utter want of attention to the little courtesies which make life agreeable to those brought in contact with a man, whether he be a great poet and philosopher, or a simple gentleman. De Quincey asserts that he was austere and unsocial, too much absorbed in the contemplation of his own greatness, to be willing to carry a lady's parasol, or perform such other trivial duty as may fall to a man in the society of the fair sex. Vanity and egotism he displayed in his works, and his conversation was a great deal about himself; he was little interested in the works of other men, and knew little of what passed in the general literary world. He was a man of extremes in his poetry as in his politics; he started the notion that there existed latent capabilities and attractions in insignificant objects, and to prove his theory he selected trifling subjects on which to weave a poem; but, as the *Quarterly Review* said, "His doctrine that the business of a poet is to educe an interest where none is apparent, engaged him in efforts to squeeze moisture out of dust."

Hazlitt's notes on Wordsworth's style are worth repeating, as they explain some of the causes of the slow progress his poetry made in public estimation :—

" Wordsworth is the poet of mere sentiment, and of many of the Lyrical Ballads it is not possible to speak in terms of too high praise. He has produced a deeper impression, and on a smaller circle than any other of his contemporaries. His powers have been mistaken by the age, nor does he exactly understand them himself. He cannot form a whole. He has not the constructive faculty. He is totally deficient in all the machinery of poetry. His *Excursion*, taken as a whole, notwithstanding the noble materials thrown away in it, is a proof of this. The line labours, the sentiment moves slow ; but the poem stands stock-still. The reader makes no way from the first line to the last. Mr. Wordsworth is at the head of that which has been denominated the *Lake school* of poetry. This school had its origin in the French Revolution, or rather in those sentiments and opinions which produced that revolution. Our poetical literature had, towards the close of the last century, degenerated into the most trite, insipid, and mechanical of all things, in the hands of the followers of Pope, and the old French school of poetry. It wanted something to stir it up, and it found that something in the principles and events of the French Revolution."

He then examines the peculiarities of Wordsworth's genius, and truly remarks that the reason that so few people take an interest in his writings is because he takes an interest in nothing that others do.

It is certain that his works have much increased in popularity since his death, and this in a great measure owing to the exertions of the very critics who were supposed to have combined together to drive the public away from their perusal. These gentlemen, on the contrary, nave erected sign-posts and mile-stones on the road, by the aid of which the general reader can go direct to delight in the beauties of Wordsworth's sonnets and ballads; or may easily discover the passages of simple pathos and tender feeling, or alight upon some of the splendours of description scattered up and down in his longer compositions, without being compelled to undertake the wearying task of toiling through *The Prelude*, *The Excursion*, or *The White Doe of Rhylstone.*

ALFRED TENNYSON.

1850.

" Who would not be
    The Laureate bold,
  With his butt of sherry
    To keep him merry,
And nothing to do but to pocket his gold ?
'Tis I would be the Laureate bold !
When the days are hot, and the sun is strong,
I'd lounge in the gateway all the day long,
With her majesty's footmen in crimson and gold.
I'd care not a pin for the waiting-lord ;
But I'd lie on my back on the smooth green sward,
With a straw in my mouth, and an open vest,
And the cool wind blowing upon my breast,
And I'd vacantly stare at the clear blue sky,
And watch the clouds as listless as I,
        Lazily, lazily !
And I'd pick the moss and daisies white,
And chew their stalks with a nibbling bite ;
And I'd let my fancies roam abroad
In search of a hint for a birth-day ode,
        Crazily, crazily !"

Bon Gaultier Ballads.

For more than a quarter of a century Mr. Tennyson has
held the title of Poet Laureate, and for the greater part of
that time he has justly been considered the real, as well as

the titular poet-king of the latter half of the nineteenth century.

His poems increase in popularity day by day, and many passages of his magnificent *word-painting* (for Tennyson is nothing, if not artistic) are treasured up as firmly in our minds, as are the sweetly thoughtful words of Shakespeare, or the sprightly elegance of *L'Allegro :*—

> " Married to immortal verse
> Such as the meeting soul may pierce
> In notes, with many a winding bout
> Of linked sweetness long drawn out."

It is, therefore, somewhat remarkable that so little is generally known of the poet himself, when other writers of far less eminence are constantly being brought before the public in biographies, sensational articles, photographs, and all the other little stratagems commonly employed to attain notoriety, if not fame.

Yet this is precisely the celebrity which Mr. Tennyson wisely avoids; many years ago, after reading *The Life and Letters of a Deceased Poet,* he wrote some vigorous lines against the needless publicity to which the life of a man of letters was subjected :—

> " For now the Poet cannot die
>   Nor leave his music as of old,
>   But round him ere he scarce be cold
> Begins the scandal and the cry :
>
> " ' Proclaim the faults he would not show :
>   Break lock and seal : betray the trust :
>   Keep nothing sacred : 'tis but just
> The many-headed beast should know.'
>
> " Ah shameless ! for he did but sing
>   A song that pleased us from its worth ;
>   No public life was his on earth,
> No blazon'd statesman he, nor king.

" He gave the people of his best :
　His worst he kept, his best he gave.
　My Shakespeare's curse on clown and knave
　Who will not let his ashes rest.''

The little that is known of Tennyson's private life and
public career is, like the tone of his writings, irreproach-
able.　In his works he has generally avoided controversial
topics, scarce one in a hundred of his readers can judge
whether Mr. Tennyson is a Liberal or a Conservative, or
can form any idea whether he prefers the stately service
of the High Church to the severely simple worship of a
Wesleyan chapel.　In a few of his earlier poems he expresses his contempt for the Papacy, and when his pen
touches upon patriotism it generally expresses some dis-
trust, if not actual dislike, of the French nation :—

" For the French the Pope may shrive 'em,
　For the devil a whit we heed 'em :
　As for the French, God speed 'em
　　Unto their hearts' desire,
　And the merry devil drive 'em
　　Through the water and the fire."

Yet these are the veriest trifles, and aged ones too,
perhaps time and acquaintance have increased his love for
our sprightly, kindly, gallant neighbours.　He has wisely
kept his private views and feelings in the background, as
studiously as Wordsworth, on the contrary, displayed his
thoughts and opinions in everything he wrote.　Not only
is this the case in his writings, but from the secluded
life he leads, it would appear that he prefers the society
of the muses in retired parts of Surrey or the Isle of
Wight, to the busy hum of men in the lion-hunting
metropolis.

Thus only could we expect to reap the fruits in his

poems, of leisurely composition and undisturbed meditation; for they are universally admitted to be most exquisitely finished productions; and had Mr. Tennyson allowed himself to be interviewed by every enterprising American journalist, or English critic, the public would probably have lost much beautiful verse in exchange for the somewhat doubtful advantage of having fuller biographical details of the author.

As a further result he has almost entirely escaped those petty enmities, scandals, and party criticisms which have embittered the lives of many of our great poets who have not had sufficient courage to shun London society and public life.

The Poet Laureate was born in 1809, at the Rectory of the village of Somerby, near Horncastle, in Lincolnshire, and received his early education at the Louth Grammar School, whence he proceeded to Trinity College, Cambridge.

His mind was fixed upon poetry at a very early period, and when only twenty years of age he wrote the poem which gained the Chancellor's medal, on the seemingly unsuggestive topic, *Timbuctoo*. Thus he describes his vision of the city :—

> " Then first within the South methought I saw
> A wilderness of spires, and crystal pile
> Of rampart upon rampart, dome on dome,
> Illimitable range of battlement
> On battlement, and the Imperial height
> Of canopy o'ercanopied.
>   Behind
> In diamond light up spring the dazzling peaks
> Of Pyramids, as far surpassing earth's
> As heaven than earth is fairer.   Each aloft
> Upon his narrowed eminence bore globes

Of wheeling suns, or stars, or semblances
Of either, showering circular abyss
Of radiance. But the glory of the place
Stood out a pillared front of burnished gold,
Interminably high, if gold it were
Or metal more ethereal, and beneath
Two doors of blinding brilliance, where no gaze
Might rest, stood open, and the eye could scan,
Through length of porch, and valve and boundless hall."

This poem has been left out of all modern editions of his works, although it contains several passages of glowing description.*

---

* Thackeray was at Cambridge at the same time as Tennyson, and in 1829 he commenced the publication of a small paper entitled " *The Snob,* a Literary and Scientific Journal," *not* conducted by members of the university. This contained the following droll poem on Timbuctoo—

To the Editor of " THE SNOB."

SIR,—Though your name be *Snob,* I trust you will not refuse this tiny " poem of a gownsman," which was unluckily not finished on the day appointed for delivery of the several copies of verses on Timbuctoo. I thought, Sir, it would be a pity that such a poem should be lost to the world ; and conceiving *The Snob* to be the most widely circulated periodical in Europe, I have taken the liberty of submitting it for insertion or approbation.—I am, Sir, yours, &c., &c., &c.

TIMBUCTOO.—PART I.

The Situation.
In Africa (a quarter of the world),
Men's skins are black, their hair is crisp and curl'd,
And somewhere there, unknown to public view,
A mighty city lies, called Timbuctoo.

The Natural History.
There stalks the tiger,—there the lion roars,   5
Who sometimes eats the luckless blackamoors ;
All that he leaves of them the monster throws
To jackals, vultures, dogs, cats, kites, and crows ;
His hunger thus the forest monster gluts,
And then lies down 'neath trees called cocoa-nuts.   10

The lion hunt.
Quick issue out, with musket, torch, and brand,
The sturdy blackamoors, a dusky band !
The beast is found—pop goes the musketoons—
The lion falls covered with horrid wounds.

Whilst at Cambridge, he formed a very close friendship with Arthur Henry Hallam, son of the historian, whose early death in 1833 called forth from Tennyson the poem *In Memoriam.*

But the first published work from his pen was a small volume, entitled *Poems, chiefly Lyrical,* by Alfred Tennyson, published in 1830 by Effingham Wilson.

This scarce little volume contained a few pieces written by his brother, and a good many poems which have been

---

Their lives at home.
> At home their lives in pleasure always flow,   15
> But many have a different lot to know!

Abroad.
> They're often caught, and sold as slaves, alas!"

Reflections on the foregoing.
> Thus men from highest joys to sorrows pass,
> Yet though thy monarch and thy nobles boil
> Rack and molasses in Jamaica's isle;   20
> Desolate Afric! thou art lovely yet;
> One heart yet beats which ne'er thee shall forget.
> What though thy maidens are a blackish brown,
> Does virtue dwell in whiter breasts alone?
> Oh no, oh no, oh no, oh no, oh no!   25
> It shall not, must not, cannot, e'er he so.
> The day shall come when Albion's self shall feel
> Stern Afric's wrath, and writhe 'neath Afric's steel.
> I see her tribes the hill of glory mount,
> And sell their sugars on their own account;   30
> While round her throne the prostrate nations come,
> Sue for her rice, and barter for her rum!   32

Notes.—Lines 1 and 2.—See *Guthrie's Geography.* The site of Timbuctoo is doubtful; the author has neatly expressed this in the poem, at the same time giving us some slight hints relative to its situation.

Line 5.—So Horace: *leonum arida nutrix.*

Line 13.—"Pop goes the musquetoons." A learned friend suggested "Bang" as a stronger expression, but as African gunpowder is notoriously bad, the author thought "Pop" the better word.

Lines 15—18.—A concise, but affecting description is here given of the domestic habits of the people. The infamous manner in which they are entrapped and sold as slaves is described, and the whole ends with an appropriate moral sentiment. The enthusiasm the author feels is beautifully expressed in lines 25 and 26.

left out of all the later editions, perhaps wisely for
Tennyson's reputation, yet every lover of books craves for
the complete works of a favourite author.

Small as was the collection, it contained such specimens
of poetical power as to convince the critics that a new
star had arisen, and the reviews were generally of a most
encouraging description. A few writers, indeed, became
almost too suddenly enthusiastic about the genius of
Alfred Tennyson, and the young poet ran considerable
risk of suffering more from injudicious praise, at the
hands of inconsiderate friends, than from the hostility of
adverse criticism.

Professor Wilson (Christopher North) saw the danger,
and came to the rescue, printing an article in *Blackwood's
Edinburgh Magazine,* May, 1832, in which playful
badinage and considerable satire, are blended with much
good advice and hearty, kindly commendation, all the more
valuable as being sensible and discriminating.

Nearly fifty years have elapsed since the article was
penned, the learned Christopher North has long been
dead, the poet has survived the critic, and his reputation
has survived the criticism. The great Poet Laureate,
honoured and pre-eminent, is now nearly seventy years of
age, and curious ideas crowd into the mind when reading
the somewhat mocking strain in which Wilson commences
his article on the "Young Poet," and proceeds, in a
fatherly tone, to "set the young gentleman down:"—

"Almost all men, women, and children are poets, except those who
write verses. We shall not define poetry, because the Cockneys
have done so ; and were they to go to church we should be strongly
tempted to break the Sabbath. But this much we may say of it,
that everything is poetry which is not mere sensation. We are
poets at all times when our minds are makers.

"All men, women, and children, then, are manifestly poets, except those who write verses. But why that exception? Because they alone make no use of their minds. *Versifiers*,—and we speak but of them—are the sole living creatures that are not also creators. They, poor creatures, are a peculiar people, impotent of good works.

"We had no intention of being so, but we suspect that we have been somewhat severe; so let us relieve all lads of feeling and fancy, by assuring them that hitherto we have been sneering but at sumphs and God-help-you-silly-ones, and that our hearts overflow with kindness towards all the children of genius.

"England ought to be producing some young poets now, that there may be no dull interregnum when the old shall have passed away; and pass away many of them soon must—their bodies, which are shadows, but their spirits which are lights—they will burn for ever—till time be no more.

"Let all this pass for an introduction to our article—and let us abruptly join company with the gentleman whose name stands at the head of it, Mr. Alfred Tennyson, of whom the world, we presume, yet knows but little or nothing, whom his friends call a Phœnix, but who, we hope, will not be dissatisfied with us should we designate him merely a Swan.

"One of the saddest misfortunes that can befall a young poet is to be the Pet of a Coterie; and the very saddest of all, if in Cockney-dom. Such has been the unlucky lot of Alfred Tennyson. He has been elevated to the throne of Little Britain, and sonnets were showered over his coronation from the most remote regions of his empire, even from Hampstead Hill.

"The besetting sin of all periodical criticism, and nowadays there is no other, is boundless extravagance of praise; but none splash it on like the trowel-men who have been bedaubing Mr. Tennyson. The worst of it is, that they make the Bespattered not only feel, but look ridiculous; he seems as absurd as an Image in a tea-garden; and, bedizened with faded and fantastic garlands, the public cough on being told he is a Poet, for he has much more the appearance of a Post.

"The *Englishman's Magazine* ought not to have died; for it threatened to be a very pleasant periodical. An essay 'On the Genius of Alfred Tennyson' sent it to the grave. The superhuman —nay, supernatural—pomposity of that one paper incapacitated the whole work for living one day longer in this unceremonious world.

The solemnity with which the critic approached the object of his adoration, and the sanctity with which he laid his offerings on the shrine, were too much for our irreligious age. The essay 'On the Genius of Alfred Tennyson' awoke a general guffaw, and it expired in convulsions. Yet the essay was exceedingly well written—as well as if it had been 'On the Genius of Sir Isaac Newton.' Therein lay the mistake. Sir Isaac had discovered the law of gravitation ; Alfred had but written some pretty verses, and mankind were not prepared to set him among the stars. But that he has genius is proved by his being at this moment alive ; for had he not, he must have breathed his last under that critique.

"But the Old Man must see justice done to this ingenious lad, and save him from his worst enemies, his friends.

" Were we not afraid that our style might be thought to wax too figurative, we should say that Alfred is a promising plant ; and that the day may come when, beneath sun and shower, his genius may grow up and expand into a stately tree, embowering a solemn shade within its wide circumference, while the daylight lies gorgeously on its crest ; seen from afar in glory—itself a grove.

" But that day will never come, if he hearken not to our advice, and, as far as his own nature will permit, regulate by it the movements of his genius.

" At present he has small power over the common feelings and thoughts of men. His feebleness is distressing at all times when he makes an appeal to their ordinary sympathies. And the reason is, that he fears to look such sympathies boldly in the face,—and will be—metaphysical."

The Professor then proceeds to examine into the merits of the following poems,* all of which he considers so decidedly beneath the level of the young author's powers, that he advises him to boldly cut them out once and for ever :—

" A National Song."

" English War Song."   (Miserable indeed.)

---

* " The critic notes are Wilson's every line,
    For God's sake, reader ! take them not for mine."

" We are Free." (That is drivel.)

" Lost Hope." (More dismal drivel.)

"Love, Pride, and Forgetfulness." (Even more dismal drivel.)

Sonnet—"Shall the Hag Evil Die ?"

" The Poet's Mind." (Most of this is silly—some of it prettyish—scarcely one line of it all true poetry.)

" The ' How ' and the ' Why.' " (This is from beginning to end a clumsy and unwieldy failure, and shows no fancy in the region of metaphysics ; though it is plain from many a page that he has deluded himself into the belief that there lies his especial province.)

"The Merman." ('Tis, after all, but a sorry affair. Should he persist in writing thus to the end of the chapter, Alfred Tennyson may have a niche in the‛ *Westminster Review,* but never in Westminster Abbey.)

"The Mermaid."

"Sea Fairies."

" The Dying Swan."

"The Grasshopper." (Conceived and executed in the spirit of the celebrated imitation by Doctor Johnson :—

> Dilly—dilly duckling !
> Come and be killed !)

" The Owl." (Alfred is greatest as an owl. All he wants is to be shot, stuffed, and stuck in a glass-case, to be made immortal in a museum.)

" The Kraken." (A sonnet requiring some interpretation.)

The Professor then observes :—

" Thin as is this little volume, 'twould yet be easy to extract from it much more unmeaningness ; but having shown by gentle chastisement that we love Alfred Tennyson, let us now show by judicious eulogy that we admire him, and, by well-chosen specimens of his fine faculties, that he is worthy of our admiration.''

" Perhaps in the first part of our article, we may have exaggerated Mr. Tennyson's not unfrequent silliness, but we feel assured that in the second part we have not exaggerated his strength—that we have done no more than justice to his fine faculties—and that the millions who delight in Maga will, with one voice, confirm our judgment—that Alfred Tennyson is a poet.''

He proceeds to quote lengthy extracts from what he considers the finest poems in the collection, and time has proved the wisdom of his judgment, for assuredly the following are amongst the most generally admired and frequently read of Tennyson's shorter poems :—" The Ode to Memory," " The Deserted House," " A Dirge," " Isabel," " Mariana," " Adeline," " The Sleeping Beauty," " The Ballad of Oriana," and " Recollections of the Arabian Nights."

The arrogant tone of the article deprives its criticism of much of its intended effect, and when the Professor deigns to speak of the friendly criticisms of Tennyson which had appeared in contemporary magazines, it is with unmeasured scorn and contempt, as where he says of the *Westminster Review :*—

" This is a perfect specimen of the super-hyperbolical ultra extravagance of outrageous cockney eulogistic foolishness, with which not even a quantity of common sense less than nothing has been suffered, for an indivisible moment of time, to mingle ; the purest mere matter of moonshine ever mouthed by an idiot-lunatic, slavering in the palsied dotage of the extremest superannuation ever inflicted on a being, long ago, perhaps, in some slight respects and low degrees human, but now sensibly and audibly reduced below the level of the Pongos."

It was scarcely to be expected that such an outspoken critique could be palatable to the poet, who had hitherto been fed on honeyed phrases only, yet, beyond publishing a few satirical lines, Tennyson seems not to have troubled himself further about Professor Wilson.

> " To CHRISTOPHER NORTH.
>
> " You did late review my lays,
>   Crusty Christopher ;
>   You did mingle blame and praise,
>   Rusty Christopher.
> " When I learnt from whom it came
>   I forgave you all the blame,
>   Musty Christopher ;
>   I could *not* forgive the praise,
>   Fusty Christopher ! "

On reference to the list of poems adversely criticised, it will be observed that about half of them have been omitted from all the later editions; trivial in subject and somewhat puerile in treatment, they merit no better fate. "The Mystic," one of these suppressed poems, which had originally appeared in the 1830 edition, was printed as a new poem by *The Atlantic Almanac* in 1870.

One effeminate lay to a "Darling Room," commencing—

> " O darling room, my heart's delight,
>   Dear room, the apple of my sight,
>   With thy two couches soft and white,
>   There is no room so exquisite,
>   No little room so warm and bright
>   Wherein to read, wherein to write,"

afforded Sir Edward Lytton Bulwer an opportunity for bringing Tennyson's name into "The New Timon," and dealing some heavy satirical strokes at "Miss Alfred," a sobriquet which long tenaciously clung to the Laureate, until indeed the reading public had become more intimately acquainted with the thoughtful depth and intensely poetical imagery to be found in most of his longer poems. Lytton's lines in "The New Timon" ran as follows :—

> " Not mine, not mine (O muse forbid) the boon
> Of borrow'd notes, the mock-bird's modish tune,
> The jingling medley of purloined conceits,
> Out-babying Wordsworth and out-glittering Keats ;
> Where all the airs of patchwork pastoral chime
> To drown the ears in Tennysonian rhyme !

> " Let school-miss Alfred vent her chaste delight
> On ' darling little rooms so warm and light ; '
> Chant ' I'm a-weary ' in infectious strain,
> And catch ' the blue fly singing i' the pane ; '
> Though praised by critics and adored by Blues,
> Though Peel with pudding plump the puling muse,
> Though Theban taste the Saxon purse controls,
> And pensions Tennyson while starves a Knowles."

Tennyson replied to this attack in a somewhat remarkable set of verses, signed ALCIBIADES, which appeared in *Punch*, in February, 1846.

This is the only known occasion when anything from the Laureate's pen appeared in *Punch ;* but it happened that Thackeray, and the wits of the *Punch* staff generally were then making attacks, more or less ungenerous and spiteful, on the writings and career of Bulwer Lytton, and Tennyson's contribution was therefore thankfully received.

The little personal fopperies of Lytton were here unsparingly ridiculed, as was indeed an easy task, but his fame as a poet and novelist was not likely to suffer much from verses such as these :—

THE NEW TIMON, AND THE POETS.

" We know him, out of *Shakespeare's* art,
　　And those fine curses which he spoke ;
The old Timon, with his noble heart,
　　That, strongly loathing, greatly broke.

" So diẹd the Old ; here comes the New.
　　Regard him : a familiar face :
I *thought* we knew him : What, it's you,
　　The padded man—that wears the stays—

" Who kill'd the girls, and thrill'd the boys,
　　With dandy pathos when you wrote,
A Lion, you, that made a noise,
　　And shook a mane *en papillotes.*

" And once you tried the Muses too ;
　　You fail'd, Sir ; therefore now you turn,
You fall on those who are to you
　　As Captain is to Subaltern.

" But men of long-enduring hopes,
　　And careless what this hour may bring,
Can pardon little would-be POPES
　　And BRUMMELS, when they try to sting.

　　　*　　*　　*　　*　　*

" What profits now to understand
　　The merits of a spotless shirt—
A dapper boot—a little hand—
　　If half the little soul is dirt ?

" *You* talk of tinsel ! why we see
　　The old mask of rouge upon your cheeks.
You prate of Nature ! you are he
　　That spilt his life about the cliques.

" A TIMON you ! Nay, nay for shame :
　　It looks too arrogant a jest—
The fierce old man—to take *his* name,
　　You bandbox. Off, and let him rest."

　　　　　　　　　　　　ALCIBIADES.

Several other collections of short poems, less ambitious in subject, although exquisite in finish and purity, appeared from time to time, and the public anxiously looked for new works of sustained interest and breadth of treatment from which a better estimate of his powers of song might be formed.

They came in due course; the publication of *The Princess* and *In Memoriam*, showed that the poet had loftier aims and aspirations than to be known only as the composer of drawing-room prettinesses, and highly wrought *vers de société*.

When, after many years of labour, Mr. Tennyson had worked out the scheme of *The Idyls of the King*, he specified a consecutive arrangement of the parts, closing with "The Passing of Arthur," the first written, yet, in some respects, the finest of the *Idyls*. After this there is an "Address to the Queen," which contrasts unfavourably with "The Dedication to the Memory of Prince Albert;" in it the poet for once ventures into the political arena, and would seem to hint that as we are wealthy, so also we should be warlike; and that it would be wiser to spend our riches in settling the affairs of other nations, than to enjoy peace and plenty at home.

Such was indeed the policy of our fathers at the beginning of the century, but the blood and treasure we so lavishly spent in assisting Prussia and Spain against the French, and the French legitimists against Napoleon, earned for us no gratitude from those for whom such gigantic sacrifices were made.

This peculiarity of national egotism, or patriotism run to seed, is to be found in a more exaggerated form in "The Revenge, a Ballad of the Fleet," in which his aim appears to have been to exalt England at the expense of Spain and the Spaniards,—

"These Inquisition dogs, and the devildoms of Spain."

To glorify useless, because hopeless, bravery, and to deify a sea captain who cruelly exposed his crew to certain death in a forlorn enterprise, may thrill the excitable nerves of a few hysterical persons with tiger-like appetites for blood and slaughter, but can scarcely appeal to the calm judgment of sober, earnest Christians, whose patriotism is not "une invention de l'homme, qui lui permet de haïr ses semblables, et de s'en faire une vertu."

Indeed, the Laureate evidently feels ill at ease on such ground, and soon returns to the realms of poetry, thus explaining the motive of his epic :—

> "But thou, my Queen !
> Nor for itself, but through thy living love
> For one to whom I made it o'er his grave
> Sacred, accept this old imperfect tale,
> New-old, and shadowing Sense at war with Soul
> Rather than that Grey King, whose name, a Ghost,
> Streams like a cloud, man-shaped, from mountain peak
> And cleaves to cairn and cromlech still ; or him
> Of Geoffrey's book, or him of Malleor's, one
> Touch'd by the adulterous finger of a time
> That hover'd between war and wantonness,
> And crownings and dethronements."

It is probable that Mr. Tennyson attaches greater importance to the *Idyls* than to all his other writings; possibly posterity will form a different estimate of their comparative worth. In the first place it is to be regretted that the labour of a lifetime should have been bestowed upon a subject having in it but few elements of general interest.

La Mort d'Arthure, of Sir Thomas Malory, is a charming and consecutive collection of old romances, forming
a homogeneous prose tragedy; but whilst Tennyson's
exquisite language, and perfect finish of detail, have
added many beauties to the narrative, he has marred the
unity of the old romance, by dividing it up into distinct
portions, each one complete in itself, having but the
slightest connection with the others, and wanting the important dramatic elements of sustained interest, and of a
continuous progression towards the final catastrophe.

How, too, is it possible to reconcile the purely ideal
beings, whom the poet describes, with the probable inhabi-
tants of France or England fourteen centuries ago?

The sunny land of fruits and flowers, the lovely, delicate
women, daintily clad in satins and velvets, and decorated
with sparkling jewels; the gallant knights, who dwell in
magnificent castles, or ride about in search of warlike
adventures, arrayed in curious and sumptuous armour,
paying the utmost deference to the fair sex, and discussing
all the metaphysical refinements of a code of honour and
chivalry, such as could only exist at a period of advanced
civilisation.

In the original romances the code of morality was
certainly not a very high one, being fashioned on the
morality of feudalism; Mr. Tennyson shows us Arthur
and his knights aspiring to a far nobler standard; the
result is indeed beautiful, but beautiful only as an ideal
and poetic conception.

Mr. Thomas Wright says, in the preface to his edition
of Sir Thomas Malory's *Mort d'Arthure* :—

"These romances differ from the *Chansons de Geste*, and the
generality of the other mediæval romances in this, that while the
former are plain and practical pictures of life in the feudal ages, these

embody a sort of mythic code, if I may use such a phrase, of the more elevated principles and spirit of chivalry, which the high-minded knight was supposed to labour to imitate."

The poet's imagination has exaggerated all the popular fallacies about the doings of a tribe of semi-barbarians who knew little, and cared less, for Christianity, who spent their time in hunting, drinking, and fighting, like the rough hardy savages they were.

Accepting the poem simply as a work of art, it is one of the most lovely productions of which our language seems capable; the grace, the elegance, the fitness of every word to its place, display the fastidious taste, and the careful revision, which, as is well known, the Laureate bestows upon all his poems, and nowhere are his perfection of ear, and choice of language, so apparent as in the *Idyls*.

Most of our early laureates were connected with the stage, and owed much of their fame to their dramatic writings; scarcely one can be named who has not attempted dramatic composition. Even Wordsworth wrote a tragedy, although, as might have been expected, the result was a miserable failure, displaying an utter ignorance of the requirements of the stage, combined with a dreary poverty of language, and uninteresting plot. Southey wrote several tragedies, or dramatic poems, so also did Whitehead and Rowe. Then Cibber, Tate, Shadwell, Dryden, Davenant, and Ben Jonson were almost entirely dependent upon the stage, as authors, actors, or managers.

It was, therefore, quite in accordance with the traditions of the office, that Mr. Tennyson should produce a tragedy, and the appearance of *Queen Mary* naturally created considerable interest and curiosity. That the Laureate possesses dramatic talent, no one acquainted with his poems can deny; but whether he had the faculty so to mould his thoughts and language round the plot as to form what is called a good *acting* piece, capable of interesting a mixed audience in these degenerate days of *opera-bouffe* and *burlesque*, was a question upon which few persons would have dared to hazard an opinion.

Mary Tudor, considered as a poem, contains some passages as beautiful as any Tennyson ever penned; and a few which might well be omitted, as, for instance, the ridiculous song of the Milkmaid, which certain critics, ready to admire anything written by Tennyson, profess to consider "pretty and bucolic." As the great aim has been to place the career of *Mary Tudor* before the public, with all the surroundings of historical personages and events, something like an approach to historical accuracy should at least have been preserved. That Mary's heart was cruel, her temper harsh, and her person unattractive, Mr. Tennyson is, of course, justified in asserting; but he makes little allowance for the virtues she possessed, her courage and her constancy, her devoted adherence to the faith in which she had been educated; once, indeed, he makes her cry, in her troubles,

> " What have I done ?   What sin
> Beyond all grace, all pardon ?
>   Mother of God,
> Thou knowest never woman meant so well,
> And fared so ill in this disastrous world.''

But everywhere the unhappy queen is unfavourably contrasted with her half-sister, the Princess Elizabeth, and one is led to forget that she, too, was violent and harsh, whilst her person was scarcely better favoured than that of her elder sister ; cruel and vindictive also was she, besides possessing other vices, which history, unfair as it always has been to the losing side, does not ascribe to Queen Mary. Her vanity does indeed shine forth occasionally in Mr. Tennyson's lines, but it is not the vanity of history, nor is her speech characteristic; gentle and meek, tearful and loving, the portrait might well have been drawn for Lady Jane Grey. But as English people have for ages indulged in the habit of speaking of *Good Queen Bess*, whilst describing Mary Tudor by a word more expressive than polite, it might have been Quixotic in a poet to attempt to set them right. It is surely, however, an unnecessary sacrifice *ad captandum vulgus* to portray an Elizabeth so provokingly and complacently good, when her greatest admirers praise her chiefly for her attachment to the Protestant religion, an attachment which was doubtless conscientious on her part, although Elizabeth well knew that had she acknowledged the Romish Church she would have admitted her own illegitimacy.

In one respect the tragedy does justice to Mary, in describing her passionate love for Philip, her anxiety to please him, even to the extent of sacrificing the lives of her people, at his request; her joy when she fondly imagines that she is about to become a mother; and her tender pleadings to dissuade Philip from leaving her, to return to Spain; these are, indeed, the finest passages in the tragedy, and, as might have been expected, are more eminently poetical than dramatic, more suitable for the study than the stage. In the last scene, where the heart-broken Mary listens to the consolation of her attendants, there is a remarkable instance of this peculiarity. Mary, bewailing her melancholy fate, asks Lady Clarence—

" What is this strange thing happiness ?
Sit down here :
Tell me thine happiest hour.

LADY CLARENCE.
                    I will, if that
May make your Grace forget yourself a little.
There runs a shallow brook across our field
For twenty miles where the black crow flies five,
And doth so bound and babble all the way
As if itself were happy. It was May time,
And I was walking with the man I loved.
I loved him, but I thought I was not loved.
And both were silent, letting the wild brook
Speak for us—till he stoop'd and gathered one
From out a bed of thick forget-me-nots.
Look'd hard and sweet at me, and gave it me.
I took it, tho' I did not know I took it,
And put it in my bosom, and all at once
I felt his arms about me, and his lips——"

Close upon this idyllic passage follows a storm of
sorrow and remorse from the dying queen, who, in a
sudden fit of passion, has cut down from the wall the
portrait of her faithless husband, Philip.

Mary, with all the faults of her cruel race, and all the
sorrows of a miserable life, is no fit subject for the modern
stage, and, even with the greatest living actor to play
Philip, the tragedy could not long keep possession of the
boards.

As a poem it has many beauties, but it has one great
and fatal defect, the character of Mary. Tennyson should
have—

           " Been to her virtues very kind
             And to her faults a little blind,"

the result might have been a better acting tragedy,
certainly one less pitiably sad and gloomy than *Queen
Mary*.

Of his drama, *Harold*, less need be said; it has not yet
been performed, nor was it, perhaps, intended as an acting

piece. The dedication to the Right Hon. Lord Lytton (son of the author of *The New Timon*), Governor-General of India, runs as follows :—

" MY DEAR LORD LYTTON,

" After old-world records,—such as *The Bayeux Tapestry* and *The Roman de Rou,*—Edward Freeman's *History of the Norman Conquest* and your father's historical romance treating of the same times, have been mainly helpful to me in writing this drama. Your father dedicated his *Harold* to my father's brother, allow me to dedicate my *Harold* to yourself,

" A. TENNYSON."

A sonnet is prefixed to the drama, and, like a tuning fork, it strikes a key-note, "most musical—most melancholy," to what follows; it is entitled —

SHOW DAY AT BATTLE ABBEY, 1876.

" A garden here—May breath and bloom of spring—
The cuckoo yonder from an English elm
Crying, 'With my false egg I overwhelm
The native nest ;' and fancy hears the ring
Of harness, and that deathful arrow sing,
And Saxon battle-axe clang on Norman helm.
Here rose the dragon-banner of our realm ;
Here fought, here fell, our Norman-slander'd king.
O Garden blossoming out of English blood !
O strange hate-healer Time ! We stroll and stare
Where might made right eight hundred years ago ;
Might, right? ay good, so all things make for good—
But he and he, if soul be soul, are where
Each stands full face with all he did below."

Sentiment and pathos Mr. Tennyson indeed possesses; but there are few traces of humour in his writings, and scarcely an attempt at wit. Some of his more homely domestic subjects would well have admitted a dash of humour, without any detraction from their simple pathos; wit, humour, and pathos alternate in the finest poems written by Byron and Burns. Although, however, Mr. Tennyson makes no pretensions to the title of a wit or humourist, there is yet a dash of grim merriment and sarcasm in *The Vision of Sin* nearly approaching that ludicrous association of incongruous ideas which constitutes wit.

" I saw within my head
" A grey and gap-toothed man as lean as death,
Who slowly rode across a wither'd heath,
And lighted at a ruin'd inn, and said :—

" Slip-shod waiter, lank and sour,
 At the ' Dragon ' on the heath !
Let us have a quiet hour,
 Let us hob-and-nob with Death.

" I am old, but let me drink ;
 Bring me spices, bring me wine ;
I remember, when I think,
 That my youth was half divine.

  *   *   *   *   *

" We are men of ruin'd blood ;
 Therefore comes it we are wise.
Fish are we that love the mud,
 Rising to no fancy flies.

" Name and fame ! to fly sublime
 Through the courts, the camps, the schools,
Is to be the ball of Time,
 Bandied in the hands of fools.

" Friendship ! to be two in one—
 Let the canting liar pack !
Well I know, when I am gone,
 How she mouths behind my back.

" Virtue ! to be good and just—
    Every heart, when sifted well,
Is a clot of warmer dust,
    Mix'd with cunning sparks of hell.

" Fill the cup, and fill the can ;
    Have a rouse before the morn ;
Every moment dies a man,
    Every moment one is born."

*   *   *   *   *

" You are bones, and what of that ?
    Every face, however full,
Padded round with flesh and fat,
    Is but modell'd on a skull.

" Death is King, and *Vivat Rex !*
    Tread a measure on the stones,
Madam—if I know your sex,
    From the fashion of your bones.

" No, I cannot praise the fire
    In your eye, nor yet your lip ;
All the more do I admire
    Joints of cunning workmanship.

" Lo ! God's likeness—the ground plan
    Neither modell'd, glazed, or framed,
Buss me, thou rough sketch of man,
    Far too naked to be shamed ! ''

Notwithstanding the care the Laureate usually bestows
upon his poems, he has occasionally published verses
remarkable for their inferiority, as compared even with
the average of magazine poetry, by no means a very high
standard.

Perhaps he never wrote weaker lines than those commencing—

" I stood on a tower in the wet,
    And New Year and Old Year met,

And winds were roaring and blowing ;
And I said, ' O years that meet in tears,
Have ye aught that is worth the knowing ?
 Science enough and exploring,
 Wanderers coming and going,
 Matter enough for deploring,
But aught that is worth the knowing ? "

printed in *Good Words*, March, 1868, although entitled
" 1865—1866." The following parody, which appeared
soon afterwards, is scarcely inferior to Mr. Tennyson's
poem :—

1867—1868.

" I sat in a 'bus in the wet,
 Good Words I had happened to get,
With Tennyson's last bestowing :
And I said ' O bard, who work so hard,
Have ye aught that is worth the knowing ?
 Verse enough and so boring,
 Twaddle quite overflowing,
 Rubbish enough for deploring ;
But aught that is worth the knowing ?
 Placards on walls were glowing,
 Puffs in the papers pouring,
 Good Words roaring and blowing,
 Once a Week blowing and roaring.''

Each new edition of his poems contains some corrections; occasionally these alterations are evident improve-
ments, but it more frequently happens that passages with
which his admirers have been long familiar, are remodelled, and the new reading sounds less pleasant than
the old.

The " Charge of the Light Brigade " is a noteworthy
instance; one verse of the original poem is now left out :—

" For up came an order which
 Some one had blunder'd—

> Forward, the Light Brigade !
> Take the guns ! Nolan said.
> Into the Valley of Death
> Rode the six hundred.

These ungrammatical and not very intelligible lines can well be spared; but the last verse—

> " When can their glory fade ?
> O, the wild charge they made !
> All the world wonder'd.
> Honour the charge they made !
> Honour the Light Brigade,
> Noble six hundred !''

which was worthy of preservation, has been replaced by—

> " Honour the brave and bold !
> Long shall the tale be told,
> Yea, when our babes are old—
> How they rode onward.''

The commencement of the fourth verse originally, stood:—

> " Flash'd all their sabres bare,
> Flash'd all at once in air.''

It now reads:—

> " Flash'd all their sabres bare,
> Flash'd as they turn'd in air.''

It is a singular instance of the perversity of public taste, that this " Charge," which abounds with faults not often to be found in Tennyson's smaller poems, is yet perhaps the most frequently read and quoted of all.

Perhaps it was from the extreme nicety in the choice of words, and the laboured finish of minute details which characterises his writings, that Lord Lytton was led to speak somewhat contemptuously of him many years ago as *Miss Alfred;* and other writers have not scrupled to question his right to a foremost place amongst our poets. Mr. Austin, in *The Poetry of the Period,* asserts that—

" He is not a great poet, unquestionably not a poet of the first rank, all but unquestionably not a poet of the second rank, and probably not even at the head of poets of the third rank, among whom he must *ultimately* take his place."

He charges him with being a puny poet, who never soars above the earth, producing nothing but pictures of still life.

" Tennyson," he says, " is a small bird, loving to sing among laurel shrubs, spicy flowers, sparkling fountains, flowery lawns, who has not one sublime passage in the whole of his works ; and what is more, there is no attempt at one."

Sublimity and passion are not Mr. Tennyson's strong points, yet posterity may decide, in spite of Mr. Austin, that he is a poet of high rank ; in fact, contemporary professional criticism has more often been reversed than accepted by posterity, especially with regard to poetry.

" The hedges around us are too high, while we are ourselves travellers through the upward slope, for us to survey the bearings of any great contemporaneous contention. But as we look back upon ages spread beneath us, so shall they that follow look back upon ours, and to them we leave such things to decide."

It has been truly remarked of Tennyson that he has never written one line of what might be termed cosmopolitan poetry, that his muse has ever been " compassed by the inviolate sea," and strictly and uncompromisingly insular.

" He is an unmitigated Englishman, apparently not aware that there is any country in the world but England, or that there exist any concerns of moment save English interests. The penalty he has

U

paid, and which his reputation will for ever have to pay, for this narrowness of survey, this insular exclusiveness, is a heavy one. It has prevented him from ever getting hold of a really great subject, or from writing a poem which shall be at one and the same time of sufficient length, sufficient completeness, and sufficient dignity. A great theme greatly executed—behold the ambition of all great poets. That Mr. Tennyson would have executed satisfactorily anything he conceived, can scarcely be doubted. Unhappily for him he has never been able adequately to conceive a great theme. When we say that he has for the most part selected small subjects and small studies we of course only use the word relatively, well aware that in themselves the poems are anything but small.

" Smallness of subject is pretty sure to entail its own special mode of treatment, particularly if he who has to treat it has a fine sense and instinct of proportion ; and no one ever had that sense and instinct more remarkably than Mr. Tennyson. He has an exquisite feeling of the fitness of things. Indeed he has it to an almost morbid degree, and is painfully solicitous that his style of composition shall harmonise with his subject. Accordingly, his writings are laboured and finished as writings were perhaps never laboured or finished before.

" But is it wonderful ? Has it not been a thousand times observed that a large house or a large garden may rely for the impression it excites somewhat upon its size, whereas a small house or a small garden depends wholly for the effect it creates on its neatness and tidiness. The park may safely scorn to be rigidly symmetrical ; but the little garden plot must be trim, the walks must be well swept, the edges sharply cut, everything in its place, everything faultless. Mr. Tennyson has instinctively felt all this, and the consequence is that his garden is not only a garden of sweets, but a garden in which no plant or flower is permitted to outgrow its place, no one pebble trespasses on the grass, no nook or corner is neglected or ignored. He is quite right. Sheridan, speaking of Burke, mentioned ' the negligent grandeur of his mind.' But to be negligent you must be grand ; and Mr. Tennyson, knowing himself to be scarcely the one, takes excellent care never to be the other. Mr. Carlyle may have had something of this sort in view when he spoke so admirably of ' the completeness of a limited mind.' But we must, at least, take leave of this delightful poet with praise. The signal excellence of his writings can be expressed only by that vague word ' charm.' There is a glamour in nearly all of what he writes. His notes may be only the middle notes, but how clear and silvery they are ! He is the most ' exquisite ' of writers."

When Wordsworth died scarcely any doubt could have been felt as to the person most fitted to occupy the vacant post, and universal satisfaction was felt at the appointment of Alfred Tennyson, as Poet Laureate. The warrant, which was dated November 19th, 1850, and signed by the then Lord Chamberlain—Breadalbane—recites that he is " to have, hold, exercise, and enjoy all the rights, profits, and privileges of that office."

When, on the accession of James II. in 1685, it became necessary to reappoint the officers of the Royal household, including the Poet Laureate, the king directed that the annual grant of a butt of sack should be discontinued, and this omission poor Dryden had to bear with until he lost his offices at the Revolution.

On the accession of William III. the grant of wine appears to have been resumed, and continued to be sent annually to succeeding Laureates, until the crowning of Henry James Pye. He, with exemplary economy, elected to accept a yearly sum of £27 in place of the wine, which amount is still paid to the Poet Laureate by the Lord Steward's department, for a " butt of sack."

The salary of the office comes under the second class of the Civil List ; it is paid from the Lord Chamberlain's office, and the amount is said to be only £72 per annum.

In 1855 the University of Oxford conferred the honorary degree of D.C.L. upon the Laureate.

In his official capacity Tennyson has not written very

frequently, a fact which his admirers certainly need not regret. In March, 1851, he dedicated his poems to the Queen, paying Wordsworth a somewhat negative compliment :—

> " Victoria—since your Royal grace
>   To one of less desert allows
>   This laurel greener from the brows
>   Of him that uttered nothing base."

The Idyls of the King are dedicated to the memory of Prince Albert, in lines which are almost as well known as any Tennyson has written.

The odes on the Royal marriages, one entitled " A Welcome to Alexandra," March, 1863, the other " A Welcome to Marie Alexandrowna," are worthy of the occasions for which they were written, but, like all poems relating to the family affairs of Royalty, possessed only an ephemeral interest.

A Welcome to Alexandra.

March 7th, 1863.

> " Sea-kings' daughter from over the sea,
>   Alexandra !
> Saxon and Norman and Dane are we,
> But all of us Danes in our welcome of thee,
>   Alexandra !
>
> *   *   *   *   *   *
>
> The sea-kings' daughter as happy as fair,
> Blissful bride of a blissful heir,
> Bride of the heir of the kings of the sea—
>
> O joy to the people, and joy to the throne,
> Come to us, love us, and make us your own.
> For Saxon, or Dane, or Norman, we,
> Teuton or Celt, or whatever we be,
> We are each and all Dane in our welcome of thee,
>   Alexandra !"

Indeed, the ode to the Russian Princess was considered a trifle too fulsome in its praise of a comparatively unknown young lady; the general public scarcely expected her appearance in this country to bring about any of the remarkable political and social revolutions here dimly shadowed forth :—

> " The son of him with whom we strove for power,
> Whose will is lord thro' all his world domain,
> Who made the serf a man, and burst his chain,
> Has given our prince his own imperial flower,
> Alexandrowna !
>
> " Shall fears and jealous hatreds flame again ?
> *Or at thy coming, Princess, everywhere,*
> *The blue heaven break, and some diviner air*
> Breathe thro' the world, and change the hearts of men,
> Alexandrowna ? "

We have been hovering on the brink of a war with Russia almost ever since the marriage, in fact, there is nearly as much poetical license as there is poetry in the ode, and the *Examiner* had a little epigram on the subject :—

> " VICTORIA, mother of the English race,
> I, Tennyson, thy poet, one thing lack.
> Long since I owed my pension to thy grace ;
> Give me its ancient comrade now, *The Sack*."

The *double entendre* is somewhat marred by the fact that the Laureate's allowance of a butt of sack is paid for in the modern form already referred to. It will be remembered that Southey and Wordsworth also preferred to take money in lieu of the wine, a small matter however,

> " For with both the muse was fed,"

as Ben says.

The ode on the death of the Duke of Wellington, and that sung at the opening of the International Exhibition, may also be considered official poems. They can scarcely be thought worthy of Tennyson's genius, or indeed greatly superior to the odes of some of his predecessors.

Tennyson thus describes the burial of the Iron Duke in St. Paul's Cathedral, close to Lord Nelson's tomb :—

" Where shall we lay the man whom we deplore ?
Here in streaming London's central roar.
Let the sound of those he wrought for,
And the feet of those he fought for,
 Echo round his bones for evermore !
  * * * * * *
Who is he that cometh, like an honour'd guest,
With banner and with music, with soldier and with priest,
With a nation weeping, and breaking on my rest ?
  Mighty seaman, this is he
  Was great by land, as thou by sea.
Thine island loves thee well, thou famous man,
The greatest sailor since our world began.
  Now, to the roll of muffled drums,
  To thee the greatest soldier comes ;
For this is he
Was great by land as thou by sea ;
His foes were thine ; he kept us free ;
O give him welcome, this is he,
Worthy of our gorgeous rites,
And worthy to be laid by thee ;
For this is England's greatest son,
He that gain'd a hundred fights,
Nor ever lost an English gun.
  Beating from the wasted vines
  Back to France her banded swarms,
  Back to France with countless blows,
Till o'er the hills her eagles flew
Past the Pyrenian pines,

Follow'd up in valley and glen
With blare of bugle, clamour of men,
Roll of cannon and clash of arms,
And England pouring on her foes,
Such a war had such a close.

  * * * * * *

Again their ravening eagle rose
In anger, wheel'd on Europe shadowing wings,
 And barking for the thrones of kings ;
Till one that sought but Duty's iron crown
On that loud Sabbath shook the spoiler down ;
  A day of onsets of despair !
  Dash'd on every rocky square
Their surging charges foam'd themselves away ;
 Last, the Prussian trumpet blew ;
 Thro' the long tormented air
Heaven flash'd a sudden jubilant ray,
And down we swept and charged and overthrew.
  So great a soldier taught us there,
  What long-enduring hearts could do
In that world's earthquake, *Waterloo !* "

To mere outsiders a kind of grim, mysterious grandeur seems to surround the solemn Laureate of these days ; he sits, like a modern Zeus, enveloped in clouds.

To only a few is it permitted to penetrate to his awful presence, and view the bard unbending from his mighty labours. This studied seclusion, which has baffled the curious lion-hunters and star-gazers, has probably often caused disappointment to ardent admirers, anxious to pay their homage to the respected bard.

On one occasion it is probable that even Mr. Tennyson felt a tinge of regret when he learnt the name of one visitor who had been turned away from his house.

The Prince, being in the Isle of Wight, and near the Poet's house, determined to pay him a visit, and, being quite unattended, meant to do so without any formal ceremony. Unfortunately the page did not recognise the features, which one would suppose few Englishmen could ignore, and, mindful of his master's strict injunctions not to admit strangers, inquired, " What name shall I say ?"

When he heard the reply, he gave an incredulous stare, and though he—

> " Expressed no word to indicate a doubt,
> He put his thumb unto his nose,
> And spread his fingers out ! "

adding, with playful sarcasm as he slammed the door, " Ha, yes, the Prince of Wales ! We know a trick worth two of that ! "

It is not known whether Mr. Tennyson laughed on this occasion, but it is tolerably certain that the good-humoured Prince enjoyed the joke, although at his own expense.

We are told, on the authority of Robert Buchanan, another poet, that Tennyson sometimes smokes a short clay pipe and drinks grog on Olympus.

Here are the lines : they are severe on Swinburne, between whom and Buchanan a paper war anent the pamphlet of the latter, entitled *The Fleshly School*, has since given rise to a lawsuit. Perhaps Swinburne is not altogether the poet for young ladies' perusal, but his reputation is not to be upset by a few satirical verses :—

THE SESSION OF THE POETS,

AUGUST, 1866.

Dî magni, salaputium disertum!—CAT. LIB. LIII.

I.

" At the Session of Poets held lately in London,
The Bard of Freshwater was voted the chair :
With his tresses unbrush'd, and his shirt-collar undone,
He loll'd at his ease like a good-humour'd Bear ;

' Come, boys!' he exclaimed, ' we'll be merry together!'
   And lit up his pipe with a smile on his cheek ;—
While with eye, like a skipper's cock'd up at the weather,
   Sat the Vice-Chairman Browning, thinking in Greek.

II.

" The company gather'd embraced great and small bards,
   Both strong bards and weak bards, funny and grave,
Fat bards and lean bards, little and tall bards,
   Bards who wear whiskers, and others who shave.
Of books, men, and things, was the bards' conversation—
   Some praised *Ecce Homo*, some deemed it so-so—
And then there was talk of the state of the nation,
   And when the Unwash'd would devour Mister Lowe.

III.

" Right stately sat Arnold,—his black gown adjusted
   Genteelly, his Rhine wine deliciously iced,—
With puddingish England serenely disgusted,
   And looking in vain (in the mirror) for ' Geist ;'
He heark'd to the Chairman, with ' Surely!' and ' Really ?'
   Aghast at both collar and cutty of clay,—
Then felt in his pocket, and breath'd again freely,
   On touching the leaves of his own classic play.

IV.

" Close at hand, lingered Lytton, whose Icarus-winglets
   Had often betrayed him in regions of rhyme,—
How glitter'd the eye underneath his grey ringlets,
   A hunger within it unlessen'd by time!
Remoter sat Bailey—satirical, surly—
   Who studied the language of Goethe too soon,
Who sang himself hoarse to the stars very early,
   And crack'd a weak voice with too lofty a tune.

V.

" How name all that wonderful company over ?—
   Prim Patmore, mild Alford,—and Kingsley also ?
Among the small sparks, who was realler than Lover ?
   Among misses, who sweeter than Miss Ingelow ?

There sat, looking moony, conceited, and narrow,
    Buchanan,—who, finding, when foolish and young,
Apollo asleep on a coster-girl's barrow,
    Straight dragged him away to see somebody hung.

VI.

" What was said ? what was done ? was there prosing or rhyming ?
    Was nothing noteworthy in deed or in word ?—
Why, just as the hour of the supper was chiming,
    The only event of the evening occurred.
Up jumped, with his neck stretching out like a gander,
    Master Swinburne, and squeal'd, glaring out thro' his hair,
' All Virtue is bosh ! Hallelujah for Landor !
    I disbelieve wholly in everything !—there !'

VII.

" With language so awful he dared then to treat 'em,—
    Miss Ingelow fainted in Tennyson's arms,
Poor Arnold rush'd out, crying ' Sœcl' inficetum !'
    And great bards and small bards were full of alarms ;
Till Tennyson, flaming and red as a gipsy,
    Struck his fist on the table and utter'd a shout :
' To the door with the boy ! Call a cab ! He is tipsy !'
    And they carried the naughty young gentleman out.

VIII.

" After that, all the pleasanter talking was done there,—
    Whoever had known such an insult before ?
The Chairman tried hard to rekindle the fun there,
    But the muses were shocked and the pleasure was o'er.
Then ' Ah !' cried the Chairman, ' this teaches me knowledge,
    The future shall find me more wise, by the powers !
This comes of assigning to younkers from college
    Too early a place in such meetings as ours !'"

CALIBAN.
The Spectator, Sept. 15, 1866.

It was Mr. Effingham Wilson, of the Royal Exchange,
London, who published in 1830, the first little volume,

entitled, *Poems, chiefly Lyrical,* by A. and C. Tennyson, which is said to be now worth its weight in gold. Since that time several firms have published Mr. Tennyson's works. A few years since it was announced that Messrs. Strahan had secured the right of publishing for the Poet Laureate, after a brisk competition with rival firms, the arrangement under which they obtained the copyright being that they should pay Mr. Tennyson four thousand pounds a year for twenty years. This arrangement seems to have been abandoned, as since then Messrs. Henry S. King have published for him. Messrs. C. Kegan Paul and Co., having succeeded Messrs. King and Co. in their publishing business, they now have Mr. Tennyson's works in hand, and to them the public owe a debt of gratitude for the last popular edition, in one handsome well printed volume, which places within the reach of every reading man all the poems Mr. Tennyson desires to be preserved.

Since the days when Dryden held office, no Laureate has been appointed so distinctly pre-eminent above all his contemporaries, so truly the king of the poets, as he upon whose brows now rests the Laureate crown; Swinburne, the nearest approach the age can produce, is he not, too, a loyal courtier of the poet king, who knowing his own worth can well afford to admire the greatness of his master? Dryden's grandeur was sullied, his muse was venal, and his life was vicious, still in his keeping the office acquired a certain dignity; after his death it declined into the depths of degradation, and each succeeding dullard dimmed its failing lustre. The first ray of hope for its revival sprang into life with the appointment of Southey, to whom succeeded Wordsworth, a poet of worth and genius, whose name certainly assisted in resuscitating the ancient dignity of the appointment.

Alfred Tennyson derives less honour from the title than he confers upon it; to him we owe a debt of gratitude that he has redeemed the laurels with his poetry, noble, pure, and undefiled as ever poet sang.

Long may he still continue so to sing in ever living verse, and when, in some yet distant time, the poet-man shall fade away, to leave the poet-work behind with us, may there be chosen out from among the living bards one to succeed him whose muse may seem the nearest to approach, in sweetness and purity, in dignity and grace, the poems of Alfred Tennyson.

INDEX.

—:o:—